Human Consciousness

The Problems of Philosophy:
Their past and present

General Editor: Ted Honderich
Grote Professor of the Philosophy of Mind and Logic
University College London

Books already published:

PRIVATE OWNERSHIP
James O. Grunebaum

RELIGIOUS BELIEF AND THE WILL
Louis P. Pojman

RATIONALITY
Harold I. Brown

THE RATIONAL FOUNDATIONS OF ETHICS
T. L. S. Sprigge

MORAL KNOWLEDGE
Alan H. Goldman

MIND–BODY IDENTITY THEORIES
Cynthia Macdonald

PRACTICAL REASONING
Robert Audi

PERSONAL IDENTITY
Harold W. Noonan

IF P THEN Q: THE FOUNDATIONS OF LOGIC AND
ARGUMENT
David H. Sanford

THE INFINITE
A. W. Moore

THE WEAKNESS OF THE WILL
Justin Gosling

THOUGHT AND LANGUAGE
Julius Moravcsik

EXPLAINING EXPLANATION
David-Hillel Ruben

Human Consciousness

Alastair Hannay

London and New York

First published 1990
by Routledge
11 New Fetter Lane, London EC4P 4EE

Simultaneously published in the USA and Canada
by Routledge
a division of Routledge, Chapman and Hall, Inc.
29 West 35th Street, New York, NY 10001

Typeset in 10/12 Times by Megaron, Cardiff, Wales
Printed and bound in Great Britain by
Biddles Ltd, Guildford and King's Lynn

British Library Cataloguing in Publication Data
Hannay, Alastair
Human consciousness.—(The problems of philosophy)
1. Man. Consciousness—philosophical perspectives
I. Title II. Series
126

Library of Congress Cataloging in Publication Data
Hannay, Alastair
Human consciousness/Alastair Hannay
p. cm.—(The problems of philosophy: their past and present)
Includes bibliographical references.
1. Consciousness. I. Title. II. Series: Problems of Philosophy
(Routledge (Firm))
BF311.H336   1990
126—dc20   89-39167

ISBN 0-415-03299-7

To Bente

Contents

Preface

This book offers arguments for believing that self-conscious action and thought play vital roles in human life. It defends the concept of consciousness in the face of current denials of its importance. So the 'problem' it deals with is rather specific and local, in the sense that the question of the concept's status has acquired a peculiar urgency in the context of recent developments in cognitive science, not least the promise shown by mechanical models of intelligent behaviour. Any success in this area immediately raises suspicions about the roles traditionally attributed to the consciousness of mental states. Physicalists welcome the suspicion because there is no clear place in the physicalist's universe for the kind of thing consciousness has been assumed to be. While those who see something intuitively correct in the traditional concept are faced with the many theoretical difficulties it gives rise to, not least the familiar mind–body problem. That problem deserves a book of its own and no solution to it is offered here. As I have seen it, this book's task is to present the issues in as much detail as space allows and let the general case for consciousness in the end speak for itself, whatever problems it leaves us with and indeed generates. Like its fellow volumes in the series, this one includes an account of the topic's 'past', though in this case in a single chapter. A fuller account would have included a proper treatment of the German idealists, but if the history strikes the reader as patchy that is because it is presented here partly as a background of philosophical resources to confront the case currently being made for the scientific expendability of the topic. I say nothing about the unconscious, but that after all is a different topic, one that also needs separate treatment, and it doesn't directly impinge on what this book has taken as its focal theme.

I am most grateful to Ted Honderich for giving me the opportunity to write this book and for his constant support and sustained confidence in my ability to do so. Among those to be thanked for helping me find my way are Pat Churchland, Paul Churchland, Hubert Dreyfus, Andrew Feenberg, Grant Gillett, Olav Gjelsvik, Geoffrey Madell, Hans Mathlein, Ragnar Ohlsson, Frederick Olafson, John Searle, Timothy Sprigge, Nathan Stemmer, Avrum Stroll, Gunnar Svensson, Torbjörn Tännsjö, and Zeno Vendler. A number of these participated very actively in a seminar course on consciousness at the University of Stockholm in 1987, the results of which became a survey article forming the nucleus of the book. Others have very generously given me the benefit of their knowledge and criticism in private conversation and/or correspondence. Many have sent me their articles and let me see drafts of work in progress. In this respect I am especially grateful to Hubert Dreyfus, Frederick Olafson, John Searle, and Avrum Stroll.

The book contains material from the survey article 'The claims of consciousness', *Inquiry* 30 (1987), and a short excerpt from a paper ('Consciousness and the experience of freedom') to appear in a volume devoted to the work of John Searle, for permission to use which I thank the respective publishers, Universitetsforlaget and Basil Blackwell.

My work was supported in part by two six-month research fellowships for which I am indebted to the Norwegian Research Council for Science and the Humanities.

CHAPTER I

The Problem

I have been accused of denying consciousness, but I am not
conscious of having done so. Consciousness is to me a mystery,
and not one to be dismissed. We know what it is like to be
conscious, but not how to put it into satisfactory scientific terms.

W. V. Quine[1]

Human beings are aware of their surroundings. Somehow they are
also aware of themselves as being in those surroundings, and for the
most part also of the contents and qualities of the ways of their being
in them. We all know what it is like to be conscious in this way, to be
thinking about something, seeing things, confidently carrying out
some task, simply coping, or stumbling, being angry or in doubt
about something, feeling relieved, and so on.[2] We also recognize that
these are not characteristics which we share with glaciers, houses, and
trees; nor, we assume, with quasars, atoms, or quarks. Whether or in
what respect we share them with other sentient creatures is less clear;
but in marking some distinction between us and them, people
commonly point to the way we are assumed to be self-aware in our
awareness, to our special linguistic capacity, and to the way we are
able to control our own behaviour by envisaging and taking
conscious and sustained account of states of affairs beyond those that
immediately confront us.

All this gives rise to many questions: Is the difference between us
and inanimate things just a matter of the way elements of physical
nature congregate to form conscious phenomena, or do these
phenomena involve the presence of some *sui generis* element or
medium, an immaterial mind? Supposing that what distinguishes us
from at least most other sentient organisms is some form of 'self'-
consciousness, what coherent account, if any, are we able to give of
this capacity? In general, how is this form of conscious engagement
with the environment to be understood in relation to the natural
world as we know it?

A common label for these and related questions has been 'the
mind–body problem'. However, the mind–body problem as traditionally conceived asks a fairly special question. It asks how sentience

1

(in general) can be in causal relation with things so radically disparate as assemblies of neurons or whatever wider aspects of the physical world are considered relevant in this context. That is clearly too narrow a focus to represent the full range of issues which questions of the *nature* of human consciousness raise. As we shall see, some of the most influential answers to questions of the nature of consciousness even imply that this is a side-issue, if an issue at all. That, it will be argued, is a mistake and an evasion. But it is true that the mind–body question has itself arisen in a context which, along with the questions most closely associated with it – the existence of an external world and personal identity – take consciousness for granted and its nature to be in the main unproblematic. That too is mistaken, not in this case an evasion so much as a distortion of perspective, or a kind of blind spot, traceable to the dualism which crystallized in the work of Descartes in the early seventeenth century.

With its notion of a realm of conscious activity (that of *res cogitans*) distinct, and for Descartes in principle separable, from that of the world upon which that activity is directed, Descartes's dualism was not just a way of dividing the universe into two distinct and separable realms; it gave epistemological primacy to subjective experience. Belief in the existence of the physical world in general (the 'external world') and of those particular parts of it which are our own bodies had to be justified on the basis of the evidence of the 'senses', which in themselves provided no direct access to the physical realm. So too with belief in the existence of a self continuing throughout a series of conscious moments (personal identity); since what is directly available on this view, in its most consistent form, is simply the presence here and now of a particular state of consciousness. According to this position, consciousness is what we primarily are and know best. For Descartes, and Locke after him, consciousness and the mind are indeed the same; consequently, in being conscious we are also enjoying first-hand access to the reality of the mental as such. But then, if what consciousness *is* is no more than a matter of how it appears to the conscious subject, the question of the 'nature' of consciousness is not a fundamental issue. This is reinforced in Descartes's own view by the implication that philosophical questions are prior to and unaffected by the results of empirical investigation. If there are any wider questions of the nature of consciousness, these can be settled by a branch of purely philosophical inquiry which Kant, in his criticism of the idea, called

2

rational psychology.[3] The thesis of rational psychology is that the self or soul is a substance of which consciousness as we know it is a first-hand manifestation.

From a first-person perspective, then, there seems to be no basic problem of what consciousness is, just because the perspective takes consciousness for granted. We know what it is like to be conscious. True, one may ask what the 'stuff' is out of which mind is composed, but what intelligible answer can be forthcoming if, as James pointed out, the only answers we can understand are those framed in terms of what normally counts as 'stuff', namely qualities of the things we experience?[4] It is also true, of course, that anyone taking consciousness for granted may be asked to specify what it is that is being taken for granted; but then again, since everything that exists from that point of view is interpreted as being available in some way or other, however indirectly, *to* a conscious subject, the question remains in an important way academic. One may wonder what this 'medium' is which one inhabits as a subject of experience, but there seems to be no way of specifying its nature other than by giving accurate first-hand descriptions of what it is like to be such a subject.

Recent years have seen a radical reversal of the egocentric perspective and preoccupations of Cartesian philosophy. The mainstream of philosophical psychology now takes its stance firmly in what a prominent representative calls the 'objective, materialistic, third-person world of the physical sciences'.[5] Given the rapid advances brought by computer science and neurobiology to theorizing about the physiology of mental processes, and the fact that of Descartes's two possibilities *res extensa* is the one in which science is most at home, it is not surprising that the dominant strain in theory of mind today should be one that pursues a strongly physicalist programme. By adding to Descartes's basically geometrico-mechanical conception the resources of recent neurobiology and cognitive science, the functions traditionally associated with the other side – *res cogitans* – are either being shelved as myths inconsistent with basic physical theory or else, as the explanatory possibilities of the gene and the excitable cell unfold, reassigned to matter. In a way this is merely a continuation of a path along which Descartes himself took the first step when he substituted a mechanistic theory of living matter for the traditional vitalizing soul. With the transfer of the soul's biological function to physical science, the way was paved for the physicalist takeover of its perceptual and ratiocinative functions too, as well as of

3

whatever else a plausible account of human behaviour may be thought obliged to include.

To many, that promise seems well on the way to fulfilment; the theoretical burdens borne on behalf of the specifically human by the traditional immaterial soul are being gradually left by the wayside or else transferred to the body. Leaning on the new resources of the computer model, some physicalists are understandably inclined to let the range of properly human characteristics (self-consciousness, volition, moral accountability, capacity to judge or appraise, have beliefs, desires, etc.) be determined by the apparently still-expanding limits of machine intelligence. If commonly-assumed attributes of the human being traditionally associated with personhood, or selfhood, prove too burdened with notions which lack counterparts in the kinds of 'self'- and environmental control exercised by computing machines, the physicalist of this bent is in principle prepared to drop them. From this perspective, the limits of an autonomous science of human mentality are set by the theoretical requirements of a grasp of the performance of abstract computer programs. On the other hand, there are physicalists who insist on the brain's being brought in as the bottom level of analysis. For them, the mind more or less straight-forwardly *is* that remarkably complex organ; and what decides whether or in what sense we have beliefs or desires, are self-conscious agents, etc., is the neurobiologist's ability in the long run to map these 'folk-psychological' categories on to determinable brain functions, whether at the abstract level of neural networks or in terms of the single cell.

Where the *res cogitans* perspective renders basic questions about consciousness otiose by taking conscious phenomena for granted, the *res extensa* perspective has to deny that they are basic because from that perspective consciousness simply doesn't come into view. For Descartes, of course, that was no problem; he had *res cogitans* up his sleeve. But physical monism does have a problem. Computers and brains are pleasingly accessible parts of a unified space–time world. They are also – on this side of any projected terminological revolution – insensate, while we, along with a large number of organisms which cannot speak for themselves, are not. The problem of consciousness, from this perspective, is what to make of it at all. Instead of facing the problem, classical behaviourism simply turned its back, redefining the mental in exclusively third-person terms. Functionalism puts a mental factor back into the behavioural equation, in the form of the informational processes that make for the organism's intelligent grasp of the environment, but that grasp is taken to be a compound product of a host of specialized functions which are themselves neither conscious nor intelligent.[6] So, apart from the difficulty of incorporating consciousness and whatever its contents may turn out to be into a unified body of scientific knowledge, there is this other potential anomaly for physicalism: its inability to give consciousness any theoretical role to play. On evolutionary grounds there is a standing expectation – a very strong one at that – that selected, i.e. surviving, mental capacities have surviving human functions. In effect, then, the more physicalism is conceded to have captured the essence of human mentality, the more mysterious the residual domain of first-person consciousness becomes.

In the Klondike atmosphere of the burgeoning cognitive sciences, the attitude of much physicalism to consciousness has been that of new owners to a sitting tenant. Admitting (though not all physicalists do) that eviction is out of the question, they are content to dispose of as much of the first-person paraphernalia as possible while keeping busy in other parts of the house,[7] concentrating for instance on the dispositional and causal properties of conscious states at the expense of the categorical nature of the states themselves. Yet the more physicalist business prospers and the better able its models are to simulate human performance without recourse to consciousness, the more anomalous this 'ghostly' remainder becomes – the less likely too, surely, that the models genuinely replicate that performance, and the more plausible the assumption that humans generate their own versions of these causal powers in significantly different ways which do involve consciousness. If, on top of this, one suspects that the significance cognitive science necessarily attaches to only certain very basic forms of causal power, or even its attachment to causal powers in general, gives at best a distorted and incomplete picture of the human mind, the ability of the physicalist programme to supply adequate models can well begin to look illusory.

If the opposed perspectives of the Cartesian tradition offer only partial views, what could provide a panoptical vision of the conscious mind? Some physicalists, secure in their faith that '[w]hatever it precisely may be, consciousness is a state of the body, a state of nerves',[8] seem to think that all that is needed is to get rid of the two-substance theory which makes it a state of an immaterial soul. However, whatever weight there may be in the claim that the immaterial soul was postulated simply to host predicates hard to accommodate in a physical universe, unless these predicates can themselves be shown to lack genuine descriptive value the question remains how bodies and nerves, as understood in the physicalist universe, can be in states of enjoying first-person points of view.

Thomas Nagel has proposed that what is needed is '[an integrated] theory of conscious organisms as physical systems composed of chemical elements and occupying space, which also have an individual perspective on the world, and in some cases a capacity for self-awareness as well'.[9] Nagel himself sees this as a distant dream, but there is a strong tendency among physicalists to believe that the outlines of that theory already exist. The apparently unlimited variety and sophistication of the relations which can obtain between spatio-temporally locatable things offers the long-term prospect of explaining everything within the physicalist frame.[10] Collectivities, institutions, languages, works of art, values, even such apparently abstract entities as numbers, may one day be intelligibly construed as properties or relations of physical things. And as far as mind itself is concerned, the well-supported belief that human mentality has its origins in natural selection, and must therefore be grasped in terms of behavioural adaptation, supports an equation of mind with some set of causal powers relevant for control of the environment. Since there are now very promising and some already successful models of some of those powers, why not suppose that these will one day simulate human capacities in a way which leaves no room for reasonable doubt that we then have all the terms and laws or principles we need for explaining human mentality?

The objection is that they will still have failed to model lived experience. One of the roots of physicalist faith is the familiarity we have with things around us in space; and the accessibility to science of the many complex structures to be found there fosters a very strong inclination to affirm that all that really exists can be located in space and time as these are straightforwardly conceived.[11] But, so the objection goes, you won't find consciousness there. It is one thing to uncover the details of the mechanisms on which conscious life depends, another to throw light on lived experience. As far as the latter is concerned, physicalist psychology is doomed to draw a blank. Whatever is learned about the processes underlying consciousness, there remains an insurmountable barrier between what the descriptions embodying that learning describe and the actual experiences (ordinary coping, seeing red, feeling angry) which those processes underlie. Bad enough that total knowledge of, say, the mechanisms of colour vision can never explain why the things we call red actually look red; much worse that it cannot even explain why they look anything at all.

The anomaly confronting the third-person point of view here is that the nature of the processes in which conscious experience is embedded can in principle be decided without mentioning the conscious experience which is what we are deeply convinced they are good for. It is as though you could give a perfect specification of what a physical thing like an eye is but without mentioning first-person seeing, an ear without first-person hearing, a tongue without first-person tasting – nerves, in short, without anything it is like to be conscious. As for that, the physicalist is forced to conclude that the topic of consciousness is one on which nothing informative can be said; which, in view of the claims of consciousness to be one of the most insistent themes of western thought from Descartes if not Plato and to this day, is a paradoxical result to say the least.

A natural rejoinder to this objection, for the physicalist, is to say that the explosive growth of our knowledge of the nervous system in recent decades indicates that the 'mystery' of consciousness can be left to itself. As far as overall human performance is concerned, it is the underlying mechanisms resulting from behavioural adaptation that we must come to grips with. So what we can and do quite successfully grasp is not only as close as we can get to the subject-matter; what we actually have in hand may reasonably be assumed to be what we were after all along, what the western tradition has been looking for but in the wrong place. It is in this naturalizing spirit that we find a proliferation of books on consciousness which in fact fail to discuss *consciousness* at all, in the sense in which it appears to resist scientific explanation. To the continued objection that there is still, after all, this thing of consciousness as lived experience, it is sometimes thought enough to assume just as a matter of faith that under certain ideal physical circumstances we will have no good reason to deny that machines are indeed sentient and in just the way we take ourselves to be. Or if that seems too obviously to beg the question, it is sometimes claimed that any 'inner life' a machine inevitably lacks plays no theoretical role in the understanding of human performance. This of course invites the objection that, even if we confine ourselves to the general area of the organism's control over its own activities, we should at least be able to hypothesize, even if falsely, that there is something that human consciousness is good for. Against this we have the recent suggestion that while conscious experience might certainly be good for some things (for instance as a guide to social relationships and a means for the retention of long-term goals), Darwinism does not compel us to postulate such functions, and in any case consciousness does not have to be thought of as providing the conscious subject with information which the *subject*, as opposed to the brain-operated body as a whole, uses in directing its own control performance. True, since it is 'posed the multifaceted task of controlling a highly active and complex body through a complicated world [the human brain] needs information about certain of its own states and activities'; but all it requires is 'certain edited sorts of information', and what we have grown used to calling 'selves', 'subjects', and 'egos', as if these words denoted some conscious consumer of the information, need be no more than recipients and relayers (to others just as well placed) of these pieces of edited information. The real work is going on backstage and invisibly, and what occurs in the conscious mind is no more the work itself than the operations of a computer program are what the computer display reveals to the user, or than the user's keyboard manipulations mirror actual performance at the machine level.[12]

A different line is taken by physicalists who do not feel constrained by the traditionally subjectivist connotations of 'consciousness' and its cognates. They simply take over the terms without the connotations. So a purely physical system can be described as conscious even if it lacks an individual perspective on the world. Conscious systems can be systems that negotiate their environments with sufficient ease for it to be plausible to assume that they encode some pragmatically adequate model of those environments. Similarly with *self*-consciousness. A self-conscious system would be one which, in addition to a model of its environment, contains a model of its own modelling of that environment.[13] Indeed, the courtesies might even be extended further to include 'individual perspective'. If it can be shown that this idea incorporates no significant additional features or powers to set it off from the kind of self-conscious system just envisioned – that is, if it can be shown that human beings have such a perspective in no more interesting a sense than some purely physical system – then machines could be said to have individual perspectives too, and perhaps even 'inner lives', in this case of a conveniently unproblematic kind since they will be located literally 'inside' the piece of physical reality in which the system in question is 'realized'.

But even here there is a limit. The unfolding of the causal powers of a system which is self-conscious in the peculiarly human way could only be adequately replicated in a machine if the machine can be said to have that kind of self-consciousness. Of course, much needs to be said before the kind can be adequately specified. But assuming it can be specified, the issue is then whether consciousness can be a state of something other than a living human body.[14] However theoretically redundant the individual perspective proved to be, however small this baby born out of physicalist wedlock, it would still be incumbent on the physicalist to find it a home in the physicalist universe. There are indeed physicalists who talk as if they could provide it, on the pragmatic grounds that you can be said to understand something if only you can systematically bring it about by producing its sufficient causal antecedents. In certain ideal physical conditions the responses of robots will leave us with no alternative but to admit that they are sentient in just the way we take ourselves to be. Obvious drawbacks of this view are (i) that we would have to be said to understand human life simply by virtue of the fruitfulness of our own propagational practices; (ii) that our command of the principles and mechanisms involved in producing suitably responsive robots should enable us to see how these responses are possible without the presence of first-person consciousness; and (iii) that for familiar 'other minds' reasons there are no compelling grounds to believe that we have indeed brought consciousness about, or that we do command its sufficient causal antecedents.

Nagel's suggestion of some fundamental conceptual revision is a distant vision and at any rate contingent upon a long-term under-mining of physicalist faith on a wider front and a gradual shift of focus on to phenomena, such as consciousness, that persistently resist accommodation within the physicalist frame. Since faith in this frame is of only recent origin, at least in philosophical psychology, it seems more likely that the problem of first-person experience will be shelved for the time being, in the hope that it will one day be solved by some conceptual or other adjustment inside the existing framework.[15] Whether a successfully integrating theory would still count as scientific, and whether, if scientific, it would still count as physicalist, are further questions perhaps themselves dependent on possible conceptual change. If it were still physicalist, it would certainly have

9

to be based on principles other than those practised by physical science today; and for the present-day physicalist to accept that such a revision would in fact solve the mystery would be to admit that all mysteries so far 'solved' are still mysterious. Recently it has been argued that the causal properties in the brain that produce awareness are endemically occult from the human vantage-point: that is, from the vantage-point of consciousness itself. The fact that the mind–body problem remains a mystery 'comes from our own cognitive limitations, not from any objective eeriness in the world'.[16] In that case, what is required is not a new, at present unenvisageable, conceptual framework, but a (just as unenvisageable) change of vantage-point.

Whatever the force of such arguments for agnosticism about the mind–body problem, they at least suggest that if there are limitations inherent in a theoretical universe modelled on Descartes's *res extensa*, we cannot count on a theoretical universe modelled on *res cogitans* doing any better. That it won't is obvious if it is taken to include the idea of mind as a second substance, for this implies that not only consciousness but also mentality *cannot* be a state of nerves. On Descartes's view the brain is no more mental than the liver. Similarly if *res cogitans* is regarded as a sealed-off area in which facts about mind can be established by *a priori* reasoning and without reference to empirical inquiry; for even if mind should unexpectedly turn out not to be a natural phenomenon, at least its existence and development depend on, and so are constrained by, whatever natural processes are needed to sustain it. Moreover, whereas Descartes's dualism gave room for a physical universe beyond the boundaries of the first-person starting-point, an integrated theory modelled on *res cogitans* alone forces the theorist into idealism from the start; and if idealism should in fact be true, that should only become evident at the end.

Richard Rorty has suggested that 'consciousness' is just a word we use to refer to a certain region of public space and time (e.g. brains and behaviour, and the relations between these). What matters is the region of space and what, if anything, we may choose to refer to there with this term. The Cartesian connotations with which the concept of consciousness is burdened should be ignored, and a fresh start made by discussing what parts of space call for description with the help of whatever distinction or distinctions the term can still usefully be employed to make. Since discourse is open-ended, here as elsewhere we may find it expedient to re-outline the region in a way that leads us to drop altogether the talk of consciousness with which we originally learned to draw up the boundaries. Rorty describes inhabitants of a fictional planet whose attitudes and behaviour, including identifications of what counts or doesn't count as a 'person', are much as ours, but who do not 'explain the difference between persons and non-persons by such notions as "mind," "consciousness," "spirit," or anything of the sort'. Instead of the Cartesian categories that infect our own vocabulary and modes of explanation, these 'Antipodeans' employ the language of neurology and biochemstry, the disciplines which brought them into conceptual contact with the phenomena. Whether they really see into their own (or each others') brains or are putting experiences like ours into the only language they have for describing them, we cannot tell. Nor does it matter.[17]

Although Rorty's suggestion sounds refreshingly progressive, on its face it is no more than an extension of the physicalist ideal and thus part of the Cartesian universe which he claims to be leaving behind. It can even be construed negatively as a counsel of despair: the 'puzzle' of the mind–body relation should be dropped because discussion of it leads nowhere. Rather than continue hammering away inconclusively at such questions as whether pains and certain brain events are or are not identical, can or cannot be explained in third-person terms as forms of the organism's control over its environment, or whatever, we are advised to let the boundaries of the mental be redrawn in ways that leave the traditional mind–body dispute behind, not letting the idea, for example, that perceptual judgments are based on the ascription of mind-dependent properties interfere with the assumption that mental and physical entities do not, after all, form two separate kinds.

Certainly, as discourse on consciousness proceeds, our ways of looking at the 'region' will surely alter and the boundaries change (expanding dramatically if panpsychism becomes the rage, or shrinking to near nothing if the ways of Rorty's Antipodeans win the day). But it seems unlikely that the term – or the notion of a first-person point of view – will become redundant. Allowance must of course be made for obscurantism, the more so that preconceived ontologies only loosely related to the *conscious* phenomena dominate a great deal of current discussion. But in the first place, discourse, after all, is carried out by subjects and they are conscious. True enough, that does not in itself guarantee a place for subjectivity in the ultimate scheme of things. But if human consciousness is central in

11

the dialogues that shape world-models at this highly abstract level, it will seem both implausible and unnecessary to argue that it does not play some essential role or roles in the 'world-modellings' that enter into the very concrete transactions human beings engage in with respect to their surroundings. And in the second place, to put the topic of the nature of human consciousness on the agenda of a discussion (the 'conversation of mankind') which deliberately turns its back on the traditional mind–body problem is to prescind from a debate which could lead to a radical revision of the physicalist backcloth against which Rorty assumes all fruitful discussion is now to be carried out.

Before going on to a detailed examination of aspects of human consciousness in the light of these doubts about Rorty's proposal, and by way of preparation for that, we shall first retrace some of the main moves in the history of the conversation of those who Rorty thinks have brought more darkness than light to our topic.

CHAPTER II

The History

That philosophers have hindered rather than advanced our understanding of human mentality is not a new idea. Well over two hundred years ago the Scottish common-sense philosopher Thomas Reid thought that philosophy, supposed 'daughter of light', might only have succeeded in shedding 'a darkness visible upon the human faculties', and cautioned it, unless it also had the power to dispel the 'clouds and phantoms' which it had 'discovered or created' in that area, to withdraw its 'penurious and malignant ray'.[1] Like Rorty, Reid saw the failure of philosophy as due to the Descartes–Locke model of an inner eye directed at no more than special mental objects or 'ideas'. From the contemporary vantage-point of the cognitive scientist, that particular model is just one typically fruitless result of the false start one makes by adopting an egocentric standpoint in the first place. But even if Reid's anti-philosophical sentiment would today find its clearest echo in cognitive science, the fact is that the more penetrating criticisms of the Cartesian–Lockean tradition have come from within philosophy itself. One only has to think of Wittgenstein and Ryle, and, especially significant for our own topic, Heidegger's deliberate abandonment of the term 'consciousness' (*Bewußtsein*) itself precisely because of its associations with that tradition.[2]

Whether from the general neglect of consciousness in modern philosophical psychology or in the light of such frontal attacks, however isolated, one may be led to wonder whether the notion itself isn't just another 'cloud' or 'phantom' which a discussion freed of the allegedly distorting projections of Cartesian epistemology can finally dispel. This chapter offers, as background to an answer to that question, a lightly critical survey of the ways in which philosophers have in fact dealt with the concept of consciousness, uncritically as

13

well as critically, and begins with a brief discussion of the origins of the terminology itself.

Relevantly to the question whether philosophy has cast more darkness than light on the subject of consciousness it is interesting to note that it is only in the last three to four hundred years that the English word 'consciousness' has acquired the sense proper to the formulation of problems in contemporary philosophy of mind. That, of course, is an ambiguous fact. It might indicate that those who claim we can do without it are right; but it could also mean that philosophy has hit upon problems of a certain very fundamental nature that require more radical solutions than we are ordinarily willing, able, or required to envisage.

To put the ambiguity in perspective let us first make some etymological observations. Earlier, the primary sense of 'conscious' was 'sharing knowledge', derived from the Latin *conscius*, while the first occurrence noted by the *Oxford English Dictionary* of 'consciousness' as denoting a state or faculty of being conscious is from 1678. Locke's *Essay Concerning Human Understanding* (1690) contains the well-known definition of consciousness as 'the perception of what passes in a man's own mind'.[3] What occur there are 'ideas' stemming from one of two sources: sensation, which is the 'great source of most of the ideas we have, depending wholly upon the senses', and 'reflection', by which Locke means 'that notice which the mind takes of its own operations, and the manner of them, by reason whereof there come to be ideas of these operations in the understanding'. Locke referred to this faculty as 'internal sense'.[4] An idea of sensation can only occur in a man's mind in the context of one or other of the mind's operations, which Locke lists as 'perception, thinking, doubting, believing, reasoning, knowing, willing, and all the different actings of our own minds'.[5] Thus thinking 'consists in being conscious that one thinks',[6] though it is only when a person 'turns his thoughts' in the direction of the operations to 'contemplate' them that he can have 'plain and clear ideas of them', just as he will fail to 'have all the particular ideas of any landscape, or of the parts and motions of a clock' if he does not 'turn his eyes to it and with his eyes and with attention heed all the parts of it'.[7]

That a faculty of inner sense should acquire the name 'consciousness' may well be linked to the secondary sense of the Latin *conscius*, 'being aware of something good or bad' not only in others but *in oneself*, which in the early eighteenth century came to be referred to as

14

possession of a 'moral sense' (cf. 'conscience' – or the Latin *conscientia*).[8] Samuel Johnson's *Dictionary of the English Language* (1755) gives 'internal sense of guilt, or innocence' as one of the meanings of 'consciousness'. And Ryle very plausibly suggests that the philosophical concept of consciousness as the mind's reflection on its own operations (later called 'introspection') is 'in part a transformed application of the Protestant notion of conscience'.[9] In a way, of course, moral sense still involves knowledge which is shared, as in the primary meaning of *conscius*, since the very idea of a specifically *moral* sense is that, on the analogy of the other senses, those who have it are able to detect right and wrong, in themselves and others, conformably with others similarly equipped; and it can be surmised that before the Protestant idea of a private conscience developed, hand in hand with that of an inner sense, the awareness of the rightness or wrongness of one's deeds was also shared in the sense that others would be just as able in principle to detect these things as oneself. Nevertheless it is easy to see how a concept of shared cognizance can leave the way open for a concept of immediate and unshareable knowledge of the contents of one's own mind. For if what is shared is knowledge of established social custom and mores, violation of these will in the first instance give rise quite naturally to a sense of social disapproval directed at the individual concerned. What began as an echo of the expressions of the disapproval of one's fellows can later manifest itself as a spontaneous deliverance of the inner mind, the focus having shifted to what are now regarded as the private promptings of an individual conscience. From there it is but a short step to the idea of a 'conscience' or 'consciousness' whose inner promptings are revelations of the mind's operations as a whole.[10]

Although this latter use of 'consciousness' departs radically from the term's classical origins, the more significant fact here could be that prior to Locke no need seems to have been felt for such a usage. This invites the reflection that the concept of consciousness may safely be dispensed with. Kathleen Wilkes points out that in spite of their sophisticated psychological vocabulary the ancient Greeks had no concept corresponding to our use or uses of the term 'consciousness'.[11] The suggestion is, first, that whatever explanatory purposes we think we need it for do not have counterparts in problems which the fathers of philosophy found it necessary to formulate, and, second, that the explanatory purposes for which we use it are spurious.

15

Since this is a point of some importance for resolving the above-mentioned ambiguity, it is worth dwelling on for a moment. First, it is not entirely true that the Greeks lacked a word for consciousness. They had both *synaesthesis* and *syneidesis*. The former only later acquired the sense of 'self-awareness' (Aristotle uses it in connection with what is now called the unity of apperception), while the latter is a counterpart of *conscientia*, though as with Johnson's (1755) sense, its application to individual knowledge was primarily ethical and its principal use may simply have been that of shared knowledge (including knowledge of having done wrong).[12] What is true is that they did not possess a concept of consciousness with the Cartesian and Lockean connotations of our own concept. But what can be validly inferred from that fact? It would be unjustified to conclude that there was nothing in ancient Greek life for such a word to refer to, even if the reference had to be made from some point of view alien to Greek culture. There is no word for weather in the native Hawaiian tongue, but people travel to Hawaii to enjoy it. And although the Eskimo vocabulary contains no word for art, that does not prevent a brisk trade in what dealers in North America refer to as 'Eskimo art'.

The analogies might suggest the following. Either the native culture has a blind spot in its self-understanding or the missing concept applies only in some alien culture (where weather is a useful or conventional topic of conversation or artefacts are marketable goods). No doubt the concept of 'art', when applied to the relevant Eskimo artefacts, misrepresents the significance those artefacts have traditionally had for the Eskimos themselves. But that is consistent with the possibility of understanding them, still in their native contexts, in ways in which the Eskimos themselves have not found it necessary to understand them, for example as expressions of psychological needs. It is also consistent, of course, with there being ways of understanding these artefacts in other (for example marketing) contexts which are not ways of understanding them in their native contexts. Grasping them in terms of the culturally alien practices of aesthetic appreciation and art-marketing is not to probe deeper into their significance in Eskimo culture.

In this latter respect the analogy would not support the view that the Greeks might well have found a theoretical use for the Descartes–Locke model; that is, that there was something there in the psychological life of ancient Greece, as perhaps wherever there is human life, that this way of talking might have effectively represented.

But Locke has indicated how the analogy, taken in the former way, might support the view none the less. He offers an explanation of why ideas based on inner sense have no strong influence on the language of everyday affairs. Before it 'turns in upon itself' and 'reflects on its own operations', the mind is first turned outward. The early years of a person's life 'are usually employed and diverted in looking abroad' and '[m]en's business in them is to acquaint themselves with what is to be found without; and so growing up in a constant attention to outward sensations, seldom make any considerable reflection on what passes within them, till they come to be of riper years; and some scarce ever at all'.[13]

Granted that the Greeks were more mature psychologists than this would allow, the point made here – and echoed two centuries later by Edmund Husserl – is that everyday life generates its own psychology and that, simply through lack of the appropriate reflection or interest, there may be fundamental concepts which it fails to take account of.

Might consciousness be such a concept? Well, if we take the first part of the above point first, it is fairly clear that ordinary psychological references manage very well without the terminology of 'consciousness'. It is true that the term occurs commonly enough in everyday language. When you faint you are said to lose consciousness and to regain it on 'coming to'. But ordinary (English) language doesn't provide for a consistent theory of consciousness. For instance, *not* having lost consciousness you cannot, in ordinary parlance, be said still to be in possession of it. The most you could say is that you *are* conscious, which on the other hand would be misleading unless there were some expectation that you might not be. In any case it seems natural, in view of the complex distinctions it has evolved to take care of, that everyday language should defy attempts to collect its terms into coherent concepts or to define neat symmetries and equivalences. Thus, though it might be a reasonable guess that 'conscious' means much the same as 'aware', you come up against the fact that you can be said to be conscious that something is wrong, unusual, or 'fishy' even though you are not aware just what it is. Or you can be said to be, or become, conscious of something you are definitely aware of, but only because up to now it has *not* been your immediate concern: a growing tension in the audience or a burning sensation in your elbow. And yet we say you can be happy in the consciousness that you have done the best you can just because

17

having done the best you can is what does currently occupy the centre of your mind.

One could conclude, then, that the terminology of 'consciousness' and its cognates has imposed itself on an everyday psychological vocabulary without particularly enriching it. These terms can just as well be replaced by others whose everyday logic better mirrors the relevant distinctions and possibilities of inference. As Ryle pointed out, the occasions when a person has lost consciousness are those in which it would be proper to say that they have been 'anaesthetized' or rendered 'insentient' in some way, so that on regaining consciousness the person is 'sentient' or 'sensitive' once more. Not having lost consciousness is not being still in possession of it, but simply to be responsive to 'slaps, noises, pricks, or smells'; while being or becoming conscious of something is more transparently described in terms of 'finding out', 'realizing', 'discovering', or 'heeding'. Similarly with 'self-conscious'. This expression is used both to refer to forms of shyness and affectation and also, in a wider sense, to 'indicate that someone has reached the stage of paying heed to his own qualities of character and intellect, irrespective of whether or not he is embarrassed about other people's estimations of them'.[14]

If we can not only cope without the terminology of consciousness but do better without it, what is to be gained by superimposing it on the rich though not overtly theoretical psychological vocabulary of everyday life? The fact that you can be 'conscious' of something in a way that implies you do *not* know what precisely it is may just show that ordinary language is far too subtle for any superimposed terminology to match, let alone improve upon. It is reasonable to assume that in the thousands of years of its evolution the vocabulary of lay psychology has generated distinctions answering to the various descriptive but not necessarily 'conscious' needs of those who have used it. Usage can have survived the needs in some cases, and along the way certain theoretical and ideological distinctions may have been superimposed on this still partly living inheritance, some being retained merely at the linguistic level out of sheer force of linguistic habit, others disappearing. But what gives the psycho-logical vocabulary its strength and flexibility may be precisely its ability to resist formalization, even at the level of the dictionary – a matter of its doing justice to a vast number of distinctions called for by a rich and complex cultural interaction. In that case, some will argue, insight into human mentality is to be found in or built upon the bedrock of daily linguistic practice, not in the alluvial deposits of superimposed theory or in any semblance of structure retrievable in the practice itself.

But the conversation of philosophers has by and large been a history of attempts of theories to exert their influence all the same. The Descartes–Locke conception of the mind as something to which the individual has direct and exclusive access is a case in point. This has become an everyday model of the 'mind' infecting our whole vocabulary. And yet we don't really know whether the fact that the conception is to be found in our ordinary ways of speaking is due *entirely* to the superimposition of theory, or whether the theory lingers because the facts as mirrored in our rich usage converge in this conception's direction. It may be that Rorty exaggerates the influence of the professionals and underestimates the weight of common sense. Be that as it may, the professionals have been busy in the last thirty to forty years putting their own weight behind the overturning of the Descartes–Locke conception.

One counter-'theory' has called for uncorrupted attention to ordinary linguistic practice. The basis for our understanding of mental phenomena is knowledge of extant mental concepts. Thus for Wittgenstein the nature of a mental phenomenon emerges through an investigation of what he called the 'grammar' of the corresponding mental-concept terms, where the reference language is that of ordinary speech untarnished by theory. The aim is to undermine the 'false pictures' that prevent people who are in their grip from understanding the subtleties of their actual use of the terms in question. Ryle campaigned similarly against the Cartesian–Lockean picture of the mind as a special kind of thing or place isolated from public view (the 'dogma of the Ghost in the Machine'),[15] insisting that '[t]o talk of a person's mind . . . is to talk of the person's abilities, liabilities and inclinations to do and undergo certain sorts of things, and of the doing and undergoing of these things in the ordinary world'.[16] Austin said that philosophical doctrines and dichotomies are due to 'an obsession with a few particular words . . . and a few (and nearly always the same) half-studied facts'. Austin's claim that 'ordinary words are much subtler in their uses, and mark many more distinctions, than philosophers have realized', and that 'the facts . . . as discovered by, for instance, psychologists but also as noted by ordinary mortals, are much more diverse and complicated than has been allowed for',[17] amounts, one might say, to a protest on behalf of the 'home' culture against sweeping conceptual innovations that lack any foundation in native ways and so distort and obscure the subtle meanings that those ways contain and which are the source of any truths pertaining to the native culture.

And yet this view might be seriously mistaken. Just as his daily preoccupations in a hard climate may make the Eskimo blind to the aesthetic aspects (and economic possibilities) or psychological meaning of Eskimo artefacts, the psychophysical subject may, by 'looking abroad' (as Locke says), be blind to facts of his own mental life. Some peculiarly philosophical form of reflection may be needed. An example is Husserl's distinction between the 'natural standpoint' which is sustained throughout 'our life of natural endeavour', and a point of view from which that standpoint is put out of action in order to bring into focus the fact that the contents of that standpoint form systems of meanings.[18] Such a shift of attention has no part in the everyday affairs of ordinary mortals; and to acquire their own data, empirical psychologists are forced to persist with the natural standpoint with its assumption of the factual existence of a mind-independent world 'out there'. It could be the case, therefore, that even if the Greeks were excellent psychologists, and their language contained all the distinctions they needed, their conception of the human mind nevertheless lacked something of theoretical importance that would have been available to them had they adopted the 'reflective' point of view which has given birth to a concept of consciousness as broad and general as our own.

Is there anything in the subsequent development of western philosophizing about mind, then, that we can say supplies what Greek philosophical psychology essentially lacked? Or, as Reid and Rorty suggest, has the effect of that development been largely deleterious? Five partly interconnected but also mutually antagonistic traditions can be discussed in this connection, which for convenience we shall term the *substantializing of the subject*, the *internalizing of the object*, the *distantiating of the subject from its mental modes*, the *empiricizing of the mental* (rather than of 'mind', that term being somewhat suspect here in view of its historical association with particularly the first two of these traditions), and the *eclipse of the first-person point of view*. A sixth possibility, which we could call the *first-personalizing of the world*, will be the focus of later chapters.

1 The substantializing of the subject

In Aristotle's hylomorphic account there is no substantial soul or mind. The human being is a special kind of organism, a rational animal; and what we now refer to as the 'mind' is the range of capacities an organism of that kind is good for. In Aristotelian terms the human soul is the form of the matter that has these capacities, and the capacities themselves, and so also the soul, can be witnessed both by observers and by the organisms themselves with no special privilege attached to the points of view of those actually exercising them. For obvious reasons, physicalists nowadays tend to regard this as a basically sound conception, since according to it mental functions are simply forms of physical activity. Subsequently, however, Aristotle's account was replaced by one in which the distinctively human features were attributed to the operations of distinct entities of which rational beings were composed. By treating what Aristotelians regarded as the differentiae of natural, living, sentient, and rational beings as actual elements in the composition of human beings, scholastic philosophers arrived at the classical substantial division of body, soul, and spirit.[19] The separation of the rational from the natural (biological and merely psychological) functions, each specified in terms of modes proper to its respective substance, placed the former in a realm of its own and gave credence to the idea of a supernatural, or spiritual, domain to which the human soul belonged and in which its essence was predetermined. In scholastic philosophy, the separable soul (and/or spirit) was conceived as a vantage-point above the natural, physical order from which a supernatural order could be imposed in thought or – in so far as knowledge of that order was not available to the 'light of natural reason' (*lumen naturale*) – at least in practice. In Neoplatonist and Plotinian versions like that of John Scotus Erigena (b. *c*. 810), the human being is an independent self, an ego, in touch with the spiritual world which is its real home and therefore eternal even when finite. Even in its finite incarnation it is not completely embodied, but with half a foot in eternity retains a transincarnational identity that allows it, in the cause of its own fulfilment, to undergo several incarnations (a belief banned by the Council of Constantinople). The substantializing of the rational faculties is usually associated with Descartes's dualism, in which (anticipating current trends in cognitive science) the biological, and also (it might be claimed) merely psychological,

functions are reduced to mechanisms belonging to physical substance, while the human spirit, the specifically human soul, becomes
the thinker of potentially rational thoughts, which if concerned with
rational ends must then be transformed by will into action against the
weight of natural disinclination.

The significance of the move from a hylomorphic to an elemental
analysis is that, by treating elements as 'substances' in what came to
be the traditional sense of what exists in its own right, it seemed
possible for human nature to retain its traditional theological
repertoire, notably freedom of choice and even immortality, in the
face of the encroachments of a mechanistic natural science. Allocating
the mind to a separate realm creates a terminological vacuum which
has to be filled with metaphors drawn from ordinary experience and
natural science. Apropos of Locke's choice of the word 'reflection' for
the mode of the self-conscious mind's operations, Ryle remarks: 'The
metaphor of "light" seemed peculiarly appropriate, since Galilean
science dealt so largely with the optically discovered world.' So the
term 'consciousness' could be 'imported to play in the mental world
the part played by light in the mechanical world', with the result that,
in this 'metaphorical' sense, the contents of the mental world could be
thought of as being 'self-luminous or refulgent'.[20] The Protestants

> had to hold that a man could know the moral state of his soul
> and the wishes of God without the aid of confessors and
> scholars . . . they spoke . . . of a God-given 'light' of private
> conscience. When Galileo's and Descartes' representations of
> the mechanical world seemed to require that minds should be
> salved from mechanism by being represented as constituting a
> duplicate world, the need was felt to explain how the contents of
> this ghostly world could be ascertained, again without the help
> of schooling, but also without the help of sense perception.[21]

Locke's notion of consciousness is that of the mind's reflective
awareness of its own operations (perceiving, thinking, doubting,
believing, reasoning, knowing, willing, etc.). This can be labelled the
mind's 'self-awareness'. But the reflective mind is understood in
another and much longer tradition as the ability of the human soul to
determine in some more deliberate way its own position in ethico-
religious space, to know where it falls short of human fulfilment. This
can be called 'self-reflection', not so much simply of the mind,
however, as of the subject itself. It is here that the light of private

conscience took over from the illumination previously thought to be available through publicly accredited bearers of revealed truth. In Hegel's *Geist*, Kierkegaard's *Aand*, implicitly in Heidegger's *Dasein*, and according to Heidegger himself explicitly in Husserl,[22] the reflexivity of the human mind is the notion of the human 'spirit' (and in Kierkegaard's case the 'self'),[23] which in general is the ability of the human being or mind to come up with specifications of its own nature; that is, 'self-understandings' in the form of appraisals of the overall standing or *worth* of its own mental and practical operations, in Kierkegaard's case not least the worth of its volitions. In general, consciousness as self-consciousness here forms a definitive cleft or hiatus in the causal structure of nature. The self-conscious subject is represented as a substance aware of its changing modes and therefore somehow separated from them and continuing through them, and also capable of actively ('freely') intervening in the world of physical processes, affecting the course of nature as far as control from the conscious level can exert an influence. In rationalist versions, the self's repertoire includes the ability also to subject its own response patterns to control from 'above' in the form of freely adopted principles, values, or goals which then govern the overall performance in a way that raises the subject (now properly an 'agent') above the deterministic influence of natural laws.

2   The internalizing of the object

However, the 'duplicate world' provided for the soul to save it from mechanism was not simply a world of substantial subjects. The 'inner world' also came to be furnished with its own special objects. The Galilean and Cartesian conception of the material world was one from which the world of the senses was excluded. According to Galileo, 'tastes, odours, colours' are nothing but 'names' that 'hold their residence solely in the sensitive body; so that if the animal were removed, every such quality would be abolished and annihilated'.[24] What we appreciate as the world of colour, sound, fragrance, the living personalities of our friends, the world of weal, woe, weather, and whereabouts, is located in subjective experience, while the physical universe itself lies impassively beyond, 'hard, cold, colourless, silent and dead'.[25] The inner light of consciousness thus came to shine on its own representation of this physical world rather than the physical world itself, on an inner world of 'ideas'. It is true that Locke distinguished between two sets of 'ideas': those that have sensation as their source and those of reflection which derive from 'inner sense', by which he meant the ability to form ideas of our own perceivings, thinkings, etc., and 'all the different actings of our own minds'. But although the former ideas are said to be due to bodies which impinge upon the senses (in the ways distinctive of 'ideas' of primary and secondary qualities), they too belong to the world of subjective experience and are properly classified as contents of our minds. One thus slides easily into an analysis of ideas of sensation which makes the having of sensation, too, a matter not of apprehending some quality of a mind-independent world, but of 'sensing' what has come imperceptibly *to* the mind.[26]

As for the mind-independent world itself, or Descartes's *res extensa*, the alternatives are Berkeley's expedient of denying its existence, Humean scepticism about the existence of an external world, or some form of representational theory like Descartes's own in which the mind-independent world is reflected in the individual mind in what would nowadays be called a world-model, a construct whose correspondence with reality Descartes himself tried to vindicate by logical reasoning from certain premisses, famously including the certainty that God exists and cannot deceive. Though not confined to Descartes's specifically rationalist form of foundationalism, this has been the conventional standpoint of philosophy since Descartes's formulation of the problem of the external world. It is a position from which it has proved difficult not to conclude that what we have in direct experience is access only to our own psychological states, which thus form a 'veil' intervening problematically between our conscious states and the 'outside' world – a world which common sense tells us is not 'outside' in that sense at all, but the directly perceptible environment with which we consciously interact. One way of reconstructing the history of modern philosophy from Descartes by way of the empiricists to Kant, Hegel, the pragmatists, and beyond is as a developing dialogue, or what Hegelians would call a dialectic, on this theme. The framework of the dialogue can be defined by its two end-points. One is the scepticism to which the *res cogitans* standpoint seems inevitably to lead when left unsupported by the scholastic principles resorted to by Descartes himself, and where the 'egocentric predicament' and solipsism stand as expressions of the radical failure of philosophy to provide a rational reconstruction of the everyday belief in the existence and availability of a common world. The other is the vindication of that everyday belief – of its coherence and truth – as part of a general understanding of the world, achieved (let it be noted) from the *res cogitans* standpoint. We shall return to this theme later.

3 The distantiating of the subject from its mental modes

Locke claims that 'the mind furnishes the understanding with ideas of its own operations' through an 'inner sense',[27] though unless one attends to those operations the ideas one has of them will be indistinct. The thesis is that a form of introspective awareness or self-knowledge accompanies every mental state. Objections to the thesis have not been wanting. Leibniz claimed that it involves an infinite regress: if every mental state is accompanied by self-knowledge, then self-knowledge, too, since it is a mental state, must be so accompanied, and so on without end.[28] If the regress is to be avoided, Locke's view must be interpreted in such a way that the awareness the mind has of its own operations is not just one more mental operation. Another objection is that, as Locke presents it, the thesis is consistent with the mind's operations existing as they are even without the accompaniment. Locke himself claims this is absurd; though, as noted above, he does allow that the awareness can be more or less cursory.[29] A third objection is to the implicit splitting of the mind into two, into the mental operation, say, of thinking about an apple, and, in addition to that and separately, that of noting the former operation. This makes introspection a second-order scanning process which again seems to imply that the first-order process could exist without it. This might lead one to conclude that the idea that there are two levels of consciousness – one the stream of ordinary experience of external stimuli, the other the monitoring of this by a second level of experience – is simply false.[30] One reason for this is that if, as seems intuitively correct, experience is unified, by being simultaneously observed the original operation is itself transformed, as presumably would also be the case in any change of the degree of attentiveness directed at it. In being observed, therefore, it is no longer the same operation, and consequently no mental operation in itself is ever genuinely noted, and introspection (as Locke's notion of an inner sense was later called) is thus an impossibility. The same difficulty may even be thought to apply if we appeal instead to something like instant retrospection, for even the very remembering of a mental operation that was not itself noted will distort the mental operation noted in memory.

And yet the facts of experience do seem to lend themselves to the kind of description Locke gives. We are indeed continually aware in some way and to some degree of the modes of our engagement with our surroundings. If we were not, as Reid pointed out, we could have no evidence of our mental states.[31] Retrospection could not give us knowledge of past mental states, since we could only retrospect that of which we had already been conscious. But then we are back where we began. If I can report my mental states only after having introspected them, what is the basis of my report that I have indeed introspected them? A further introspection? But then we have an infinite regress once more. However, if no further introspection is required it seems that the introspected mental state does not require a separate operation of introspection in order to be reportable.[32] But in that case what is it that reveals to us the content and cognitive mode of our engagement?

If, as seems clear, there is no future in an analysis of the mind's self-awareness in terms of a secondary mental operation of introspection, it seems that if we are to talk of conscious mental operations at all, the fact that they are conscious must be understood (as Sartre claims)[33] as some inherent feature of the operations themselves. Thus if we are to retain the idea of introspection as a distinctive mental operation, it can only be as just another form of engagement with the world, or more properly a form of disengagement or reflection, but as such a mental operation like any other. It cannot be an operation which brings the forms of our engagement to light, for these are already conscious in their own right. The mind can indeed reflect on its own operations, as Locke says.[34] But when I focus attention on what I am doing (e.g. running for a bus) I cease to be doing it in the same way, even if the action continues more or less automatically as before. What I can do when I reflect on my own mental operations is bring some relevant psychological scheme to bear on what I was and may still be doing though more or less automatically. Although the previous activity was not introspected, it was conscious all the same in the only sense, however we explicate it, in which any human operation can be conscious.

This is the gist of Sartre's notion of consciousness's inherent 'non-positional' awareness of itself;[35] functionally, it can be expressed negatively by saying that in order to know what you are doing at any time you do not have to find out, because – and this is the apparent peculiarity of conscious states – the information is already dispositionally present in an implicit form even when, and however single-mindedly, a person is 'looking abroad', whether engrossed in a novel or running frantically for a bus. Consciousness just is the presence of such information in some categorical form; that is, in some form other than that of data recoverable from an external source. What Locke calls reflection is, then, either one or both of two quite different things: the presence of such information already within our focused engagement with external things, whether traffic on the road or moves in a game of chess (the mind's self-awareness); or the focus we can bring to bear on our own mental operations in driving and playing chess (self-reflection). The latter can involve further self-reflective operations, some perhaps even more deserving of that name, for instance applying, and at an even higher level, critically appraising and perhaps revising, the conventional modes of describing the operations Locke refers to as perception, thinking, doubting, believing, reasoning, knowing, willing, etc.; but also – as in the 'spiritual' reflexivity noted above – appraising the overall patterns of our own purposive and moral performances. These two latter examples suggest that the proper model for analysing inwardly-directed modes of consciousness may be explication, or articulation, rather than reflection.[36]

Granting that the consciousness we have of our own mental modes is not something additional to the modes themselves, there may still be some common feature of conscious states, whether inwardly or outwardly directed, which distinguishes the consciousness we have of these and that of which we are conscious. Moore, concerned to oppose the idealist turn that makes the contents of consciousness features of consciousness itself, argued in this vein. Although Moore thought it unlikely that we can find some common element of consciousness, or a unitary act of consciousness, covering all that comes within that range, he thought there was a unitary notion covering some cases. If we take, say, consciousness of colours, there is something in the case where I see blue that occurs in just the same way when I see red:

> There is nothing more certain to me than that I do constantly
> see one colour at one time, and a different colour at a different
> time, and that, though the colours are different, I am conscious
> of both in exactly the same sense.

27

Moore concludes that '[t]here is . . . always a distinction between *what* I am conscious of and *my consciousness* of it'.[37] From this he inferred that colours themselves are not mental, the word 'mental' being reserved for the consciousness that is distinct from what it is consciousness of. Although Moore himself resists the suggestion, there seems no reason, if cases of seeing two colours involve consciousness in exactly the same sense, why seeing any two different things at all, say a sunset and a bottle of beer, should not also involve consciousness in exactly the same sense. From there one might go on to include objects of different sense modes, as different, say, as someone's listening to Beethoven's Ninth and a ballet dancer's proprioceptive awareness of his own body configuration. One could then postulate a unitary factor, a single sense of 'consciousness', in all conscious activity.

A reason for not extending the range in these ways would be that consciousness, although to be distinguished quite generally from its objects, has modes of its own, as Moore himself implies in referring to specific 'mental acts' and 'acts of consciousness' (e.g. believing something, thinking about it without believing it, being pleased or displeased about something, deciding to do something).[38] It would then be to abstract beyond the empirical contents of acts of consciousness to talk of a unitary *consciousness* present in every case. On the other hand, it might be argued that it is already an abstraction to talk of the consciousnesses of red and of blue as involving a common element of consciousness, for all that there is in the experiences themselves to indicate a common feature of any kind is the fact that their objects are both instantiations of the abstract notion of colour. In that case, even if acts of consciousness can be classified in terms of their modes, there is just as good a reason for saying that two acts of consciousness in different modes are acts of the same, unitary consciousness as there is for saying this in the case of two acts in the same mode (e.g. colour) but with different objects (e.g. red and blue).

Another way in which acts of consciousness may be unified, also discussed by Moore,[39] is in respect of an alleged sense in which each such act is experienced as being an act of the conscious subject in question: the 'mineness' of my acts of consciousness. In this case the unifying principle obviously transcends all differences of mode of acts of consciousness. But the question again arises: Is there anything in an act of consciousness that provides a purchase on the idea of such a

28

resemblance? According to Hume the answer is no. Whenever he consulted his own experience he always found a 'perception' but never anything more than that, not for example a substantial ego in which the perception inhered or to which it belonged.[40] Hume's empiricism, of course, commits him to having to look for his self among original, discrete impressions, and that restriction logically guarantees that no substantial self will be found behind these. However, since the empiricist tradition treated consciousness as a composition of elements (ideas), which the mind worked on much as computers work on isolable data, it lacked the resources to find a self within the domain of conscious experience. Thus empiricist psychology creates insuperable problems for any account of what our actual impressions may incline us to describe not in the punctate terms of atomic ideas but as an unbroken continuity and seamless whole. How can 'moments' of consciousness relate to or constitute a 'flow' of consciousness? How indeed do the parts of a moment of consciousness form a whole moment? Are moments aggregations, i.e. with 'parts' as 'elements', or are the parts internally related to one another – so that they are what they are only in virtue of each other and the mutual relations of the parts?

Kant provided one kind of answer. At first sight a substance in which individual 'perceptions' can inhere might seem the only option available for an atomist psychology, as far as accounting for the unity of consciousness is concerned. But Kant, who accepted Hume's criticism of the notion of a mental substance as well as inheriting his atomist psychology, came up with an alternative: the formal 'I think' that must accompany all 'representations' if the latter are to amount to contents of thought.[41] Kant agreed with Hume that the deliverances of inner sense were 'merely empirical, and always changing': 'No fixed and abiding self can present itself in this flux of inner appearances.' What Kant was looking for was a *necessary* numerical identity in the flux, and since with Hume he rejected the idea that necessity can present itself in experience, 'to render such a transcendental presupposition valid, there must be a condition which precedes all experience, and which makes experience itself possible'.[42] This Kant found in the 'universal proposition "I think" ', in the form of an 'I' that accompanies all thought.[43] This, the transcendental unity of apperception, performed both the functions Hume's theory failed to provide for: it collected the parts of a moment of consciousness into the whole that the moment must be if it is to have

29

the structure needed for it to count as a moment of conscious *thought*; and it seemed to provide a formal unity of the moments of thought accompanied by the same 'I think'.[44] It did the former by showing how experiences are possible only because they are syntheses formed with certain structures (employing categories such as substance and causation which Hume had notoriously found no room for); and it did the latter by collecting the otherwise causal and quite contingent sequence of conscious contents under the same formal principle, which once the experiences are there provides the self-identity of a subject of experience. Kant's reply to Hume is, in effect, that when I consult my own experience I am already under the formal unity of the bare concept of consciousness.

The 'I' of Kant's 'I think' is not a thing or substance; 'we cannot even say that [the simple, and in itself completely empty, representation "I"] is a concept . . . only that it is a bare consciousness [the mere form of consciousness] which accompanies all concepts'.[45] Clearly, such an empty, merely formal subjectivity cannot distinguish you from me; the ego here is transcendental and the unity it is alleged to provide too abstract to separate actual biographical sequences of experience. The same is true of Husserl's transcendental ego, the subject of all first-hand experience (mental contents) revealed as a 'new realm of transcendental subjectivity' to phenomenological reflection in the '*epoché*' in which the actual world is treated as 'transcendent' to a sphere of meaning, so that the objective existence of things, persons, etc. in the surrounding world is taken not as a fact to be argued or assumed, but as part of what is meant or 'intended' by 'things', 'persons', etc. With the Cartesian 'cogito' and Descartes's methodological doubt in mind, Husserl says we mustn't assume that 'with our apodictic pure ego, we have rescued a little *tag-end of the world*, as the sole unquestionable part of it for the philosophizing Ego. . . . This Ego, with his Ego-life, who necessarily remains for me, by virtue of [the] *epoché*, is not a piece of the world'.[46] On the contrary, the world – the phenomenological world of meanings – is 'inside' the transcendental ego; Husserl describes this ego, from the point of view of whose 'new realm' the 'transcendence' of the world is 'part of the intrinsic sense of the world', as bearing 'within him' (*sic*) the world 'as an accepted sense'. The ego is transcendental because necessarily presupposed by this latter.[47]

There is an important parallel between Kant and Husserl. For both, the immediate object of consciousness is some analogue of

Humean perceptions in which it is possibilities of an abstract ego that are realized rather than of the natural world. For Kant the world of experience is still only a world of mind-structured phenomena; the things-in-themselves are radically 'transcendent' as pre-structured and thus inconceivable causes of the pre-synthesized manifold. While, though, Husserl's 'transcendent' reality is closer to home, so to speak, in that it is in some sense a product of the contents of the 'realm of transcendental subjectivity', the 'being of the pure ego and his [*sic*] *cogitationes*, as a being that is prior in itself, is antecedent to the natural being of the world'.[48] Behind this bias in favour of the subject is Hume's observation that experience in itself discloses neither a subjective nor an objective principle for unifying discrete experiences (in the form of personal identity on the one hand and causal necessity on the other). For Kant these are indeed provided in the form of principles of synthesis prior to and necessary for experience itself; while for Husserl experience is transformed in the *epoché* into a realm of meaning which is assumed from the start to be correlative to a subject whose meanings they are, and out of which the world of things-in-themselves is 'constituted'. Consciousness is now the lens through which the world becomes manifest, and the forms of its manifestation are necessarily 'mental' in some sense other than that in which the mind and the operations whereby it grasps the world are the topic of scientific psychology.

The primary exponent of this kind of view is of course Hegel. But Hegel's philosophy contains a revolutionary amendment in relation to the Kantian and Husserlian versions. It says that experience does indeed disclose unifying principles and that these are no less properly regarded as principles of natural being than as principles projected on nature by the acts of an ego. Indeed they are the same. Hegel's *Geist*, though it preserves the transcendental status of Kant's 'I think' and Husserl's 'reduced' and 'purified' ego, is the specification of a project which has as its goal the realization of the essential identity of substance and subject, or in Hegel's terms, of the 'in-itself' and the 'for-itself'. Substance – lost to philosophy since Hume, although retrieved by Kant in the form of a pure concept of the understanding[49] – was restored to concrete reality by Hegel but now in the context of the Aristotelian contrast between possibility and actuality. The subject in Hegel is not a substantial self from the start; indeed Hegel doesn't usually talk of individual subjects of experience but of subjectivity. And when he does talk of the particular 'I' it is in negative terms as something abstract.[50] Substances in the human sphere are socio-political orders, or organizing principles capable of self-subsistence in the face of 'subjective opinion and caprice'.[51] Typically their self-subsistence or substantiality is founded on institutions which are their external expressions, though in the case of some institutions such as married and family life substantiality is expressed only inwardly in the form of a spiritual bond.[52] The crucial substantiality for Hegel is that of the state, of which two radically contrasted kinds are the despotic state, which exerts absolute power over its subjects, and the modern, diversified state in which subjects, now citizens, by learning their relationship to it, realize its role in conserving universal interests. In this, as Hegel characteristically puts it, the *state* 'knows what it wills and knows it in its universality, i.e. as something thought'.[53] In this way socio-political reality, composed of Hegelian substances, becomes subjective, though of course in the process the subjectivity expressed in individual (educated) minds has ceased to be merely capricious and the subjectivity of substance is inherently rational. The process encapsulates Hegel's notion of *Geist* as the goal of history: namely 'Substance [being] essentially Subject'.[54]

The significance of Hegel's revolutionary amendment is first of all that it offers one way of vindicating the everyday belief in the existence and availability of a common world. Kant's noumena are brought in from the cognitive cold of inconceivability, and the world no longer 'transcends' the level of meanings in any more problematic sense than that in which objects in the world do not depend for their existence on the presence of individual minds. The solution looks far-fetched in so far as it depends on a form of knowledge (Hegel's 'science' – really just a substitute for the guarantee of knowledge given by Descartes's God) in which the 'antithesis' of subject and object is in principle (at least in its epistemologically problematic respects) dissolved in a kind of return of both to the status of unmoved mover;[55] but an advantage of the framework in which the closing of this circle is described is that it at least provides a possibility of an account of human knowledge in terms of the involvement of consciousness within, rather than inescapably apart from, the world of its objects.

But there is another important aspect of Hegel's treatment of consciousness. For Hegel consciousness becomes self-consciousness when it sees itself as a centre of control over the body (thereby becoming a substantiality), and thus by extension no longer in continuity with the environment and 'externality'.[56] Consciousness is conscious of *it*self in the sense that its relation to the environment is something it can, and in a sense must, ask questions about. This is a form of reflection properly so called which, as noted above, adds to Locke's 'inner sense' the capacity to identify and judge the status or worth of its current mental operations, in other words its forms of engagement with the world. For Hegel the emergence of such questions heralds the opportunity to arrive at satisfactory answers in terms of 'science' or the self-knowledge of substance; but in post-Hegelian philosophy (characterized most generally by a criticism of Hegel's 'scientific' ideal of a substance that is 'essentially subject') this capacity for self-determination acquires a different significance. In Kierkegaard, for example, Hegel's notion of spirit as reflection becomes the basis of the trials in which the subject is exposed to and tries to efface the challenges of absolute individuality before God.[57] In Heidegger it becomes 'existence', a structural feature of *Dasein*, an 'entity which does not just occur among other entities [but r]ather . . . is distinguished by the fact that, in its very being, that being is an *issue* for it'.[58] And in Sartre it is the *pour-soi* (Hegel's 'subject') which lacks substantial being but in bad faith perpetually seeks to present itself to itself as having such being.[59]

With Sartre our historical sketch of the role provided for consciousness in the context of the mind's 'duplicate world' comes full circle. The duplicate world, according to Ryle, was invented to safeguard freedom from the encroachments of mechanistic science. In the absence of sense perception it needed the inner light of reflective consciousness to illuminate it. For Sartre there is no duplicate world of the mind for the light of consciousness to shine upon. The world of common experience is the only one there is, and there is no substantial self, or ego, whose product the duplicate world could be. The 'self' indeed becomes just another 'object' *for* consciousness and no longer its subject.[60] That means that self-consciousness is not the consciousness a *self* has of itself but the consciousness that consciousness has of itself. But since consciousness, because it lacks a nature, is nothing, neither can it – any more than Kant's purely formal 'I think' – be an object of, or for, itself. As noted earlier, consciousness for Sartre is only 'non-positionally' aware of itself in its engagement with the world, or reflectively in its engagement with that engagement. That, for Sartre, is the truth of what Locke described in terms of the mind's perceptions of its own operations. For Sartre consciousness is nothing also in another sense: it exists only in its engagement with the world. Consciousness is not an independent dimension of reality, a level proximal to the first-person point of view and in problematic relation to a distal world; it is how the world itself is made to appear from particular first-person points of view. As for the 'I', there is no need for consciousness to embody this first-personal reference; consciousness is 'pre-personal' and emerges only 'at the level of humanity' as but one aspect of the 'me', what Sartre not too perspicuously calls the 'active aspect'.[61] On the other hand, freedom *is* preserved. Having no nature, consciousness, in radical opposition to the inert in-itself (Hegel's substance) of the world, is unlimitedly spontaneous. Though constrained by the 'facticities' of its confinement to the real world, at least its interpretations of the situations it finds itself in are entirely its own responsibility. In a way there is also still room here for the metaphor of light. The world as it is for the for-itself of consciousness is the in-itself illuminated by the classifications and evaluations that the for-itself imposes on it in its constitution of a world of its own activity.

4 The empiricizing of the mental

Sartre's account, like Hegel's, can be seen as part of Reid's project of ridding philosophical psychology of 'clouds' and 'phantoms' due to the inner-eye model and the compositional kind of analysis that stems from the substantializing, internalizing, and distantiating tendencies outlined above. However, far from putting consciousness itself in that category, these philosophers treat the notion as fundamental. Hegel's Absolute is the merging of subjectivity (consciousness) with the independent being of things, while a demythologized consciousness's continual confrontation with an independent world is the basis of Sartrean philosophy. But some philosophers, notably Heidegger and James, have treated consciousness itself as another cloud or phantom. There is a sense, however, in which both, sensitive to the distorting influences we have mentioned, overstate their case. We shall examine Heidegger's rejection of the terminology of 'consciousness' later, merely observing here that since he considered the term itself a product of the inner-eye model, he felt the associations it gave rise to were bound to be misleading.

The same is partly true of William James. James praised empiricists (especially Hume and the German philosopher and psychologist

Johann Friedrich Herbart) for making 'the Self an empirical and verifiable thing', but complained that they had 'neglected certain more subtle aspects of the Unity of Consciousness'.[62] Not the unity of the concept, be it noted, but of consciousness itself. James was in effect arguing that the empiricists had not been empirical enough. He argued against the 'pulverization' of experience in British empiricism, its atomistic 'ideas' being intellectual abstractions. In experience itself we have no sense of isolated parts but of indeterminate continuity. Moments of consciousness occur to us as continuations of narratives that have begun in the past.[63] And because consciousness is a continuous stream, no phase in it can be separated entirely from its predecessors and successors. Although James wrote: 'I believe that "consciousness" . . . is the name of a nonentity and has no right to a place among first principles', he meant not that the term had no empirical reference but that it had come to mean 'a mere echo', a pure consciousness behind the verifiable facts, or, if you like, a kind of medium this side of the facts into which the facts do not reach and so lose their verifiability – that one should look instead to 'its pragmatic equivalent in realities of experience'.[64]

James believed that these realities could best be captured by introducing the conception of a 'primal stuff', to be called 'pure experience', so that 'knowing can easily be explained as a particular sort of relation towards one another into which portions of pure experience may enter', and where the relation itself is 'a part of the experience'.[65] The position closely resembles Hume's in aiming to eliminate entities not analytically reducible to portions of experience-in-relation, except that for James the relations can just as well join as separate the elements, and the relations themselves are as much matters of direct experience as the elements.[66]

> All the experiential facts find their place in this description unencumbered with any hypothesis save that of the existence of passing thoughts or states of mind.[67] . . . It is impossible to discover any *verifiable* features in personal identity, which this sketch does not contain, impossible to imagine how any transcendent non-phenomenal sort of Arch-Ego . . . could shape matters to any other result . . . than just this production of a stream of consciousness, each 'section' of which should know, and knowing, hug to itself and adopt, all those that went before, – thus standing as the *representative* of the entire past stream . . . [68]

Since the physical world had to be dealt with in the same way, the procedure parallels the view that came to be known as 'neutral monism' (shared by Mach and Russell), according to which the physical world and the mental are *sui generis* constructs out of experiential atoms (sensations) that are neither physical nor mental.[69] Actually, in spite of his reference to a 'primal stuff', James denied that experience itself formed a level of some basic kind of neutral material out of which mind and matter proper are constructed. In this he was furthering his criticism of the empiricists for being insufficiently empirical. But formally his view follows neutral monism in that object and subject are different organizations of the 'primal stuff' or 'pure experience' which forms 'the instant field of the present'. In one organization you can get a personal biography, in another the history of, say, a house.[70]

Consciousness, on this view, is not the same as experience. The notion of consciousness seems perplexing because there is a tendency to think of it as something special or substantial, 'a special stuff or way of being' – something that gets in the way of the things we perceive. Instead James says that consciousness is 'a kind of external relation'. 'The peculiarity of our experiences, that they not only are, but are known, which their "conscious" quality is invoked to explain, is better explained by their relations – these relations themselves being experiences – to one another'.[71] The common-sense belief that our experiences are our own in a sense captured by the metaphor of ownership improves on Hume's account, in which all we can say we are is a bundle of perceptions. But it suggests an 'arch-ego' behind the perceptions, the non-empirical substance of which they are accidents. James thinks he can improve on the common conception. The owner is present

> in the shape of something not among the things collected, but superior to them all, namely, the real, present onlooking, remembering, 'judging thought', or identifying 'section' of the stream. This is what collects, – 'owns' some of the past facts it surveys, and disowns the rest, – and so makes a unity that is actualized and anchored . . . [72]

James's view is 'Cartesian' in the sense of seeing lived experience as the closest kind of reality we have access to. Indeed in a certain sense we *are* such experiences. But unlike Descartes's view it is essentially monist, though the monism is not of the substance

36

variety. The conjunctive models available to the first-person vantage-point are taken to apply to all of reality. The view is therefore also idealist; though unlike Hegel's idealism it is reductive. One way of putting it is to say that James adds an ontological primacy to the epistemological primacy already conferred on consciousness by Descartes, both world (or matter) and self (or mind) being composite concepts generated out of the more fundamental notion of experience itself. This too might be called a way of vindicating the every-day belief in the accessibility of a shared world from the *res cogitans* standpoint. It ascribes to conscious states a fundamental role both in the knowledge of reality and in the constitution of reality itself.

We must be cautious, however, about calling it a first-person view. If what is implied by calling an approach first- rather than third-personal is that it takes the subject of experience to be epistemo-logically and also perhaps ontologically prior, then since the point of James's view appears to be that the subject of experience is a derivative notion, as also that of an object of experience, on his view these labels will mark a distinction made within the view and so not available for characterizing the kind of view itself. Indeed the same might be said, though not in quite the same way, of Hegel's and Sartre's views. After all, Hegel's 'subject' is a generalized subjectivity, and Sartre's consciousness is pre-personal, not a transcendental ego but a 'transcendental field'.[73] The fact that the notion of personal identity is, respectively, transcended in or eliminated from their specifications of consciousness makes it at least less apposite to call their views first-personal.

But two provisional points can be made here. First, it might be argued against James (as Kierkegaard argued against Hegel) that the 'purity' of the foundation upon which his account is based is itself just a new 'phantom', literally empty in the sense of being an abstraction from what is genuinely present in experience from the very start; that the domain is already constituted in a way that from the outset renders appropriate the ordinary use of personal pronouns and indexical terms. Where there is experience there is a subject of experience, and there is something the experience is of: presence is necessarily presence *for* and presence *of*.[74] Similarly, Sartre's attempt to remove the first-person pronoun from its position as the logical subject of consciousness and to let it first appear in the guise of an object of reflection is exposed to the objection that in spontaneous experience there is nevertheless a sense of awareness of the self right from the start.[75]

Second, and regardless of these objections of over-abstraction, there is a distinction to be drawn between a first- and a third-person approach which places the above accounts firmly in the first-person camp all the same. However fundamental or absolute you take the concept of experience to be, the concept does carry with it the notion of its opposite. How that opposite is to be characterized is another question. One way is to say that it is the object of experience; another would be to say that it is simply what lies beyond experience, and that might mean – as it typically does – what we do nevertheless experience but which being objective also transcends experience, or it might mean simply what transcends experience in a way that implies that it is never experienced. Given this rough conceptual opposition, we can say that a first-person approach to the human faculties is one that takes the perspective of experience, with or without an I, as providing access to facts and categories essential and sufficient to an adequate account of the nature of human mentality and of its relation to nature. The first-person approach enters the arena through the door marked 'experience'. Having done so it stays there. Typical of the outcomes of the conversations of the philosophers, most of whom have entered the arena through this door, is that they find it hard, if not impossible, to do justice to what lies beyond. Their problem is epitomized in Fichte's conclusion that the 'not-I' is something the self-conscious ego itself must posit.[76] Neutral monism, in spite of its attempt to get behind the I–other distinction, can only bring the other in on the I's own terms; and even Sartre's attempt to make do with a rock-bottom analysis that sets *pour-soi* and *en-soi* in permanent confrontation with each other looks like a refusal to face a residual issue about the status of the world in which human faculties arise.

5 *The eclipse of the first-person point of view*

Radically opposed to approaches which only begin once the door of experience has been entered is another and increasingly more potent source of innovative theory which denies that it has to enter that door at all: namely scientific psychology, or more generally the collection of diverse investigations now called cognitive science. Here, we have unambiguous third-personalism. If philosophy may be said to impose theory on ordinary discourse from 'above', cognitive science is out to subvert it theoretically from 'below'. The goal here is to arrive at a unified theory of human mentality based on models which simulate purposive behaviour. Theoretical as well as technical advances in cognitive science challenge not only the Descartes–Locke tradition in philosophical psychology, but also the everyday assumption that the primary explanations of human behaviour are those that non-specialist people themselves give in terms of desires, fears, beliefs, hopes, goals, passing moods, and so on. For, of course, on the common-sense view the causes and therefore explanations of human behaviour are events or states which are quite obviously 'conscious', even if that rather special term is not one that people would commonly think of applying to them. Actually, what the models that are so successful in cognitive science enable students of human behaviour to do is recreate in a purely physical medium, from scratch, and with all the explanatory tools on the table, performances that invite serious comparison with the way human beings cope in general with their environments, as well as with the way some humans cope with certain very specialized and rule-bound activities, as for instance in playing chess. Within that range, it can look as if the middle ground of ordinary, 'conscious' believing, desiring, hoping, and so forth – the area of the so-called 'propositional attitudes' or 'intentionality' – can simply be dispensed with for the purposes of a scientific psychology, or of whatever science eventually provides the relevant basic concepts and principles.

Once you have mastered the principles of purposive response in general in purely physical terms, and then shown that they can be applied to quite specific tasks, it might look as if there were no explanatory role left over for these conscious states; or, as those who follow this line would probably want to put it, there is no explanatory role left over for whatever it is that makes us want to say that the states in question are conscious. There are several kinds of consideration that physicalists may appeal to in support of this view of things. First, they may argue that if there are such states then they are at least also physical, and if they are to play any part in scientific explanation it will be in regard to that aspect, and not to their being 'self-luminous' or 'refulgent'. Second, they may argue, more conservatively, that although lay psychology may indeed function quite adequately for the kinds of explanation needed in everyday life (explaining why someone has gone to the doctor, is looking pleased, is sulking, and so on), there is nothing here of interest for a scientific psychology once you see that the principles governing purposive or responsive behaviour in general can be exemplified in non-conscious mechanisms. A third, behavioural argument says that, whatever limited access persons may have to their own mental processes through introspection, the fact that they can introspect these states has no explanatory role since the states themselves are primarily dispositions to behave, and it is behavioural responses to publicly determinable stimuli that provide the empirical content for our mental concepts.

What may be granted in the light of developments in cognitive science is that intelligence is not as closely linked to consciousness and the propositional attitudes as has traditionally been supposed. Some may even hypothesize that there are forms of intelligence – pure intelligence perhaps – which are only hindered if filtered through consciousness and the propositional attitudes. A science devoted to intelligence might then regard human intelligence as an inferior example, and ignore the conscious and propositional versions in the interests of uncovering the basic principles of intelligent performance. But then we are no longer interested in *human* psychology. It is quite another thing, of course, to claim that consciousness and the propositional attitudes are not crucial features of human intelligence. Prima facie it is unlikely on evolutionary grounds that the existence of conscious mental states plays no role at all in the production of human (or, in general, animal) behaviour. The ascent from simple sensation through emotion and feeling to the (themselves hierarchically structured) propositional attitudes looks, to minds attuned to things evolutionary, very much like an ontogenetic series rehearsing the stages of a phylogenetic development. If it proved possible to reproduce the human's power of control over its environment mechanically, that in itself would not show that human beings themselves control their environment according to mechanical principles. All it would show is that the same results can be achieved in that way, which still leaves unanswered the questions of why nature selected the conscious way, what specific contributions the consciousness of (some) mental states have made to the survival of the species, and what contributions they still make to sustaining human control over the environment, as well as how they make these contributions.

While physicalist psychology, for the kinds of reason mentioned above, tends nevertheless to be confident of its ability to capture the essentials of human intelligence, or 'sapience', it is otherwise with 'sentience', or more generally the fact of lived experience. The qualitative aspect of human mentality seems to stand stubbornly in the way of a totally physicalist vision, and for this reason sensations have become the focus of much intricate debate. Physicalists naturally tend to treat this area as the ground where the issue between physicalists and dualists or other brands of mentalist is finally to be fought out. And their approach has been to show that sentience or lived experience plays no basic role in the explanation of how humans cope with their environments. They may or may not be right in this. But the approach underestimates the repercussions for our general view of things of the kind of analysis we give of the sentient aspects of human life, amongst other things our view of what constitutes an environment. In that case, sensations may be very far from being the hopeless last ditch from which dualists and their ilk defend a dying cause.

Since our own approach here is to take up and assess the challenge of those who deny the importance of the first-person point of view, we can appropriately begin our review at the point where the challengers themselves believe their case is to be decided.

CHAPTER III

Quality of Experience

The mentalist is often portrayed as defending his position by means of a 'hollow shell' strategy. This says that however well computers perform *as if* they really grasped, meant, or cared about things, they do not genuinely do so, because a necessary ingredient for doing these things, for example consciousness, is missing. Other candidates for the missing factor are intentionality, a first-person point of view, free will, and emotion.[1] One view that protagonists of these ingredients may take is to say that this concedes too much to the opposition, on the grounds that computers are still a long way from reproducing human performance *in vivo*. They may therefore propose the 'poor substitute' strategy. This claims that computers are just unable, as a plain matter of fact, to emulate human performance.

But both strategies have their weaknesses. The former exposes the mentalist to the charge of fetishism. As the principle of computer modelling proves increasingly fruitful, physicalists demand to be shown what it is about consciousness, or whatever, that fails to be captured by current theories of cognitive ability, or why such an elusive factor should undermine the strong claims of these theories already to provide convincing explanations of human cognitive performance.[2] When so much within this province seems explainable without recourse to conscious mental states or processes, those who still insist on there being some explanatory role for such states to play are suspected of 'an obsession which, at least since Freud, we have no reason to honor'.[3] As for the alternative, this, although it may seem to have the universally applauded result of exposing either party to empirical refutation, commits the mentalist to the view that the mentalist position will actually have been refuted by some determinable degree of isomorphy between computer and *public* human performance, whereas a mentalist may reasonably want to insist indefinitely, as the hollow-shell approach helps him to, that what is to all outward appearances a human performance need not necessarily be genuinely so.

However, rather than risk the charge of apriorism by reverting to the hollow-shell approach, the mentalist may choose a third option. Both the hollow-shell and the poor-substitute strategies are consistent with the assumption that computational models of the mind have got it right so far. A bolder strategy is simply to deny this and claim that the modellers have been wrong from the start.

A full-scale implementation of this strategy would require two things: on the one hand, a critique of the computational approach itself, exposing its own apriorism, for instance, and the generally speculative nature of inquiries into the nature of mental design; and on the other, a positive case for the claims of the missing ingredient. The aim would be to strengthen the case for the ingredient as a structural component of human mentality (whether one wants also to call it 'genuine' mentality is perhaps another and not immediately relevant question). My own strategy in the remaining chapters of this book will be to focus exclusively on the second of these requirements.

I emphasize the strategic, even tactical, nature of the enterprise. There is clearly no room in a work of this size to argue anything like a comprehensive case for the importance of consciousness in an adequate conception of the human mind, even less for a detailed criticism of the sophisticated arguments that exist for the computational and other physicalist approaches. What this and the following chapters aim to do is to flex the theoretical possibilities of the concept of consciousness in order to make it less obvious that the mentalist case is based on an obsession with notions that are being increasingly shown to be theoretically redundant. We shall begin here with sensation, which may be regarded as a minimal form of consciousness, and then proceed via the claims made, first, for the unity of consciousness and, second, for its representational function, together with questions of the ontological status of conscious experience, to the unfashionable and anti-functionalist idea of human performance itself being unified by conscious control 'from the top'. Then, finally, we shall consider the role of conscious experience within social reality and its implications for moral life.

Sensations provide a convenient point of entry to the problem of consciousness as I have chosen to address it. They are, in the first place, strangely ambiguous in their subject–object polarity. It is not just that what we might properly call sensations range from objective phenomenal properties of 'outside' things (taste, colour, pitch, cold, heat, pain, fragrance, hardness, softness, roughness, etc.) to properties which have a merely phenomenal being (pleasures and pains, passions such as anger and fear, moods of sadness, rejoicing, restlessness, listlessness, bodily cold, hunger, thirst, etc.); but rather that considered in themselves they may be taken to form a single category of, let us say, modes of sentience, which are in themselves indeterminate as to whether the properties in question are or are not to be assigned to 'external' objects. Facts or not, they are at least categorical. This is not to say that they cannot be analysed partly as dispositions, or as being in this or that causal relation to something else. But it is to say that, whatever dispositional or causal properties they may possess, there is still some subjectively determinable episode, event, or period which is the occurrence of whatever has those other properties. William James used the Latin 'quale' (plural 'qualia') to refer to a determinable quality of feeling or sensation.[4] A quale is a quality as it appears to consciousness – the redness that is part of our experience when we see something red, the painful feeling we have when in a state of pain. Qualia are a problem for functionalist psychology.

Unlike behaviourism, functionalism postulates mental states in causal interaction with environmental stimuli and behavioural responses. In this it seems evidently an improvement on behaviourism. But by defining mental states in terms of causal relations, functionalism seems to avoid any essential reference to those categorical events, such as felt pains, which are the instantiations of modes of sentience. Functionalism defines, that is to say identifies, pain with a certain complex, 'functional' state defined in terms of its causal relations to 'inputs, outputs, and other mental states'.[5] It is not clear where the causal links specific to a given mental state are held to begin, but they will include in the case of pain such things as bodily trauma (e.g. damage to tissue) and reactions including any remedial behaviour, as well as whatever mental states combine to cause the organism to make that response follow from the input, including presumably also those fairly stable states which make the organism sensitive to this among other environmentally available stimuli. The main problem, however, is that the qualitative aspect of the functional state, or the experience itself, seems, to put it somewhat paradoxically, to fall between the stools provided by the analysans. Paradoxically because you would think that an analysis of sensations would put the stools firmly under the experiences and leave the *relations* to fall between them.

The crux and potential crisis of functionalism, then, is its theoretical indifference to the nature and constitution of whatever it is that stands in the defining causal relations. In terms of the hollow-shell metaphor, we are asked to ignore the inside and look to the shell in order to pick out the mind and its states. That the consequences are critical emerges in what have been labelled the 'absent qualia' problem and the problem of 'inverted spectra'. Take the former. In the human case, suitably located bodily injury elicits its typical behavioural responses to the accompaniment of a feeling of pain. But conceivably the relations defining the mental state of pain could remain the same with some other accompaniment, for instance a non-located sound or perhaps a smell, but also with no qualitative accompaniment at all. The problem of 'absent qualia' is, then, the implication of functionalism that the kind of organization it defines as the essentially mental can be realized in physical systems that lack the qualitative characteristics of human psychology. According to one thought-experiment, the kind of organization functionalism takes to be the quintessence of mind, including the human version, can be realized in a population the size of China's, individuals being linked in suitable ways to each other and to an artificial body.[6] The idea of a unified conscious state finds no home in this conception. If China can be in pain, it must be without the benefit or accompaniment of the *feeling* of pain. As for the second problem, if the only properties relevant for defining mental states are the causal relations mentioned, then the visual sensation that is normally reckoned part of what it is to see a ripe tomato may in my case depart radically from yours. Thus, although the stimulus conditions which evoke in me the quality I call 'redness' may evoke just the same verbal response in you, the quality could be what I would call 'greenness', since our chromatic responses are determined by a mutual inversion of the colour spectrum.

These difficulties may remind us at first sight of the problems facing Cartesians in connection with the existence of other minds, and Wittgensteinians in dealing with the loopholes of lying and mimicry in trying to do justice (e.g. with the help of Strawson's notion of behavioural criteria that are 'logically adequate') to Wittgenstein's famous remark that '[a]n "inner process" stands in need of outward criteria'.[7] But the situation is in fact quite different. With Descartes's dichotomy it was still possible to postulate the unaccounted-for or unknowable item (on Descartes's view the essential mental factor); what we were left with was doubt about whether in the given case there was such an item, or, if so, whether it was just the one we were led to believe. Here, however, since what we *are* able to account for in terms of causal roles is what *defines* the mental, the qualitative aspect drops out of the picture altogether.

For the general run of mental performance, functionalism might seem a very plausible approach. It ensures that mental states are revealed for what they are in (to use Sprigge's useful phrase) their causal ambiences.[8] And it is certainly true that for a wide range of cases mental states are appropriately defined in terms of their input–output patterns. Perceptual beliefs can be identified by their causal roles in maintaining appropriate matchings with their 'objects'. Beyond their simply occurring, as behaviourists would have it, functionalism sees the matchings as manifestations of a state of the organism which has the relevant cause-and-effect pattern as its 'essence'. To perceive a tree is to be in the relevant causal matching circumstances in regard to a tree. That might seem to make sense. Moreover, as far as sensations, our present topic, are concerned, these can hardly be said to play a central part in the overall causal context. Their own aetiology lies in the circumstances that give rise to the various modes of sentience; they are at the outside edge of mental life, one could say, caused by circumstances that the organism's cognitive economy is equipped to respond to in various ways but not part of the internal workings of that economy itself, and it is these latter that are the proper topic of a scientific psychology.[9]

There is however something deeply unsatisfying about an approach to psychology which implies on the one hand that it is possible in principle for a system to satisfy its requirements for, say, seeing a tree even when (as where the system is the Chinese population) there is no basis for postulating a unified subject of consciousness in which an *experience* of a tree might occur, and is forced on the other to admit that questions of the causes and effects of sensations fall outside its province.

Someone sensitive to these scruples might try to recapture sensations for psychology by pursuing the following path. One could begin by treating qualia as 'adverbial', a variable 'how' qualifying the essential 'what'. If the objective physical properties of a given ripe tomato (the objective 'what') can be agreed upon, the supposed fact that the sensations may differ (the variable 'how') can be accepted without affecting the view that functional roles define our mental states. What they define is the interaction between environments, organisms, and their responses, including such verbal reactions as 'I see a red tomato'. The quality of the visual sensation itself will be irrelevant, and the question of inverted spectra can be safely left alone. The principal difficulty, the possibility of absent qualia, would be solved by insisting that there must be some sensation in the right mode causing the utterance. For the sensation to occur there must be a subject of consciousness, and this in itself will bring the range of possible instantiations of the sets of causal circumstances defining types of mental state within something close enough to human limits.

But this is still unsatisfactory if you expect functionalism to be a general human psychology. For in that case it would have to take account of the whole spectrum of human performance, complete with its characteristic modes of sensation and experiencing, and show how it lends itself to a taxonomy of mental types based on functional roles. One way of achieving that end would be to ignore the problematic possibilities and let functional roles, based on agreed identifications of stimulus conditions and responses, define a sensation as one, say, of red whatever its 'subjective' quality. Functional roles would then define the types of (e.g.) our visual sensations whatever the first-person facts may be for the individual perceiver who has them.[10] That solution, however, introduces a new 'subjective'–'objective' distinction within the original subjective domain; a distinction, moreover, that has no basis there and is drawn simply to save the letter of the theory at the expense of its spirit, which again is surely to be able to give a basis for the type-identities of the visual sensations we do in fact have.

A way of satisfying the spirit as well as the letter of the functionalist goal might be by hypothesizing lawlike correlations between certain functional-role sets and 'normal' visual experiencing, letting the causal roles determine the types of visual sensation and presenting the anomalies of the thought-experiments in the guise of straightforward, though not straightforwardly confirmable, empirical falsehoods. If, confirmably or not, there happened actually to be cases of absent qualia or inverted spectra, either these should be taken as invalidating the hypotheses or else *ad hoc* hypotheses should be introduced to explain the anomalous results.

47

Among the difficulties of this alternative would be the old dualist point that nothing in a set of physical circumstances implies the presence of one rather than another, or indeed any, quale (the 'blank wall' problem mentioned in my opening chapter), so that the choice of the norm here, and consequently any typology, will be fundamentally arbitrary and its paradigm instances, if any, in principle inscrutable. That, however, might be avoided by allowing that the visual sensations we do have, broadly and with explainable exceptions, are in certain ways functionally relevant. The sensations can then be parts of functional-role sets which provide the essentials of their definitions or identities as mental states. This would bring the type-identities of our visual sensations within the province of the spirit of functionalism.

The problem here, however, would be to assign causal relevance to determinable quale-kinds. Apart from the difficulty of isolating such kinds, the causal picture would then also have to include relations between publicly observable and exclusively first-person mental events, thus destroying the scientific integrity and thereby much of the point of functional analysis as a brave attempt to achieve unity of theory within the framework of a monistic materialism. And, of course, we would still have failed to provide an account of sensations as being mental states *in themselves*. For by admitting sensations into the causal complex of relations between inputs, outputs, and other mental states which are supposed to provide the definitions of our mental states, we have simply allowed that they can function either as inputs, outputs, or as one of those other mental states. If they are to be either of the first two, then they are not mental states; but if they *are* mental states, then, as such, they in turn must be defined in terms of their causal relations to inputs, outputs, and other mental states, and so on indefinitely. In view of this regress it is indeed doubtful whether functionalism can claim to possess a coherent concept of 'mental state', except heuristically in the abstract form of flow charts or other graphic representations of the causal relations functionalism appeals to in its explanation of the organism's behavioural repertoire.

The idea of a sensation's being a mental state in itself suggests yet another line of approach. It is to claim that sensations form an autonomous domain of types. On this view, colours, sounds, smells, tastes, feels, and proprioceptive qualia too, just are what they seem to be; or as Sprigge puts it, they are 'as clearly present to our consciousness as anything can be, each in its distinctive nature, and . . . cannot turn out to be in their own selves something other than what they seem to be'.[11] Initially, however, there seems to be a major objection to this approach. It looks suspiciously as if what a given sensation-type is could be determined without reference to any causal ambience in which a token of the type occurred. In adopting this line, then, one would either be assuming from the start that sensations do not play any causal roles, or else supposing, implausibly, that the causal role or roles which a mental phenomenon does play have no influence on what is finally to be said about the nature of that phenomenon.

I shall argue in a moment that this objection is ill-conceived because founded on a false dualism which excludes sensations from the causal network. But before doing that it is just as well to note how such dualism is at work even in an avowedly non-dualist theory which does try to implicate sensation in psychological causation: namely the mind–brain identity theory.[12]

According to this theory, mental states are actually identical with things belonging in certain causal contexts, as what tends to produce x or to be affected by x. Mentality, on this account, is a feature of nature consisting of states with the unusual property of being double-aspected, subjective and conscious on the one hand and objective and material on the other. The mental vocabulary refers to states that are also physical and thus secures its basis in the third-personal public world as the apparatus we need for describing human performance. Pains are identical with brain states. Experienced pain is a brain state, and some brain state is experienced pain. It is to be characterized by its tendency to be caused by something and also by its tendency to cause something in turn. This idea is generalized to all other mental states. Desire, for instance, is a state which gives rise to behaviour with a tendency to produce a certain result, the precise behaviour being continually modifiable in response to sensory inputs relevant for achieving the result. Belief is a state which also gives rise to behaviour, but in its case any sensory inputs which tend to modify it do so by affecting the belief itself and not just the behaviour it gives rise to.

A theory of this kind takes mental states to be targets of two non-equivalent definite descriptions: one and the same state is both a brain event and a conscious event. The mentalistic vocabulary of pains, sensations, fears, beliefs, etc. applies directly to brain states, and the states which are describable in terms of the theory's synthetic identity

49

claims are conceived as, and only as, elements in causal interactions. The significant feature of the theory is that the 'nature' of the state is not to be found in the qualitative aspect alone but in some specific capacity, or set of capacities, for physical activation – that is, in terms of causal roles played out in the publicly accessible physicalistic third-person world. On this view the qualitative aspect taken by itself is an abstraction. It doesn't do anything on its own; it can't, because on its own it is nothing. Aspects are not substances. So it implies a denial of the view noted above according to which colours, sounds, feels, etc. cannot turn out to be 'in their own selves' something other than themselves. They do, in the sense that what they are in themselves is not merely a matter of how they appear to be to the subject of consciousness, for that takes us no further than their capacity as qualitative aspects of causal processes which necessarily transcend the phenomenological appearances. In its origin, the mind–brain identity theory is a direct response to Cartesian dualism: the view that mind (as consciousness) is one thing and the nervous system and body with its behavioural repertoire another. For Descartes, as noted earlier, the brain was no more mental than the liver. By taking the mental to be but one aspect of a state which includes naturally based cognitive and motivational aspects, the identity theorist integrates the conscious mind with the physiology of the brain and thus finds a causal role for mental states.

At least on the surface, then, the identity theory does not, as behaviourism does deliberately and functionalism by default, deny the qualitative aspect. It is guaranteed a place by the theory's synthetic identity claims. Still, as we saw, the aspect taken by itself is, on the identity theory, an abstraction, a descriptive layer removed from the thing itself. The dialectic of the position is that if the layer did indeed describe something 'in itself', then Cartesianism would *have* to be true; but since Cartesianism is false, the layer must describe something physical. What the identity theory claims, in effect, is that there is no in-itself of the qualitatively mental for reflection on the mind's operations to reveal. That is what is implied by taking the non-equivalent modes of description to be descriptions of one thing or process.

The theory faces the familiar objection that pains can be sharp, thoughts amusing, and desires burning, but brain states none of these things, while brain states for their part are electrochemically locatable and measurable and can be explained by neurophysiological laws, none of which is possible for pains, thoughts, and desires. But let us focus here on what proponents of the theory consider its main positive feature: that it is only in terms of the traditionally physicalistic properties of these dual-aspected states that they possess their causal powers. The 'mental' aspect, although its identity with the brain allows the latter also to be mental, consequently provides no foothold for the idea that conscious states might occur causally in their causal ambiences by virtue of their being conscious. There is nothing in the mind–brain identity theory that can support the view that the consciousness of our conscious states and attitudes is a causal factor in the production of behaviour.

In a way, functionalism is a cleaner approach. It is more consistent in that it makes the quale not only redundant but also eradicable, since systems replicating the functional aspects will be mental even if thay are demonstrably not conscious. The same can be said for eliminative materialism, since it hypothesizes that the mental vocabulary, with its inheritance of folk-dualism, will be replaceable once the brain sciences get their chance to explain in full something the mental half of which dualism once made extramural. Although the eliminative materialist can allow that conscious states exist, once they are properly understood, answers about what colours, sounds, feels, etc. are 'in their own selves' will be given in a taxonomy 'more penetrating' than one based merely on how they seem to be from the point of view of the subject of consciousness, because the taxonomy will then be 'drawn from a completed neuroscience'.[13]

Why should one not say the following? Mental states are situated in their causal ambiences by virtue of their being *conscious*. This does not say that there are states which are merely conscious and whose natures, anomalously, can therefore be determined altogether on the basis of how they seem; all it implies is that the property of their being conscious is itself a causal property. The states may also be physical. The point is that if they are physical, then the properties whereby they play causal roles in mental contexts are properties that are to some degree 'realized' in consciousness. Put differently: the causal properties of states which have both purely physical and also conscious aspects are causal also, perhaps necessarily though not exclusively, by virtue of their conscious aspects.

If not always openly dismissive of qualities of experience, causal-role and functional-role analyses of mental concepts are at least peculiarly evasive about them. They leave one asking: But what *about* the qualitative aspect? What about the fragrance of a rose and the whole variety of sentient life in all of its modes? This evasiveness may be traced to two circumstances. First, owing to the unlocatability of sensations in public physical space, such entities, if they exist, cannot participate on their own in the world of physical causation. For that reason, they have to derive whatever causal powers they may possess from some kind of formal or factual linkage with physical, e.g. neural, processes. Second, since sensations have essentially an occurrent aspect, they are not exhaustively analysable in terms of sets of causal relations to inputs, outputs, and other mental states. As mental episodes they are just themselves, the fragrances, hardnesses, restlessnesses, listlessnesses, etc. that form the continual flux of lived experience. So even if causal-role and functional-role analysts were prepared to expand their frameworks to permit entities not locatable within the physicalist universe to have causal roles, and even if they were able to specify the causal relations in which such entities stand, they would still have nothing to say about the entities themselves in their qualitative aspect.

In spite of Hume it is at least plausible to assume that if things stand in certain causal relations, that has something to do with the things themselves. But if we ask in any particular case what that something is, causal-role theories have no answers, for the only answers they have must be given in terms of further causal relations. It is tempting in the case of sensations, however, to propose that an answer can be given in terms of the nature of the sensation itself. Thus the right answer in the case of sensations might be: They stand in those relations because they are *in themselves and of their nature* prone so to do. That is to say, sensations do indeed have causal relations, or more properly causal powers, both to occur and to cause other things to occur, and this is a fact of their nature. Moreover, it is an ascertainable fact, though perhaps Wittgensteinian scruples might lead us to qualify that claim – strictly, it needs no ascertaining; it is 'ascertained' in the sentient moment. In other words, sensations can well be (typically, one must say, to fend off premature counter-examples) themselves, in their essences, causes and effects, and *consciously* so.

But is there any phenomenological evidence for that? Theoretic habits may incline us to expect the answer no. We are inured to the thought that sensations are the typical 'givens' of mental life, its data rather than its causally implicated components. That this is the case, however, is far from clear, and even if what we take to be close attention to experience itself inclines us to the view, that may simply be due to an inherent tendency in our reflective grasp of experience to represent the moving picture of sentient experience in isolated 'stills' abstracted from its causal ambience. If we were to introspect our own sentient states clearly, we would see how they are woven into the fabric of our consciously active engagement as an integral part of the causal ambience. Of course, if, as with Condillac's thought-experiment with the marble statue, one thinks of a solitary sensation, with no relation to any other and separated from any possible interaction with an environment,[14] its causal influence will be of vanishing proportions. But if, to pursue that rather strange thought-experiment, sentient experiences accumulate, they acquire the status of knowledge,[15] knowledge by acquaintance both of things other than the sensation itself and also of the subject's own modes of response to these. If we look to our own actual experience, we note that some specific sensations are obviously causal. The unexpectedness of a feeling causes one to recoil, the latter itself being a response with a clearly sentient aspect, just as anticipated sensations may cause contentment, which too has a sentient aspect. And so on. Not only common sense but experience tells us that the qualitative aspect of mental life is inextricably bound up with the overall activity of the human organism.

Physicalist psychology doesn't want this to be true. But that, as we have just noted, is because there is no place in the physicalist's causal nexus for the kinds of states sentience consists in. That being so, physicalists have usually responded to the challenge of 'qualia' by seeking to undermine arguments purporting to show that the fullest physicalist description of reality excludes any significant causal factor.

One of these arguments concerns Mary, a brilliant scientist specializing in the neurophysiology of vision. Mary is forced to conduct her investigations of the world from a black-and-white room through a black-and-white television monitor. We are to assume that she acquires all the physical information there is to obtain about, for example, what wave-length combinations from a ripe tomato stimulate the retina, and how this, by the mediation of the central nervous system, produces the vocal utterance 'The tomato is red.'[16] There is still, so the challenge goes, something about redness for her to learn if released from her non-chromatic environment.

In an attempt to rebut the argument, Paul Churchland has first presented it in the following 'conveniently tightened' version:

(1) Mary knows everything there is to know about brain states and their properties.
(2) It is not the case that Mary knows everything there is to know about sensations and their properties.
Therefore, By Leibniz's law,[17]
(3) Sensations and their properties [are not identical with] brain states and their properties.[18]

Churchland maintains that the argument is invalid because it exploits an equivocation between knowledge by description and knowledge by acquaintance. 'Knowing about' in (1) involves mastery of a set of sentences or propositions, while in (2) it is a matter of having a representation of redness 'in some prelinguistic or sublinguistic medium of representation for sensory variables'.[19] Thus it is possible to argue that *what* Mary knows both during her confinement to a non-chromatic environment and afterwards is the same thing; what differs is *how* she knows it. And materialism does not preclude the possibility that there are ways of having knowledge other than storing sentences.[20]

Churchland reinforces the objection by claiming that if the argument is interpreted in the way its defenders really require in order to defend the notion of 'emergent qualia', then if premiss (1) is true, premiss (2) must be false. For if Mary did in fact know all there was to know about the brain and the nervous system, then the information available to her would include the conceptual tools available to a matured neuroscience, such as the 'spiking frequencies' in the relevant layers of, say, the occipital cortex, which would tell her what the states of having sensations of black, white, grey, or red really were, and from which information – even if one of those states was one she had never been in – she might still *imagine* the relevant experience.[21]

There is indeed no reason to suppose that a matured neuroscience would not allow finer distinctions to be drawn between the brain states underlying qualia than are possible on the basis of the experiences themselves, and therefore – if mental states are treated as having both conscious and purely physical aspects – more accurate distinctions between the mental states which have the relevant qualia as an aspect. One possible outcome of this could be a more subtle discrimination of qualia, supported as it now becomes by better-informed expectations. It may also be possible for Mary to create the sensation of red in imagination on the basis of the knowledge thus available to her – though that may reasonably be doubted, and if she does so a plausible explanation would be that the the neuro-physiology itself, without the benefit of her knowledge, had caused her to 'dream up' the new experience. But can we conclude that sensations themselves, whether stimulated in the brain or by the external environment, are kinds of acquaintance with facts which can form part of a full physicalist description of reality?

That we cannot so conclude might be argued as follows. If the general category of 'modes of sentience' is to be incorporated within a physicalist account of the universe, then everything that falls within that category must itself be physical. But in that case it must be capable of physical description. This principle will then apply to whatever it is we call 'acquaintance' or 'imagining', as much as to the brain and its properties. In that case, as Madell has pointed out,[22] there is no real distinction between a kind of propositional knowing that covers brain states and their properties on the one hand, and kinds of prelinguistic and sublinguistic knowing in the form of representations on the other. 'Acquaintance' and 'imagining red' will have to be knowledge that is necessarily propositional. Assuming sensations and their properties to be properties of brain states, then premiss (1) in Churchland's version of the argument will imply, incompatibly with premiss (2), that Mary already knows everything there is to know about sensations and their properties.

This, of course, is a result that the physicalist would be happy to accede to; but the implication depends on the intuitively false assumption that the actual experience of seeing or imagining something red can be given a physical description. The best the physicalist can do is to offer a causal account linking facts about the brain with certain utterances and behaviour; but, reverting to a point made above, and as Madell correctly says, 'such an analysis departs from our ordinary conception of awareness as an intrinsic state of consciousness . . . which cannot be analysed purely dispositionally'.[23] Once again the categorical nature of the conscious state slips through the meshes of the causal net.

The physicalist may argue that it should simply be let slip. There are several possibilities here. One is to deny that there are any facts of a matter for Mary to know when she is introduced to a chromatic world. The argument could be based on an alleged conceptual connection between being a fact in this matter and having explanatory value. The physicalist will of course allow that when Mary first sees something red there is a new underlying neurological fact of this matter, relating her experience to underlying neurophysiological circumstances in a causal way. But this fact is part of physical knowledge of the brain and its properties; and as far as any explanation of her now increased discriminatory repertoire is concerned, the physical account covers all the evidence the physicalist needs. There is no call to summon any putative further facts of conscious experience. Furthermore, assuming that the only facts concern physical entities and physical connections, and that knowledge of physical nature is all there is to know, if Mary really does have universal physical knowledge she must already possess universal knowledge of facts. If in addition to this knowledge we were to talk of a knowledge of redness etc., we would have crossed the boundary of myth and in effect be talking, as a proponent of this argument puts it, as though 'things' like angels and Zeus' thunderbolts were causally operative in the universe.[24]

But there are several objections to this. In the first place, the categorical status of conscious mental states will not go away just because (if it is possible) a sufficient explanation of the occurrence of a mental state can be given in purely physical terms and on purely physical, i.e. behavioural, evidence. Second, unlike angels, conscious mental states do actually exist and no behavioural-cum-neurological evidence of Mary's having had the experience in question logically entails (the fact) that she has indeed had it; so whatever conceptual limitations there may be on the notion of a 'fact', there is still *this* possible fact, additional to the evidence, that indeed she is or was in the sentient state in question. Third, if the physicalists insist on denying that there is *this* fact of the matter, then they are either merely drawing again on their conceptual assumption and begging the question of whether qualia can have causal properties, or else they are taking facts in a wider sense and just flying in the face of the only kind of directly confirmatory experience there can be.

A second strategy is to accommodate facts of qualia by allowing a domain of facts of no interest to scientists. Thus it has been suggested that room may be offered to qualia by distinguishing a 'semantic level', at which states of functional systems can be identified as equivalent in terms of functional roles, from a 'sense-mode' level or 'point of view of (flavoured) manner of presentation', in which the problematic 'being something it is like to be' 'escapes the scientific net' but can still be something 'worth knowing about'. If there are cultural and experiential differences between us and, say, Martians, these will show up functionally to the extent that they are physically grounded, while 'the information conveyed by a functional or a physical account of... Martians will not give us their sonar-flavoured aspect on the world, and so will not convey to us what it is like to enjoy Martian experience, and so will not tell us everything there is to know about their minds'.[25] According to this account, differences of sense-modality are 'accidental' to the substantial goings-on occurring at a level where cultural and experiential differences *are* able to get a grip on the underlying physiology. However, apart from the question-begging nature of its way of marking the distinction between what is accidental and what substantial, an added defect of the account is that it offers no grounds for assuming that the fact that experience has a sonar rather than a visuo-spatial 'flavour' is something we can afford to let slip through the scientific net.

If we can say that for this approach not all psychological facts are scientific ones, another would be to say that the facts in question are not psychological either. Thus it has also been claimed that although functionalists must of course account for all psychological concepts, qualia are not psychological, so that functionalism is not required to explain them.[26] Pain qualia, to take the favoured example once more, are features of the external world, of animal bodies, rather than of the mind; they are *objects* of motivation and cognition, not qualitative items to be placed on the same level as the latter. As qualities they qualify (are 'adjectival' to) the body.[27] So there is as little reason for functionalists to take functional account of pain qualia as there is for their analyses of the perception of, say, trees to include functional analyses of trees. Pains, like trees, are not psychological.[28] And similarly, in principle, for all other qualia.

There are several points to be made about this approach. In the first place, it has some apparent advantages over the alternatives already mentioned. Although taking qualia out of psychology as well as science may seem at first glance a more extreme position than the immediately preceding alternative, unlike the latter it does in fact secure a place for qualia in scientific explanation. For despite the fact, according to this view, that qualia themselves play no part in psychological theory, just like any other cognitively and motivationally significant objects (e.g. tigers and trees) they can certainly enter into scientific explanations of specific behavioural events in the form of initial conditions. Thus the approach does justice to the fact of sentience, but without putting that fact in a scientific limbo. Moreover, treating pain qualia as 'objects' in this way, or more accurately as qualities of bodies or of parts of bodies, places them in the same category as 'external' sensations, such as coldness, hardness, and fragrance; and this seems correct both phenomenologically and theoretically: phenomenologically, because the distinction between inner and outer sensation is itself a theoretical distinction not based in the mere occurrence of sensation itself; and theoretically, because even if our learned reactions to sensations do discriminate between inner and outer sensation, both forms are equally 'objective' in the sense that in respect of the intentionality of the states in which they occur they both occupy the object and not the subject position.

But there are also objections. Although from one point of view treating pains as bodily characteristics excuses functionalist psychology from having to deal with them, from another removing qualia from the mind is clearly also a strategem that opens the way for an exclusively 'sub-personal' account of the mind's cognitive and motivational functions, an account which does not require these functions to be instantiated in conscious organisms. By being located in parts of our bodies, pains are apparently being offered a habitat in the physical universe alongside whatever complexes can instantiate the type of functional organization which it is the job of a scientific psychology to explain. The prospect being offered is that of the third-person world of physical science. First, however, if pains and other qualia are put in the 'object' position, they must be correlates of a subject; there must also be a subject of consciousness. Of course, the subject of consciousness need not figure in a scientific psychology as itself a bearer of causal properties; but their correlation with a subject does take qualia beyond the limits of the third-person point of view. Second, for familiar reasons the correlation suggests that the objects in question are in a sense mental, or mind-dependent, and that for this if no other reason they should be regarded as constituents of psychological facts. Third, although the position has it that pain qualia, for example, are not themselves implicated in the cognitive and motivational functions which for functionalism are the proper study of the mind, it is at least an initially plausible assumption that if they were so implicated, that would necessarily be in part by virtue of their being qualia for some subject. Fourth, there are grounds for supposing that if pains are located in bodies, are 'adjectival' to them, then it is in a way that implies that the bodies also are themselves for a subject. One might see the notion of a subject here as in itself a threat to the functionalist assumption that the mind is a cognitive and motivational system with no essential connection with a first-person point of view, and as suggesting a basis for a way of talking in which pains, however located in bodies, are still in a sense mental.

But beyond that, it is misleading and pre-analytical to treat the tree as analogous to the pain in the context of this argument; for the tree can be found in public space while the pain in my toe will *not* be found in my toe, even though that is where I myself feel it. This is one ground for taking the pain to be psychological: it exists in a different 'space' – that of first-person experience. Finally, in whatever space and whether or not it is psychological, if the pain quale on the offered account is an object of cognition, analogously to trees and tigers, then there is still the lived experience *of* the pain quale to account for; that is to say, we still lack an account of there being the cognition of the quale-as-object, as a specification of 'what it is like to be conscious'. One way with qualia would be to treat them as specifications of this formula; in which case there would be qualia for seeing tigers and trees too, and in general for lived experience in all its variety. The usual way, however, is the one we have adopted, namely to identify qualia as determinate qualities of feeling or sensation. As we noted at the beginning, in the context of functionalism it is sentience as a kind of sheer givenness that has been thought to present the main difficulty. The strategem of treating qualia as objects is designed to place them outside the functionalist's domain. But in doing so it appears to defeat its own ends by having to invoke the notion of a subject-correlate which threatens to reduce all 'objects' – tigers and trees included – to modes of subjective experience. In doing that, in turn, it opens the way to the thought that the real problem with functionalism may not be sentience or 'raw' sentient experience, but the wider first-person category of subjectivity itself.

Within this wider category it may be that sentience does not play such a major role after all. Indeed sensations may go largely unregarded – in a not necessarily paradoxical manner of speaking, our sentient lives may be something of which we are largely *in*sensible, in the sense that the flux of sensory experience is not routinely focal in our characteristically goal-directed forms of activity. Dewey and others have argued that attention and conscious thought arise only when routines are interrupted.[29] If so, then the roles that sensations play in their causal ambiences may be at best supporting ones. However, if we now return to Mary and her transition from a non-chromatic to a chromatic environment, it is still incumbent on us to ask why the additions to her sensory repertoire should *not* play any causal role.

Since the cognitive and motivational aspects of human psychology are in fact supplemented with a qualitative one (perhaps one among conceivable alternatives), the natural assumption is that they do play just such a role. In that case we should want to regard qualia as part of the functional context and expect functional analyses to be forthcoming.[30] However, functionalism analyses human mentality in terms of management of the environment, and this means that the analysis has to be given in cognitive and motivational terms. For functionalists these refer *ex hypothesi* to parts of observable physical reality. Qualia are not physical observables, so in one sense – as the analysand – the qualitative aspect is analysed away, while in another – as what resists such analysis – it simply drops out from the start. In practice it becomes indifferent whether functionalists 'accept' qualia or not. If they do, it is because qualia can be talked about in cognitive and motivational terms. If not, as in Dennett's case, it is because what may strike the conscious subject as being some kind of 'inner' life is really only the subject's 'having a certain sort of functional organization' whose states are essentially dispositional ('current capacities and past activities').[31] To be conscious is no more than to catch oneself in 'propositional episodes' about whose origins 'we have not the faintest idea'.[32] And having a pain, for example, is not there being some specific conscious episode, but an event of a kind we may one day have 'a good physiological sub-personal theory' about, something of a kind which even robots could in principle instantiate.[33]

Those who make such claims often insist that disagreement with them is mainly a matter of cultural or theoretical inertia and that phenomenology in any case provides only a very superficial and partial view of what actually happens. In the end, one is told, we will see, even phenomenologically, why we should stop playing Cardinal to their Galileo.

There is almost certainly a good deal of inertia in our theorizing about mind, as about anything else, and certain pictures which hold us captive no doubt do get in the way of improvements in understanding. But the functionalist promise of improvement seems to be itself no more than a picture, indeed just the old picture turned upside-down. The surface plausibility of the functionalist way with qualia is itself due to an artificial and abstract way of talking which places dispositions uncritically in the world of observable, inspectable facts, and treats qualia, the 'inner' life, or 'what it is like to be conscious', as something non-dispositional, and in cognitive and motivational terms essentially superfluous. But why should qualia not be both episodic and dispositional? Why should they not, on occasion, be conscious dispositions? If one pays more heed to the character of one's own experience, the causal properties of sensations, widely construed as in the earlier reference to James, may be describable in active or passive terms. Rather than being something it is like something to *be* (e.g. just having this or that sensation), the phenomenological event might be better described as one of being something it is like being about to *do* or *become*, or having done, or not done, or of having been done to, and so on. The 'inner' life is, on this picture, the life of the organism as a whole in its more or less active and more or less passive engagements with the world it is familiar with. That world is not, of course, a sub-personal world in which the aetiologies of propositional episodes can only be speculated about; nor is it an 'inner' world whose episodes are revealed to the light of consciousness. It is the world of a more or less collected past, present, and future in which the present can be seen to be leading on from past to future in sequences of (more or less) propositional episodes, each of which can in principle have an origin traceable to its predecessors, all on the 'personal' level. This continuing process is one in which sensitivity to colour, sound, heat, cold, texture, taste, smell, and the proprioceptive sense of being sheerly bodily claim their rightful place.

So when we ask how conscious states are embedded in the cognitive and motivational contexts in which they occur, the right phenomenological answer might well be that they are embedded in it causally. If possessing an inner life is to possess a certain sort of functional organization, the question of what sort of functional organization it is could then be answered by saying that it is the kind in which the functional organization itself can be, and more or less is, *conscious*. And the question of how, or to what extent, sensations can play functional roles could be answered by considering how much of the functional organization is 'represented' in the sentience that accompanies the actions of the organism. If pain qualia, for instance, are to be analysed functionally, that does not mean that they dissolve into a complex of sub-personal and behavioural causes and effects. Pain qualia will be parts of functional organizations to the extent that the behaviour of organisms whose organizations they are can be shown to be responsive to distinctions in qualities of pain. And similarly for the rest of their quale-tative lives. The range covered by this formula may even include such extensive and hard-to-specify qualia as what it is like to be a successfully or indifferently conating being, striving, shirking, suffering setbacks, giving up, getting back to the task, completing it, and so on, and in general what it is like to be an embodied subject with these characteristics among others.

The moral about sensations is this. Even if pains are treated as kinds of object (a view which may be preferred to the standard account which takes pains to be mental states and so – along with unfocused anxiety – exceptions to the rule that mental states refer to something beyond themselves), having pains, like seeing trees, is part of the flux and content of lived experience; and just as there is something it is like to see (climb, circumvent, fell) a tree, so is there something it is like to have (be concerned about, stoically endure, half ignore) a pain. These are among the typical 'episodes' of lived experience and as such part of the subject-matter of psychology. It may be argued on behalf of functionalist psychology that lived experience falls outside the scientific net. But the attempts to show that it does so look like pieces of defensive gerrymandering. Although that word is not as old as 'casuistry', the activity itself is certainly an egregious example: a casuist is someone skilled in the art of resolving *casus conscientiae*. If 'conscientia' is read as 'consciousness', we have a rubric here for much current debate.

But, as I shall argue later, there are grounds for concluding that any scientific psychology which hopes to explain the causal powers manifested in the kinds of functional organization we are must refer to the kinds of objects that these powers are designed to encounter and cope with. It must do that because these objects enter essentially into descriptions of the capacities in question. And that goes for pains as well as trees, or perhaps one should say for trees as well as pains. In that context, it is not clear that functional explanations should not also have to account for trees. The standard functional analysis of perception is in terms of the tendency to form certain kinds of belief and purpose based on what is grasped in the form of sensory input interpreted in a way that the perceiver's mind (or self-correcting mental economy of causally interacting internal states) has learned through interaction with the environment. The beliefs and purposes themselves are analysed in terms of their causal roles in speech and action. But the actual practices involve perceptual beliefs and judgments and their background in sensation.

CHAPTER IV

Subjects

From one point of view, treating pains, tingles, and itches – or 'raw feels' in general – as objective entities on a par with tigers and trees (along with the sensible qualities of these) may seem an effective strategem for a theorist who wants to relieve psychology of unwanted first-person impedimenta. The picture speciously offered is one of safely public facts: the physical instantiation of some functional organization on the one hand, and on the other the (both internally and externally) sensible universe in which that organization functions. Here, at least so long as pains and their 'internal' kindred are treated as spatially locatable, everything seems neatly placed in a third-person universe. What we have conforms pretty well with what Brentano understood by 'physical phenomena', amongst which he listed 'a color, a figure, a landscape which I see, a chord which I hear, warmth, cold, odor which I sense', though Brentano went so far as also to include mental images of these.[1]

But then Brentano set off his 'physical phenomena' precisely in order to distinguish them from the 'act of presentation' of any such phenomenon.[2] Which raises a question of the subject for which or whom the phenomena in this world *are* presentations. If at first as just a matter of form, presentations are presented to subjects. Moore, we remember, classified colours as non-mental precisely to distinguish *what* we see, remember, want, etc. from our *consciousness of* whatever it is we see, feel, imagine, remember, want, etc. – that is, from the mental as what Moore chooses to call *acts* of consciousness.[3] So unless one can somehow also rid the things in question of their status as objects, we are faced with the need to make some account of the subject-side. Could there be something here that will prove just as problematic for the functionalist as absent qualia and inverted spectra, or even worse? An active subject, in some more full-bodied sense than that implied by Moore's 'acts' of consciousness? A control capacity with executive power, perhaps, or even overall direction of the organism's performance? A rational and intentional agent? At what cost to their claims to provide the full range of principles of that performance could functionalists afford to omit this kind of item from their stock-in-trade?

In fact, today, functionalists are less likely to feel threatened by such possibilities than if they had offered their accounts in the heyday of liberal individualism. The autonomously active ego is now widely discredited as a mere cultural artefact, an invention of the Enlightenment,[4] a grammatical illusion, even just a piece of defensive wishful-thinking on the part of those who have grown used to the role of autonomous actor and don't fancy the thought that they might be subject to disintegrating forces of which they are unconscious and over which they have no ultimate control.[5] If the subject-side is simply a preconstructed arena in which various unconscious forces are at work, and it cannot even – as schizophrenia and brain-bisection show – lay claim to being a single and unified focus of such influences, there seems little there to endanger the simplicity and integrity of the functionalist's third-person framework.

On the other hand, it may be questioned whether the arguments offered for the impotence or non-centrality of the ego really have the trajectory required to reach their intended target; or, if they do, whether that isn't just because the target they should really be aiming at is further away than the one they choose, namely the Cartesian idea of an immaterial substance. To wage a convincing and not merely rhetorical campaign against the idea of an active and centred self, more qualified notions of self and of unity may need to be taken into the reckoning, notions not at all affected by the denial of substance-dualism.

That there is a subject-side is unquestionable, whatever conceptual or causal significance we may or may not eventually feel justified in attaching to the notion. One way of seeing this is to try to imagine what it would be like for there to be a sensation, for instance a tingle, without it being *for* some conscious moment. Perhaps some very rudimentary form of sensory episode could occur in something without there being anything remotely like a point of view on it, just a kind of 'having' or 'being' it; and sensory episodes might occur sequentially in certain organisms without the organism having any sense of the sequence, the episodes flowing into each other, or even occurring in total isolation from each other, each one being for the organism all the sentience it knows – though not even that would be something it had the sense of its being. If all this is provisionally granted, we may accept that there are more rudimentary ways of being subjects of experience than those to which we ourselves are accustomed. We are perhaps more at home with the idea of a subject for which a sensation is not something we feel ourselves wholly to be, though there are certain all-encompassing moods that fit that description, but something which is an object *for* something that we experience ourselves as wholly or centrally being, it being this latter which counts as the subject. One may even think of a rudimentary form of *this* form of sensory experience in which, say, a tingle is treated as an object which has an existence independently of its occurring for this subject – just as one might think of headaches waiting in line to afflict one. There is at least a kind of prising open of a subject–object opposition in which sensations assume the latter position and thereby provide a minimal basis for talking of a subject.

However, the subject–object schema does not apply smoothly to conscious episodes in general. For in the case of thoughts – or the so-called propositional attitudes, i.e. beliefs, desires, fears, hopes, and so on – the objects we speak of are those (possible) objects which correspond to a propositional content, and that content itself is only in an extended sense referred to as itself an object for a subject. The true 'objects' are the possible states of affairs that count as what are called the 'conditions of satisfaction' of the mental contents, and it is the contents themselves that must now be thought of as related in some way to the subject.

A complication here comes to mind if we recall Moore's argument for distinguishing colours from the consciousness of them and his conclusion that what counts as 'mental' in the most fundamental sense of the word is the latter and not the former.[6] One is conscious of seeing one colour at one time and a different colour at another time, and although the colours are different, Moore claims that one is 'conscious of them both in exactly the same sense'; so that, 'since the colours are different in the two cases, whereas what I mean by my consciousness of them is in both cases the same, my consciousness of a colour must be something different from any of the colours of which I am conscious'.[7] The complication is that it is less clear that propositional attitudes – considered here as actual representational episodes – are not mental. Nor is it clear in the typical case where we do talk of sensations, for instance colour experiences, that this is not also part of a propositional episode, a perceptual thought, for instance about whether to pluck the rose that has that colour; in which case the colour will feature not as a non-mental object for a subject but as a constituent in a thought-episode of a subject and thus as part of the subject's mentality.

In characterizing the duality of conscious mental episodes we find ourselves resorting to a duality of subject and content rather than of subject and object. This duality has a number of problematic features, the first of which Moore focused upon. We recall that Moore noted that there is a part of a conscious episode that remains invariant through changes of content. About this it can be said, in the case of any conscious episode, that it *would have been* the same even if the content had differed, and furthermore, in a given sequence of such episodes, it can be said that it actually does remain the same.[8] Let us call this the continuity feature. The problem is to be able to specify what it is that remains the same. Moore's own remarks indicate some of the difficulty. He is willing to call every act of consciousness a 'mental' entity, but this does not tell us what acts of consciousness are; that is, what it is that is the same through changes in content. Moore's suggestion is to classify them in terms of propositional attitude. Thus seeing something is one kind of act, instantiated by all cases of seeing; remembering is another; and so on. So there is no guarantee, on any two occasions of being conscious of something, that one is conscious of it in the same sense.[9] Yet one wonders, if we are conscious in the same sense when on one occasion we see red and on another blue, why it should not be equally acceptable to say, when on one occasion we see something red and on another we imagine or remember something red, that here too we are conscious in just the same sense. That is, why should differences of propositional attitude imply corresponding differences of kind of mental act when differences in the object of a particular kind of propositional act do not?

One answer could be that, since propositional attitudes correspond to types of psychological mode and the acts in question can be said to have the character of the mode, the subject of the acts – the empirical agent of consciousness, so to speak – can be identified as the person whose conscious life consists of sequences of such acts. The reason why differences in propositional attitude betoken differences of kinds of conscious act, while differences of object within one kind of propositional attitude do not, is that it is among the psychological attitudes that you find the biographical materials of the living, experiencing, environment-negotiating subject. Acts of consciousness, classified by their attitudinal types, belong to the subject-side and give us specifications of the living agent.

An alternative answer puts the psychological mode together with the propositional content and places the subject, identified as the agent of consciousness, outside. This takes us once more in the direction of a transcendental ego. If in seeing a tiger I am afraid, then the fear belongs with the sighting of the tiger on the 'content' side of the subject–content duality. The subject transcends the content in the sense that, as content, it is still necessarily content *for* a subject. But now the subject remains the same throughout all content change. An argument sometimes proposed in favour of this view is that there seems to be an unavoidable sense in which all the conscious episodes belonging to one biographical sequence are episodes – or in Moore's term, 'acts'[10] – of the same person or mind. All the conscious episodes I myself enjoy have the characteristic of 'being mine'. But in principle one might carry this line of thought further and put the property 'mine' on the side of content, too, thus treating the term indexically; so that we find ourselves talking of an ego transcending particular biographical sequences of contents, a kind of Platonic Ego in whose contents particular minds, with their indexically specifiable 'mine's', can participate.

Zeno Vendler, a recent proponent of the 'thoroughly transcendental ego', argues on the one hand that experiences are 'owned', but on the other that this is an aspect of experience which scientific explanations of mental phenomena cannot account for. Although Vendler concedes the claims of physicalist psychology to the point of subscribing to an identity theory, he argues that the truth of that theory is to be deduced philosophically by way of a transcendental argument which also guarantees a place for the self.[11] He begins with a conception (or 'representation') of the world bereft of all subjective experience, inner life, or consciousness, but not of animal and human organisms. This insensate world is the topic of science. But over and above this world there is consciousness; we know it in our own case. We know it initially, however, only from the viewpoint of a dislocated, transcendental 'I' capable of projecting experiences anonymously as to whose they are. That the 'I' is in this particular case the subject of *my* (this body's) experiences, rather than, say, Napoleon's, is a matter of fact to be discovered in the special access one has to this fact, yet one which makes no difference in the world itself – certainly not in the insensate physical world of our objective conception, but not even in the sensate world we 'project' by endowing all 'deserving' bodies with consciousness.[12] 'By showing that there might be . . . soulless worlds [e.g. in which evolution didn't get] beyond trees . . . you do not show that the transcendental self might not exist; all you show is that in such worlds it would not find a home.' The 'I' isn't in the world, or in time, and 'in general [it is] not subject to the categories governing the manifold of experience'.[13] Echoing Kant:[14] what 'I' marks (but can't be said to 'denote') is the 'ultimate subject of all representations' which 'defies representation'.[15]

Suppose I try to imagine a world without subjective points of view. Some would argue that I must be frustrated in that attempt since, by having to imagine it from my own subjective point of view, I must imagine it as containing at least that point of view. Vendler's argument is based on a denial of an inversion of this kind of conclusion. If my attempt to imagine Napoleon's subjective states were necessarily frustrated because I could only imagine myself being Napoleon, the result would be solipsism. Since solipsism is false, I must be able to imagine Napoleon's experiences without imagining myself having Napoleon's experiences. Vendler concludes that the 'I' is logically free of its association with *this* body and its experiences, and the question 'How do I know I am this?' is therefore one that can be posed. To answer it I have to pick out the actual 'this' from all the other 'deserving' bodies with which I (am necessarily in principle able to)[16] populate the world.[17]

A weakness in the argument is the premiss that solipsism as Vendler describes it is false. Of course, solipsism as the denial that there can be other subjects of experience is open to several objections, including the pragmatic objection that defending the position implies its falsehood. But in another sense there may be more to solipsism than Vendler allows. Even if only on psychological grounds, it can be argued that it requires feats of exceptional insight and imagination to entertain the thoughts or mental 'sets' of other subjects. Residues of solipsism may be dispensed with only in rare cases; and perhaps in the ordinary course of our fantasies or sympathies they tend to be ignored rather than overcome. In that case, the connection of the 'I' to its world-factual 'this' may be closer (and potentially more solipsistic) than the premisses of Vendler's transcendental argument suppose.[18]

This is a point we shall return to. What calls for special attention here is Vendler's conception of his own programme. 'My main concern', he writes, 'is with the epistemological, or rather transcendental, grounds for such statements as ["I am Zeno Vendler"], which express one's location in a "centreless" world-representation'. He thinks he must be able to explain the fact that the body with the name 'Zeno Vendler', and which is the 'seat' of the consciousness he 'actually enjoys', is *his* body and the seat of *his* consciousness, because this fact is not a fact about the space–time universe.[19] Primarily, the 'his' in both occurrences refers not to the particular set of embodied experiences about which it *is* a fact of this world that it is the set belonging to a person called 'Zeno Vendler', facts about whom are also facts about the space–time universe, but to the 'I' about which it is a contingent fact that *it* is enjoying the unfoldings of that particular embodied consciousness.

But do we have to pose the question of the identification of selves in this way? Certainly, it can be said that in representing the centreless world of physics to ourselves we cannot determine which of the deserving bodies in that centreless world is ours on the basis of the representation. But that could be because to represent the world as devoid of subjective viewpoints ('objectively', that is) is to represent an abstraction in which the information you have that you are the subject of the experiences of *this* body is artificially excluded. Subjectivity and the 'ownership' of experience (along with its hereness and nowness)[20] might turn out to be entailed by the notion of experience itself. In that case, of course, if experience is as body-bound as Vendler – agreeing with the physicalists – assumes, the subjective viewpoint poses a greater threat to the integrity of the physicalist universe than it does on Vendler's transcendentalist account, with body-tied experience conceived as one thing (e.g. the mere presence of qualia) and their ownership (the mineness of experience) another. For while in the latter case the subjectivity of experience (e.g. the pain as an episode in *my* experience) remains antiseptically 'aloof from the causal processes of nature',[21] in the former case subjectivity, or the first-person point of view, will be there threatening contamination of the physicalist's picture from the start.[22]

But perhaps the picture *should* be contaminated. Why not look for the subject-side in the processes themselves? Not of course in sub-personal processes, but in the flux of conscious experience, in the *content*? That will sound absurd if the content is limited to 'propositional' content and propositions are defined in terms of their objectively identifiable truth-conditions; the passing show of perceptual objects and events is perhaps the most fluid element of all in the flux of experience. And similarly even when psychological modes are included; we would look in vain for some propositional attitude repeating itself like a ground bass under the varied attitudes we take to the world around us. What the view requires is that, for any propositional content in any psychological mode, there is – in the experience itself – an experience of continuity. And of course there is. Each such content is part of a total conscious episode part of whose content is also the sense of that episode's having followed upon a previous such episode and of its being about to be followed by another. What we have here, then, is the content-side actually containing the subject-side.

What this view brings out is that conscious episodes are complex entities: they are not just representations, nor just these with accompanying attitudes; they contain certain background awarenesses which include the sense of their being episodes in a continuing series. It could be said that, just as conscious episodes contain the awareness that the objects of their representations are continuing things in space and time – this being part of what we all know it to be to represent something, or simply 'have some object or event in mind' – so do they also contain the awareness that those things in space and time are accessible to renewed representing in conscious episodes in the same continuing series.

That may be thought to misrepresent the actual form of the relation of a subject of consciousness to the content of its consciousness. But the suspicion may be due to distortions brought about by certain analytical preoccupations. The notion of a subject of consciousness, combined with the idea that what is interesting about conscious states is their ability to carry propositional content, and that in turn combined with the view that such contents are universals, and so objective in the sense of being available identically to a plurality of subjects – all this may lead one to think of those subjects, individually, as standing outside the shareable thoughts for which their consciousnesses are the vehicles. Thus it is very easy to begin to think of the universal here as finding its opposite, the particular, in isolated acts of consciousness; and then there arises the question of how to grasp what seems to be the fact that such acts are collected into separate sequences corresponding to individual subjects.

A proposal which effectively counters that misleading result is to be found in Sprigge's suggestion about the nature of personal identity. Sprigge seeks to capture the intuition we have that we are the same individual throughout our changing experience by describing the self as a universal. A universal in the ordinary sense is not tied to particular spatio-temporal locations, nor therefore to any particular series of such, and so does not give us the notion of a continuant. In this sense universals are abstract. But continuants, such as particular houses, can be called 'concrete' universals, where this means that identically the same house is present in a single, uninterrupted temporal series (usually it will be a single spatio-temporal series, but the fact that houses can be dismantled and rebuilt in the same or, usually, another location raises problems of their continuing identity). A self is a concrete universal, wholly present in each conscious episode. There are, of course, problems. Houses and selves do change to some extent throughout their histories, and selves are ordinarily thought to persist during gaps between conscious episodes. Regarding the former difficulty, Sprigge proposes that it should be possible to pick out some 'more specific universal . . . realized all along the series', and in the case of persons he refers to a 'distinctive way of consciously cognizing and dealing with the world' as what constitutes a 'personal essence'. Regarding the latter difficulty, which as Sprigge notes is not peculiar to personal identity, he suggests we can talk of a concrete universal's being 'in the offing'.[23] Given these qualifications, however, we can say that in any conscious episode part of what is present is the self, in its entirety, into whose characteristic style of cognizing and dealing with the world any particular propositional content in its attitudinal context is integrated.

There is still a problem. Sprigge talks of individuals in terms not of individuated particulars but in relative terms that allow the possibility or even likelihood of duplication. Thus personal essences may be more or less individual. But in that case the former notion is still left unaccounted for. Technically it is taken care of by calling the universal in question 'concrete'; but while houses, like all things physical, acquire their particularity by monopolizing determinate areas of real estate (in accordance with Aristotle's idea that matter is the principle of individuation), the 'concreteness' of a given subject of consciousness can be accounted for in that way only if the subject is treated as a physical thing. But if the subject is part of the content of 'its' consciousness, that option seems to be excluded. So even if we accept that '[a] genuine continuant is a concrete universal present as one and the same thing in different momentary instances',[24] we are still left looking for the basis of its concreteness and particular presence. A possible answer, and perhaps Sprigge's, is that conscious episodes naturally form streams and monopolize the streams they form as exclusively as houses monopolize the real estate (and volumes of space) they occupy. If consciousness could be said to be a property of suitably organized matter, then that would be intelligible as well as possible. Conscious episodes would be physically based points of view, liable to physically supported continuation, and in whose development selves of a more or less distinctive nature become established. So the basic continuant is a particular set or series of conscious episodes. Each episode contains the universal 'consciousness' not just in the abstract sense in which two separated walls can have the same wallpaper, but in the sense in which a particular wall, whatever wallpapers come and go on it, remains at each instant the same wall – in Sprigge's terms realizes, and that means actually *is*, the same *concrete* universal 'wall'.[25]

If each episode contains that particular continuant which is your or my consciousness, then by the same token it contains you or me. A consequence of the subject of consciousness's being contained, wholly contained, within consciousness in this way, is that the conventional subject–content formula is dispensed with. It can, of course, be retained if the subject is understood as sufficiently transcendental; but there seems no conceptual or explanatory reason for this. True, on some accounts the transcendental ego has been given the task of universal generator of all content; but it may be argued that the intuitions we have about contents being necessarily for subjects are better captured by the notion of a subject in some sense fully realized in each conscious episode than by that of a subject authoring each content in some way from 'behind'. Of course, neither would it be correct to say that the way in which the subject is fully realized in a conscious episode is one in which the subject stands 'before' consciousness. Conventional wisdom says that conscious contents, in the form of audible and visible signs, or even just plain objects, must be before the mind, but what the above account implies is that whatever is before the mind is not before it in some absolute sense; objective contents are to be conceived holistically as bearing some inherent relation to, or possessing some property deriving from, a distinctive cognitive and motivational style. It is only in so far as that style is itself in some way a feature of what is (let us say) objectively present to the mind that the subject itself can be said to be present in that connection.

And yet the mind is able to reflect upon itself, and there is the claim already noted that, even when it does not do that, it is in some sense aware of its own acts of awareness. Let us turn to this 'reflexivity' feature. As we saw in Chapter II, analysed in one way the claim that conscious episodes are aware of themselves as such implies an infinite regress. Assume that every conscious mental episode is one which the subject is conscious of having. Thus for a subject to have x (e.g. 'pain' or 'red') as its content, its having that content must itself be a content for the subject. But then this content – the subject's being conscious of x – is the content of a further conscious mental episode which again must have its corresponding subject-side. Since, according to the initial assumption, every mental episode is one which the subject is conscious of having, this conscious mental episode too – consisting of the subject's consciousness of its consciousness of x – must be the content of yet another conscious mental episode, again with its subject-side, and the subject's consciousness of that in turn is a conscious mental episode, and so on infinitely.[26]

The traditional solutions are single-act solutions. They include Brentano's single-act-with-two-objects account (no additional mental act or episode is needed since each mental act, apart from its being an awareness of, e.g., a tingle, a tiger, etc., is also aware of itself as, e.g., the act itself of feeling a tingle, seeing a tiger, etc.).[27] This has its Sartrean 'non-positional' variant (consciousness is conscious of itself but not as an object, except in reflective awareness involving short-term memory).[28] And then there is Ryle's behavioural version (there is no accompanying 'monitoring or scrutiny of our doings and feelings, but only the propensity *inter alia* to avow them, when we are in the mood to do so').[29] Another version attacks the premiss that the mind is aware of all of its acts. It claims that the one and only act always in (the conscious) mind is that of experiencing, and that the mind is unaware of precisely that act.[30] Although formally satisfactory, that proposal has the paradoxical consequence that conscious episodes are themselves blind spots in the conscious mind. What the account is driving at, and is undeniable (as Sartre and Ryle agree), is that the mind does not attend to its experiencings. But that in no way implies that experiencing does not occur consciously; nor, on pain of contradiction, could it. Suppose I am running to catch a bus. Even when all I am attending to is the bus, or, more sharply focused still, the handrail as I despairingly lunge at it, it cannot be said that my act of experiencing is something of which I am not conscious. To say that it is would imply grotesquely that experiencing is something I might do without my ever knowing it.

Indeed the qualifications 'conscious' and 'consciously' are redundant in respect of 'experience' and 'experiencing'. All my experiencings are acts or events of which I am aware. The crux is that the manner in which I know my experiencings for what they (consciously) are is not the same as that in which I am conscious of what they are experiencings of. The difference can be put graphically by saying that the conditions of satisfaction of my knowing, say, that I am seeing a bus or hankering after a Martini are *in* the mind without being *before* the mind. The conditions do not correspond to presentational states of affairs, as do those for there being a bus before me or a hankering for a Martini 'within' me (an actual Martini in the hand satisfies the hankering but is not, of course, what makes it true that I am hankering for one). Nor are the conditions straight-forwardly behavioural as in Ryle's account: the self-knowledge is not merely a matter of what I am liable to say if in the mood; the knowledge is a continual feature of the experiencing. It could be called a dispositional feature, but what that means is that the concurrent knowledge can be reconstructed as the topic of a later act of experiencing, not that I have a propensity to bring it to mind or utterance, of which propensity I am no more aware than any third person.

So far, it looks as though we are saying that self-conscious acting and feeling is a matter of knowing that p, in some propositional sense, but without attention to the circumstances that are the conditions of satisfaction of p. If not directly incoherent, that is at least obscure. What more positive account is available? Perhaps concurrent self-knowledge can be linked to an acting subject's ongoing sense of the place of its doings and feelings in a wider context, a matter of the continuity of the subject from its own point of view. If the subject is continually present in experience, and there is enough short-term memory to establish the 'specious present',[31] then any conscious episode will include not only what is focally 'before the mind' (the bus I am running to catch or the lack of physical form which makes it look as though I'm not going to catch it) but also the immediate past (e.g. my already having started to run) and the salient future (what will happen if I miss the bus) with which the present activity is intrinsically connected. If conscious episodes are related to one another internally, not externally as the 'act' terminology suggests, the sensible cohesion of the immediate past with the present will allow the subject quite ordinarily to 'bring to mind' or 'avow' its own doings and feelings.[32] It can do that without having to look over its own shoulder to catch itself in the act; or without having had to do so in order to be able to recapture the requisite experience.

Further support for such an account might be sought in the fact that human responses occur within an articulated thought-structure. Traditionally, human beings were distinguished from 'brutes' by the supposed absence in the latter of a capacity for introspection, the 'spiritual' aspect.[33] But since introspection, as a form of reflective awareness as opposed to the concurrent self-knowledge we are discussing, is just a special case of human-type awareness, this attempt to mark the distinction leads straightaway to the infinite regress. What is common in all cases of such awareness, however, is its exemplifying some conceptual structure. A current way of putting this is to say that a subject of consciousness is necessarily conscious of something 'under a certain description'. Since descriptions have conceptual links with other descriptions, these links may then be considered to enter at least incipiently into any conscious episode. What sets human consciousness apart – if not so obviously from that of all other organisms, then at least from 'mere responders and information processors', is that in the human case conscious episodes involve *conceptual* acts.[34]

It is unclear, however, just what feature of conceptual acts can supply the basis we need. Take, for example, the generalization feature. If what is required of a response involving a conceptual act is that the response can be generalized to an indefinitely large variety of conceptually determined situations, although this has obvious consequences for communication and co-ordination of response, as well perhaps as for the richness and articulateness of which human response is capable, it has no obvious implications for the alleged self-consciousness of ordinary human action. True, such responses are selective in a way that, arguably, mere responding and information-processing are not. That is, the response is not directly to a stimulus 'given' to experience in the sense of being selected for a subject by a cognitively attuned but non-conceptual analysing process which has no part in a subject-side, a stimulus that simply occurs as *the* salient aspect of the environment to whatever sensorium an information processor may be thought to possess. In the case of conceptual response the selectivity is due to the system of concepts or rules which form the subject's experiential repertoire. This in itself can be thought of as forming a rift or hiatus between the world of situations and those centres of response which subjects of consciousness, on this picture, begin to appear to be. However, even if this much cleavage is established, it is not clear that it contributes to our understanding of the self-consciousness of the selective responses themselves. Similarly with the flexibility and adaptability of conceptually mediated response; for the changes in pattern of response that occur as the human organism learns new ways of responding, although they may indicate the superior flexibility of this kind of response over that of straightforward information-processing, do not require the postulation of acts of deploying or refashioning concepts which are themselves self-conscious.

And yet, as subjects of consciousness, we do grasp ourselves as distinct and continuing centres of activity with the ability at least to deploy and refashion *ourselves*. We also think of the world in which we act as external to and independent of us, and as experiencers we also have the *concept* of 'experience' as implying a contrast between how the world at any rate appears and how it may actually be in itself. As subjects of consciousness we conceive of ourselves as subjects opposed to a surrounding world which can demonstrate to us that our responses are inappropriate and in need of correction. But we also conceive of ourselves as pursuers of projects of which our particular pieces of attentiveness are parts. So there is something more heavily weighted on the subject-side than the mere fact that the selectivity of responses is due to a system of concepts or rules which the subject's experiential repertoire instantiates. There are the projects which form the background and rationale for what shareable concepts and rules a particular environment will press into service in the case of *this* subject rather than that.

Whatever accounts for the subject's self-awareness in acts of consciousness must be more than a continuing awareness of a goal or project under which a current piece of attentiveness is 'subsumed'. We don't always have such goals, and when we do we may temporarily lose sight of them. But whenever we attend to something, and it seems that in fact we nearly always do,[35] our attentiveness is always subsumed under some concept or rule. It is said that the form in which concepts and rules are known need not be propositional; it can be a form of practice, just knowing 'how to go on'. But this disjunction may well be false: knowing how to go on could be a propositional aspect of the agent's or feeler's own experience. In that case knowing how to go on might be, from the agent's point of view, not just being prepared to see how it goes on, but concurrently knowing that the right way of going on is under way. Taking our cue from the phrase 'knowing that', we can call this a propositional theory of the subject. It is not propositional in the sense of there being a set or series of representations. The knowledge exists even when the circumstances which are the conditions of satisfaction of *p* are not the point of focus. But they can *become* the point of focus, and that is the dispositional aspect of this knowledge. Here, then, we have a possible interpretation of the claim that the subject's 'acts' of consciousness are conceptual acts, an interpretation which links that claim with the previous one that the mind is aware of all of its acts.

Whether or not the view bears further analysis – and as presented it does admittedly look suspiciously like a mere paraphrase of the earlier claim – it has at least some significant consequences. If all our conscious episodes are conceptualized, and subjects or 'selves' are fully present within them, then there is no 'raw' self that has them; just as there can be no 'raw feels' if by that is meant some aspect of conscious experience that has bare particularity. The human subject is as constitutionally propositional as its objects. It is bound to sort, classify, or 'conceive' things, including itself and its own activity. But is there any 'it' thus bound? It seems that any subject 'of' such acts of classification would have to be transcendental – what Wittgenstein calls the metaphysical subject, at most 'the boundary (not a part) of the world'.[36] But a psychological self wholly present in each phase of its own projects and practices would be 'immanent' in the solipsistic series or sequence of knowings *that* something or other is going on or being done.

The notion of being 'wholly' present implies not only that everything that pertains to the subject is there, but also that what is there is present in some unified way. Traditionally, the problem of the 'unity of consciousness' has to do with how the mind 'synthesizes' separate inputs to produce such fully-fledged multimodal objects as sweet-smelling tasty red apples, and (for instance in Brentano's case) how acts of consciousness can have several 'objects' at a time; whether, in view of the multiplicity of mental phenomena in a given act, 'there is still a real unity which encompasses them all'; and whether, say, the words of a sentence may be more intimately connected than simultaneous sensations of different senses.[37] Recently, however, the question of the unity of consciousness has been raised in connection with the underlying physiology of the mind. Thomas Nagel has argued that in trying to discover the neurophysiological basis of mind, we come across facts which are in conflict with the belief in a single subject of experience; that is, with what is perhaps the central component of the notion of a mind whose basis we are out to find. A central case in point are the data from brain-bisection patients; that is, from epileptics who have undergone operations involving the severing of the higher connections, or commissures, between the two cerebral hemispheres. Nagel's argument, in synopsis, is as follows.[38]

The brain-bisection data (which we shall not rehearse here) appear to give functional evidence of the existence in commissurotomy patients of two distinct minds. Granted that the patients have a fairly normal mind associated with the hemisphere controlling the production of speech (nearly always the left hemisphere), there is still too much apparent purposiveness in the responses of the other hemisphere to conclude that these are simply automatic; and furthermore, there is enough alertness, organization, and intermodal coherence in those responses to support the attribution of a distinct mind. This despite the fact, for example, that the subject denies awareness of the activities of the second hemisphere, as well as the fact that these activities are not particularly intelligent and do not include speech. On the other hand, since in non-experimental situations the surprising normality of the patients' overall behaviour suggests that they are as mentally integrated as we are, there is no real evidence outside those situations that they do not possess only one mind. However, the argument goes on, it is implausible to suppose that the experiments actually produce any fundamental change in the patients, for example establishing a second mind just on those occasions; and in view of the depth of the split they reveal – deep enough to make it impossible for us to imagine what it is like to be both parts simultaneously – the plausible supposition is that they do indeed lack the psychological unity we require of individual subjects of experience.

But then, continues Nagel, since this shows that mental activity is possible without a single mental subject, what grounds have we for assuming that we ourselves are such single mental subjects? May not our own unity be 'merely another case of integration, more or less effective, in the control system of a complex organism'? And in the final analysis, he urges, 'what we call a single mind consists of an enumeration of the types of functional integration that typify it', types that can 'be eroded in different ways, and to different degrees'. To invoke the notion of a single subject to explain our own, apparently unified, functioning is 'an illusion':

> Either this subject contains the mental life, in which case it is complex and its unity must be accounted for in terms of the unified operation of its components and functions, or else it is an extensionless point, in which case it explains nothing.[39]

But consider. That a psychologically involved self cannot be, in Wittgenstein's metaphor,[40] an extensionless point is clear enough. But the alternative need not be to say that it is no more than a product of the manner or degree of integration of its components and functions. So long as a split-brain patient is aware that there is some functional anomaly in the organization, then there is still a reason to say that she or he is a single subject.[41] There is nothing transcendental or extensionless about this subject so long as it is actively or passively engaged in whatever puzzlement and annoyance the failures in its own performance give rise to. Writers on the split-brain data have a tendency to leap to the conclusion that functional disruption at the conscious level indicates a rupture in the self, with correspondingly separated streams of consciousness. Often they prejudge the issue by talking of the hemispheres themselves as subjects; Nagel, for instance, has them 'guessing', 'complaining', etc., while whatever 'smiles', 'frowns', or 'guttural exclamations of disgust' emanate from the patients are treated as pieces of inter-hemispheric reaction rather than intelligible responses of a single subject.[42]

But if, as Gillett points out, the states of informational disruption are only transient and the patients 'tend to "get their act back together again" albeit gradually', the question we should ask is not how many separate streams of consciousness there are, but whether there isn't 'some single subject of experience who is making and is aware of these mistakes'.[43] If there is, then whatever illusions attend the belief that complete functional integration can actually be *explained* by the presence of a single subject, at least belief in the potentially significant presence of a numerically single subject will not be an illusion *even in the case of functional disruption*. Gillett mentions one way in which the presence of such a subject can be significant, namely as a factor in rehabilitation.[44] But this would indicate that its presence has a wider significance as part of the explanation of the brain-bisection data themselves. In any case, to approach the question of the existence of such a subject one has to focus on the right spot. According to Nagel, what undermines attributions of unity of consciousness are such things as 'lack of interaction in the domain of visual experience and conscious intention' and lack of intramodal and cross-modal connectedness in experience.[45] But these are things we can very well imagine as contents *of* experience. The impossibility of imagining what it is like to be 'both hemispheres' simultaneously may well be a conceptual illusion due to the assumption that unity is to be accounted for in terms of the 'components and functions' of the subject's mental life.

In conclusion, let me briefly diagnose that illusion. It has at least two origins. One is the belief that unity must imply lack of contradiction. Now thought-ascription involves attributing relevant inferential patterns, and evidence for the presence of a subject will include whatever behavioural grounds there are for supposing that such patterns are being instantiated. What makes it appear evident in these cases that there cannot be just one mind is that the patient simultaneously performs contradictory tasks. But before reaching that conclusion, caution indicates that one should compare such allegedly incompatible tasks with complex performances which we ordinarily regard as quite normally accommodated within a single mental moment, and search the data with other interpretations in mind than those that most obviously suit the hypothesis of mental separation. It may look as though the split-brain patient loves and hates his wife at the same time, because with one hand he embraces her and with the other pushes her away; but apart from its not being self-evident that love and hate are incompatible states of the same mental moment, the fact of brain-bisection might lead one to suppose that the two hands are dealing with quite different and not obviously incompatible modal aspects of the loved or hated (or both loved and hated) one.[46]

Second, there is the point made at the beginning of the chapter. The unity sought but not found here is of the ambitious kind inherited from Descartes's substantial ego. Not finding this unlikely feature, the theorist who faces the messy area of actual content without some alternative model for the ego will be left with the classificational schematisms of psychology and neurology, with their distinctively 'modular' picture of the processes underlying behaviour. The mind then seems in some absolute way to be a collection of separate, specialized functions, and 'unity' to be a concept applicable only at the functional level, where the human organism demonstrates or fails to demonstrate a consistency of appropriate performance. At the level of basic modular processing, there is of course no unity in any apperceptive sense. So only the ability of these processes distributively to produce a co-operative performance can justify the attribution of unity or singleness of mind. But if we could place the subject in rather than above or behind its conscious episodes, the theorist would indeed have an alternative: one in which unity or singleness are provided by an apperceptive form of control exerted at the top and which, so long as that form of control persists, imposes *its* unity on the separate and specialized functions. In that case, and it is an argument we shall return to in Chapter VII, the alternative Nagel gives us to a non-explanatory extensionless point would not be the only one. For it would not be the components and functions that determined the unity of the complex mental life that the subject 'contains'. If the components and functions of a mental life issue in a unified operation, that would be due to there being a subject which 'contains' them in a more active sense, by being present in the operation itself.

CHAPTER V

Objects

Often what a current theory claims to be its problem is not the one it really faces. Earlier we considered the proposal to treat pains as objects. We did that because we saw that physicalist theorizing about mind, satisfied in the main that the operational core of the mental is amenable to functionalist (as once also to behaviourist) analysis, finds sensations – for reasons we mentioned in Chapter III – stubbornly resistant. To be able to conclude that pains, as sensations, really are in, say, the neck seems to promise a solution to the problem of qualia in general, which for much current philosophy of mind – as noted in Chapter I – is *the* problem of consciousness.

But the real problem facing much materialist philosophy of mind is to vindicate the token-identity theories with which it tries to combine an ordinary mentalistic vocabulary of thoughts, desires, fears, etc. with a physicalist explanation of the events to which that vocabulary applies. The impossibility of actually translating mentalistic predicates like 'wanting to visit Paris' into the vocabulary of, say, neurobiology is not in question. It is clear that so long as psychology, even a scientific psychology, employs mentalistic predicates, there is no possibility of describing psychological events in purely physiological terms. For physicalists, however, my wanting to visit Paris must just be a form of physical, typically a neural, event. So the problem they face is that of admitting this possibility even though the language of mental states and events cannot be part of the language of physiology.

Davidson's way of putting this latter point is to say that the mental and the physical are regulated by incongruent sets of constitutive principles.[1] Mental states are related to one another (either succeed or fail to go together) in terms of rationality, coherence, and consistency, while physical states are related to one another in (enter or fail to enter into) relations of lawlike causation, and unlike mental states they are also susceptible of various forms of quantitative analysis. If mental and physical terms are used in explanations, or perhaps even just descriptions, of events within their respective domains, then it must be the case that the mental and the physical vocabularies each contain words for 'kinds' or general types of events. But if Davidson is right it will be impossible to correlate kinds of mental event, described in a normal mentalistic way, with kinds of neurological event, described in the precise language of neurobiology. Type–type identity is excluded. Mind–brain identity theories are, historically though not necessarily, attempts to preserve the belief that physicalist science is self-sufficient, without abandoning the belief that mentalistic predicates are true of real events. (Not necessarily, since in a different theoretical climate they might be attempts to assert mentalistic theories without implying a reversion to substance-dualism.) But given the desire to preserve the principle of physical sufficiency, if type-identity theories are excluded for Davidson's reasons the only alternative is token–token identity. For the token-identity physicalist (as opposed to a putative token-identity mentalist) no psychological type can be mapped on to a neurological type, but any possible or actual psychological event is also a neurological (or, more widely, physiological) event. This, as in Davidson's 'anomalous monism', allows mental events to be described in neurophysiological terms which bring them under a closed system of causal laws. Describing them in mental terms is not to do so. The anomalism is both vertical and horizontal: on the one hand there are no strict laws connecting my thinking about visiting Paris with the neurological events that occur as I do think of visiting Paris (psychophysical anomalism); and on the other there are no laws strictly connecting my thinking this with other mental states (psychological anomalism).[2] The vertical anomalism preserves an opacity between the two ways of describing the same event, thus guaranteeing the closure of the physical system, while the fact that there are no psychological laws ensures that the physical way of describing it has no competitor. However much one may legitimately speak in normal mentalistic terms of the event of my thinking about visiting Paris, it is still a neural event which we could describe in strict neurological terms if we knew enough about the specific case and its mechanism. In short, under their physical descriptions, mental events, just like any others, are susceptible of total explanations of the kind afforded by physics; that is, in terms of physical laws and other physically described events.

The promise of token-identity theories, then, is their offer of a non-reductive physicalism. Mental events can be a species of physical event in spite of the fact that psychological descriptions are untranslatable into neurology. But the problem is that in ascribing psychological predicates we are left offering what certainly look like, and are conventionally intended as, a genuine if special form of explanation (in which rationality, coherence, and consistency play a special role) of something whose behaviour can nevertheless be predetermined by concepts of another and totally disparate kind. There are plenty of indications that token-identity physicalists are in two minds about the psychological domain having no genuinely explanatory value at all, or about there not being any authentically and autonomously mental reality corresponding to whatever descriptive resources it may possess. An example is Dennett's use of the notion of an 'intentional stance', officially an instrumental concept enabling the observer merely to make sense of behaviour, but at times verging close upon being a means of access to objectively existing patterns not accessible to a purely physical stance.[3]

Token-identity physicalists often obscure the issue by pointing to certain kinds of activity, such as monetary exchange and time-keeping, which can be performed in numerous different ways and with different physical 'realizations'. They regard these as unproblematic for physicalism, and suggest it is a mistake to see any further difficulty in the case of psychology. There is an objection to this, well put by Madell. It is that the analogues themselves can be understood only against the background of human purposes and interests which economic or chronometric conventions serve; it is these purposes and interests that allow 'any of an indefinitely large class of physical items which exhibit no common feature at all' to be identified in particular instances (tokens) as the activity in question. But how can the claim that each token of a psychological state is identical with some physical arrangement be established if the explanatory categories of psychology are not reducible to those of the physical sciences? You cannot appeal here to the background of human psychology to bring the disparate descriptions to bear on the same event, 'since in this case we are concerned with the explanatory categories of psychology itself'.[4]

The crux of the problem is that a psychological description of an event applies explanatory concepts which are *sui generis*. It is this, in a way, that makes theories like anomalous monism themselves anomalous. All identity theories lose credibility to the degree that the domains they try to unite project disparate forms of explanation. It is only if mentalistic categories could either be part of or, alternatively, reduced to the categories of some suitable physical science that physically based identity theories would begin to be credible and the goal of a unified theory of nature with man in place a realistic one. The same point can be made in another way. For various reasons, claims have been made for a weaker form of relation than identity, e.g. correlation, or 'union'.[5] Although correlation is a weaker form of psychophysical connection, it implies something much tighter at the level of explanation. Indeed, if the coincidence between each of our thoughts or feelings and some neural event turned out to be general enough to be of a lawlike character, it would be hard to see what argument there could be for the mutual autonomy of the psychological and physical domains.[6]

That perhaps they are not mutually autonomous might be a thought in the right direction. But clearly it is one that can point in two opposite directions. One direction is eliminative materialism. Obviously that view offers a cleaner and more consistent programme than the non-reductive form of physicalism to be found in token-identity theories. If the problem facing materialist philosophy of mind is to combine an ordinary mentalistic vocabulary of thoughts, desires, fears, etc. with a physicalist explanation of the events to which that vocabulary applies, the best way out is the outright elimination of mentalistic terms or, for any that resist elimination, their reduction to a purely physicalist vocabulary. This removes the fundamental weakness of token-identity theories, namely the retention of a set of referential terms that lack any function or role in explanation.

But among the reasons for favouring a correlation account of psychophysical connection over identity, there are some that point in the opposite direction.[7] One of these will occupy us in a subsequent chapter: it is that there are indeed reasons for retaining mentally referential terms; that psychological events really do hang together on non-causal rationality principles; and that there is reason to surmise that there are non-causal principles of explanation, or at least principles which, if causal, are not of the kind paradigmatically afforded by physical science. Of course, if such principles are taken to compete with strict physical explanation of the same event we are back with the anomalies of token-identity. The way in which this feature of psychological events supports correlation in favour of identity is that it ascribes to the mental a structure which physical events in themselves are incapable of possessing on any current account of the physical. It is the same sort of reason as was once brought against type–type mind–brain identity theories: brain states would have to have properties (e.g. the 'burning' quality of a pain) which are no part of any possible neurological description of the brain; and mental states would have to have properties (e.g. the firing of certain C-fibres) which no mentalistic vocabulary could conceivably contain.

There are two ways in which physicalism might fail: by not exhausting the explanatory vocabulary we need to explain human behaviour, or by not being able to absorb the mental in its genuinely mentalistic form. Our focus in this chapter is on the latter. In particular we shall look at what is usually referred to as the 'intentionality' or 'other-directedness' of conscious experience. The ability of a mental state to refer beyond itself looks, at least at first glance, fairly convincingly like a residual anomaly of the mental which will survive any merger with the physical on the explanatory level; that is to say, it promises to be a feature of reality which physicalism is unable to absorb in any case, and independently of any incongruency between the psychological and the neurological as modes of explanation or of any possible intrusion of either of these upon each other's domain. Apposite here is Brentano's well-known claim that intentionality, or the directedness (*Gerichtetsein*) of mind upon its objects, is the mark of the mental. What he called the 'intentional in-existence' of the mind's objects, or 'the reference to something as an object', is 'a distinguishing mark of all mental phenomena'. And Brentano claimed that '[n]o physical phenomenon exhibits anything similar'.[8]

Classically, the mind's objects have been grasped as being somehow within the sensing, thinking (etc.) subject, or 'within consciousness'. Brentano himself insisted that the objects were real things, in respect, naturally, of the mind's concern with them. But there are notorious difficulties in arriving at a satisfactory analysis. Take, for instance, the traditional epistemological argument based on the possibility of illusion. Dreams, or faithful visual hallucinations, and ordinary veridical experience can be mutually indistinguishable, at least on the basis of the experiences themselves; consequently the actual content of the (in this case) visual experiences must be identical. But then, since what is seen in the former case is not something external, it follows that what we directly see in ordinary veridical experience cannot be external either. So perceptual experience as experience of a world of real – that is, mind-independent – objects, if possible at all, must be indirect, and the objects that are directly before the mind are mental objects. This, together with other arguments, for instance that no visual (etc.) experience bears on its face any trace of its causal origin, lent support to the strongly first-person stance of classical Cartesianism, with its belief both in the foundational role of first-hand experience and in the inner transparency of the mental.

At the opposite pole we find a thoroughly third-person view of intentionality which analyses the mind's 'other-directedness' in purely behavioural terms. Recall, however, that the formula which best expresses the duality of conscious episodes is that of 'subject–content' rather than 'subject–object'. This suggests that any account of intentionality will have to do with the way in which words apply to the world. The way in which they do that is commonly accounted for in terms of the relations that utterances bear to specifiable 'truth-conditions' or 'conditions of satisfaction', corresponding to publicly identifiable states of affairs. The behaviourist analyses intentional activity against a pre-hung backcloth on which the objects of the organism's various forms of engagement are fully represented. The relations between utterance and world are then taken to be manifested in behaviour. On one version, the behaviour may actually consist in words of some natural language; the objects a person has 'in mind' can then be identified by noting correlations between utterance and backcloth. For functionalists, however, there is something more basic. As we noted earlier, 'mind' for functionalists does not break down into actual and possible behaviour; it is something inherent to the organism – something inside, or at any rate about, the organism that initiates goal-directed behaviour. But when it comes to saying what it is inside or about the organism that does this, the functionalist finds no need to refer to conscious episodes or their content. Intentional meaning is introduced in terms of relations that can be inferred from the behaviour of the organism just as if that behaviour were the output of a machine. All you need is an appropriately interpreted formal system for making sense of the machine's input–output relations.[9] Here, ascriptions of semantic content are not made to any representational function in the machine itself, nor indeed to anything 'about' the machine. They are merely ways of construing the 'system' from outside. The only conscious mind that the analysis presupposes is that of the interpreter.

This view has been vigorously contested by John Searle, who urges that conscious mental states are essential to human activity and that we must 'always insist on the first-person point of view'.[10] Searle has recently been concerned to rebut claims that no 'mental entities' intervene between stimulus and response, e.g. 'consciousness, intentionality, thoughts, or any internal "meanings" connecting the stimuli to the noises'.[11] And in arguing the need to 'analyze . . . the level of semantics [which] involves a level of intentionality', he characterizes this level as one at which 'we express beliefs and desires . . . mean things by sentences and mean quite specific things by certain words inside of sentences'.[12] The burden of Searle's argument is to show that conclusions drawn by Quine about the indeterminacy of translation and by Davidson about the inscrutability of reference can just as well be taken as refutations of the respective premisses.[13] In fact it is a comprehensive attack on what might be labelled the 'evidential' approach to attributions of content. The important thing is Searle's insistence on invoking first-person, common-sense intuitions against the kind of restrictions Quine and Davidson put on the empirical basis for assigning specific contents to utterances.[14] Roughly, *we* know what we mean even if under publicly observable conditions the sentences we use or hold true provide others with insufficient evidence for ascribing a determinate content.[15] In the case of functionalists the point is rather that unless there is a first-person 'place', there will be nothing for you to ascribe a determinate content to.

It is worth noting that Searle's first-person view of the intentionality of mental states is not as radical a departure as it might have been. Searle assumes that the only *conscious* mental states which could 'intervene' between stimulus and vocal response are 'propositional'. There are two ways in which this can be seen to impose unnecessary limitations on the notion, and hence the explanatory potential, of consciousness. One has to do with what Searle has to say about 'literal meaning'; the other concerns his distinction between, on the one hand, the propositional content of our thinking, by virtue of which an intentional state *represents* objects and states of affairs, and on the other hand the 'psychological mode or manner' in which the representative content occurs.[16]

Consider the first limitation. Searle doesn't claim that 'intentionality' and consciousness are coextensive; one can have beliefs which one isn't currently entertaining, and there are conscious states, e.g. 'forms of nervousness, elation, and undirected anxiety', which lack a definite object.[17] More important, Searle argues that the actual content of a mental state cannot be given independently of its relation to other mental states and also to practical background knowledge which is of a non-propositional nature.[18] To ascribe a conscious intention to someone, e.g. 'marry Jocasta' or 'make a sandwich', one must also ascribe a whole network of beliefs or assumptions which the given expression contextually implies (for instance that Jocasta is not the person's mother, or that gravitational forces will keep the cheese from flying off the bread), but which need not, typically do not, and could never in their entirety, enter the person's mind. They are accordingly outside consciousness. Indeed some of these implied assumptions will be so general in character, and so embedded in social custom, as in all likelihood never to have entered the person's mind as conscious thoughts at all.

An important argument is built on these considerations. In order to account for the 'quite specific things' which the words used in actual expressions of conscious intentions mean, one must invoke a background of understanding that 'goes beyond meaning'.[19] Take the word 'open'. This, according to Searle, has a literal meaning common to its use in a variety of contexts, e.g. 'open the door, 'open your eyes', 'open the book at page 37'.[20] What it means in each case, however, corresponds to a set of conditions of satisfaction specific to the context in question. In other words, the literal sense does not express a specific action of opening common to all of them. What determines the conditions that the action must satisfy in each context is a 'preintentional' background. Without appealing to that background you cannot supply the definite set of conditions corresponding to the verb 'open' specifically in, e.g., 'open the door'. Therefore if what does enter a person's conscious mind is expressible in words understood exclusively in terms of their literal meanings, the person's actual intention in a given instance will have to be found in some mode of understanding that 'goes beyond' what that person literally and consciously means. Searle identifies this mode of understanding with preintentional 'capacities and social practices': knowing *how* to open 'doors, books, eyes, wounds, and walls'.[21]

Now, although Searle's main point, that intentional content depends on preintentional capacities, may be granted, and one allows that the level of meaning that intercedes between stimulus and noise has this foreground/background character (or, rather, that it *is* the foreground in respect of a preintentional background), there is room for doubting whether the account accurately captures the *extent*, or perhaps *depth*, of what may count as content, even if this is more closely identified as intentional content. In fact I believe that Searle's propositional account of conscious states underrates the semantic resources of these states. Consider the claim that there is a level of literal meaning which remains the same even if one alters the preintentional background. Why shouldn't the primary sense of 'meaning' in connection with mental content be that specified by the contextually relevant conditions of satisfaction themselves, so that 'literal meaning' can be shelved as some lexicographical abstraction? Indeed, unless that were so, if (i) the content of an utterance is a function of the literal meaning of its components, (ii) literal meaning is indeterminate at the level of consciousness, and (iii) what we are conscious of is confined to what is immediately known to the first person, occupancy of the first-person point of view will put you in no better position with regard to the meanings of your own utterances than that of a Davidsonian observer. The first-person intuition that you straightaway know what you mean, in the sense that you know *that* you mean it, still remains unaccounted for. The solution is surely to say that one is conscious of intentional content to whatever degree is required to distinguish first-personally the specific 'conditions of satisfaction' of one's utterances. Where 'opening the door' expresses what I consciously believe myself to be doing, then what entered my mind would be what I took to satisfy this case of opening something. Of course, as Searle points out, nothing representational with regard to what it means to open things need enter my mind at all as I burst into my office or wander, deeply preoccupied, into the corridor. But this does not mean that there is no sense in which I am aware (in some diminishing degree) of the truth-conditions of the quite specific thing that I mean by 'opening the door'.

In that case one may speculate as to whether any consciousness that intervenes between stimulus and vocal response might not also include what for Searle is the preintentional level. In a discussion of Searle, Richard Aquila has suggested that, '[i]nstead of thinking in terms of things done "against" a certain background', we might regard

91

a set of non-intentional capacities as 'comprising part of the *material* of any psychological state that has the "form" of intentionality'.[22] This could be a fruitful suggestion. At least it has the conceptual advantage of placing background 'skills, stances, preintentional assumptions and presuppositions, practices, and habits' unambiguously, as Searle too intends, among *mental* phenomena.[23] But the metaphor of hylomorphism also implies the inseparability of psychological matter and form. So, assuming for the sake of argument that intentionality is indeed the form of this matter, the model would allow us to think of intentionality as applying on some scale or other to anything that counts as a psychological state.

But now let us apply this thought to Searle's distinction between representative content and psychological manner or mode. This corresponds to a common-sense model of the subject's active contact with the world. There is, first, a referential core of our thinking, a propositional part which either represents or fails to represent those segments of reality which form the targets of our anticipations, surmisings, and recollections. Surrounding that core there is a mental state or attitude corresponding to the psychological mode of our thinking, whether hope, fear, expectation, relief, belief, disbelief, or whatever. If, as Searle has put it, intentionality is 'that feature of mental states . . . that enables those states to represent other things',[24] then the psychological mode forms the practical 'how' of our engagement while the referential core forms the cognitive 'what', with perception functioning as a testing ground and continuing control.

There are two ways of understanding the distinction. According to one, the world is, roughly, a unitary space–time continuum containing assorted and, at the level of perception, fairly unfugitive matter. The matter provides common vistas for suitably placed perceivers, and the basic form of access to these vistas is direct acquaintance with whatever public objects, states of affairs, and events a view of them affords. Perception, thus conceived, is like viewing things from a window, viewing things which others can view from other windows, windows from which anyone can look. A description of those things provides the 'what', while the 'how' is accommodated in a separate 'non-cognitive' category which, though it may be called mental, does not affect or invade the cognitive core.

The other way of understanding the distinction is as a theoretical categorization abstracted from the actual phenomenological situation in which the two are never entirely separable. To find a model for this version, one need only examine visual experience itself, without introducing any psychological modes. The visual 'how' is not usually accounted for in philosophical analyses of perception. The reason for that may be linked to the naïve assumption that the 'what' is the province of scientists, journalists, and photographers, while the 'how' remains a kind of window-dressing, on the analogy of what Frege refers to as the 'colouring and shading which poetic eloquence seeks to give to the sense' and which is 'not objective' because it must be 'evoked by each hearer or reader according to the hints of the poet or the speaker'.[25] But the significance of the visual 'how' is that it is a 'how' whose specification necessarily enjoys the referential position. It does so simply because any specification of the visual 'how' is a specification of how some public object appears to be but at least in part only because that is how some particular mind grasps it. It is a plain fact of experience that visual characteristics not true of things in their strictly public space and status nevertheless appear to be true of them.

This fact gives rise to a question which the recent linguistic tradition in philosophy contrived to conceal. It is the question of the true identity of the bearer of these aspects: is there still an incorruptible core to the corruptible 'what', or does the possibility of the invasion of the 'what' by the 'how' somehow reduce the referential core of perception as a whole to 'subjective' or 'mental' status? It is not that the phenomena or the distinctions are ignored, but simply that they are dealt with at a level where the crucial problems do not arise or else are susceptible of merely linguistic and therefore facile solutions. Thus there is talk of two *languages* of perception: the language of 'appearing', in which the object-phrases of verbs of perception are specifications of things that exist outside minds; and the language of 'appearance', in which verbs of perception (perhaps the very same verbs but with different uses) have as their complements specifications not necessarily applicable to whatever (if anything – it may be pure imagery or 'empty' hallucination) appears in the former sense.[26] This may give rise to the ontological problem of the status of the merely intentional (i.e. unreal) objects of appearance-descriptions, but then one seeks to eliminate these rogue references by treating the object-phrases corresponding to them as 'oblique' references to public things not presently appearing: they are references contained in clauses specifying how some presently appearing object 'looks'. Thus the true description 'I see two pennies', when there is only one penny to be seen, is elliptical for 'I see what looks like two pennies'.[27] The result seems to be that one can go away satisfied that all descriptions of visual content are 'ultimately' descriptions of how publicly perceivable objects appear or look, and that no descriptions of how they appear or look include specifications of things which are not publicly perceivable.

The message of the visual example is that there are good phenomenological grounds for denying any sharp categorial distinction between a psychological 'how' and a cognitive 'what'. The psychological modes 'infect' the propositional contents, so that a *full* set of truth-conditions for a given content may have to include the psychological mode in which the 'what' presents itself ('credible', 'untrustworthy', 'captivating', 'frightening', as the case may be). This is most apparent in volitional experience, the most central and concrete form of experience there is, and in which the way we experience an object depends on how we are going to use it, or how we could use it.[28] Thus things and situations assume a variety of kinds and degrees of subjective importance, depending on whatever relations of interest (involving also time and distance) they stand in to subjects of experience. The experiences themselves, their content, and so also their sense, vary correspondingly.

What is wrong is the intellectualist assumption that consciousness and intentionality add nothing significant to what we are already allegedly given in the idea of propositional content. It is a fallacy that gives undue credence to several influential views. Concentrating the idea of human mentality in the ability to manipulate sentences in natural languages has clear ideological advantages for those who aspire to master the principles of the human mind by developing computer programs capable of processing such languages. It also helps to make observational accounts of meaning, like Quine's and Davidson's, which are based on forms of assent to sentences stimulated by events in the world,[29] look like full-fledged theories of the mind. What falls through the net of responses can then be dismissed as psychological incident.[30] Taken to extremes, this leads to the illusion that the evidently true notion of a thinker's actual thought as something 'expressed' by certain audible and visible signs, but which cannot itself be 'perceived by the senses',[31] drops out of view altogether. If one abandons the first-person vantage-point, it falls between the two observable stools of inscription or utterance on the one hand and stimulus- or truth-condition on the other. The idea that meaning is captured in use and that use is behaviourally determinable is no doubt due to several powerful impulses in modern thought: respect for the concepts and methods of natural science, a post-Wittgensteinian focus on the publicity of language, and not least the obsessive anti-psychologism that led Frege to give an account of objectivity in terms of an abstract world of thoughts into which minds, or subjects, in their various particular ways enter. The 'how' of the individual mode of access is thus eclipsed by the status attached to an ideally extensional 'what', and we are left with the illusion that nothing to which the thinking subject may have special access need play any role in an account of human mental performance. In general, the propositional paradigm of intentionality ignores the (contingent) idiosyncrasies which render the visible and audible signs intelligible to observers only if the latters' modes of perception or 'grasp' are similarly idiosyncratic; it tends in any case to focus on those contents which are in fact shared, because that is what communication requires, thus incorporating a bias towards the exclusion of subjective meanings. The indications are that we should treat consciousness as a much wider concept than the propositional paradigm implies.

We noted Searle's insistence on the first-person point of view, coupled with his criticism of the view that no 'mental entities' intervene between stimulus and response. The general position is one in which conscious mental states play an essential part in the identification of intentional content. We have followed Searle in this but expanded the range of what might be included in that content. In doing so, however, we come up against some well-established counter-intuitions. One of these confines consciousness to contemplative or attentional states of 'awareness'. Hearing, seeing, tasting, or smelling something are typical examples, or catching oneself in the act of doing or thinking something.[32] To be in a conscious state is then to have some 'object' fairly definitely in mind. But our suggestion has been that whatever it is of which the subject is aware is intrinsically related to other, non-intentional features or capacities. One can, of course, simply decide to call these 'unconscious'. But that implies a categorial distinction which fails to do justice to the *phenomenological* facts of conscious experience. A better approach may be indicated by Aquila's suggestion that any non-intentional capacities or features be treated as part of the *material* of any psychological state that is intentional in *form*. Still, even the intentional/non-intentional distinction may not be such a clean one.

Once we allow that intentional objects are qualified by their subjects' concerns, we cannot assume that these qualifications will correspond to properties which the subjects themselves would be ready to attribute to them. Take an intentional predicate like 'familiar'. The familiarity of a place may be a feature of it which the subject is not aware of except retrospectively, when made to see it in some way that empties it of that quality. This, as well as many other different kinds of example, suggests that intentional objects can have properties of which the subject is currently unaware but which are nevertheless bound up with the manners or modes of the subject's engagement in a way which it would be misleading to describe negatively as unconscious and which must in any case be accorded some role in the the specification of the subject's *mental state*.

Similarly with our second counter-intuition: what might be called the essential publicity of language. We are used to hearing that languages are forms of regulated social engagement, and that understanding must be manifested in practice and actual behaviour. This Wittgensteinian position suggests that momentary mental states are not the place to find meanings. Where then should we look for them? In practices, comes the answer. Yes, but practices can be grasped from a third- or a first-person point of view. The counter-intuition begins by saying it would be wrong to take behaviour and utterance as mere outward tokens of the real thing that lies within, as if nothing in behaviour and utterance counted and what did count was the hidden mental state. It goes on to say that, if the behaviour and utterances don't tell us enough, instead of looking behind the phenomena we should look for more phenomena or place the phenomena in a broader setting. But it should be obvious that phenomena can only be placed in settings at all within mental states, whether these are mental states of people interpreting others' behaviour and utterances or mental states of those behaving and uttering. The trick, it seems to me, is to balance two apparently opposed insights: the social nature of language, and the individually sited occurrence of meaning or content. The illusion is to talk as if meaning emerged from behaviour and utterance, which would be the same as supposing that the imperceptible thought emerged of itself from audible and visible signs. What we need is some idea of meaning or content as intentional structure 'informed' not only by some 'theory of the world' but also by abilities and practices. The notion that best captures this is that of the subject's 'world'.

Before going on to discuss the relation of practices to consciousness, let us conclude this chapter by considering one particularly prevalent kind of argument used to cast doubt on the notion of intrinsic intentionality as a property of mental states. The argument is part of a general campaign to clear the mental decks of first-person protuberances, and its strategy is to enumerate a set of features essential to mental states, and then to show that the same features can be ascribed unproblematically to machines. Thus it is pointed out that a given semantic entity, say a sentence-token as it occurs in a thought-episode, cannot 'represent' reality on its own, but only in conjunction with a language of which it is a part. Since a sentence (or any other representational device) has meaning only in the context of a language, it can be regarded as a representation on its own only if we presuppose the language to which it belongs. Properly speaking, it is only the system as a whole that can be called representational. Since, however, it is impossible as well as phenomenologically unjustified to say that this entire system is present to the mind, in the form of conscious content, the presence to the mind of a sentence (as expressing a thought) or the occurrence of any isolated conscious mental state is no indication of the occurrence in consciousness of a representational ability. On the other hand, although the system itself is not present to the mind, it is indeed present, or 'realized', in the human organism's general ability to manipulate things in the world, including symbols. Thus any system evincing this ability is representational, whether or not it has a conscious component; and if there is such a component its presence is not what tells us whether the system it belongs to is representational.[33]

The argument can be made more pointedly by appeal to the idea of a Turing machine. In a Turing machine, not an actual construction but a theoretical model, there are two sets of items: a list of tokens interspersed with blanks, and changing internal states of a scanning device. The latter scans one token at a time and, depending on its current 'internal state', just reads the token and moves on to the next token (or blank) or else writes another in its place (or fills the blank) and moves on; or it just comes to a halt either leaving the token (or blank) as it was or after having changed it.[34] Tokens are just shapes, and they acquire 'meaning', so to speak, in the relation they bear to the current internal state of the scanning device. Since scanning of the internal states of the scanning device plays no part in the process, and all that is given to the scanner is an isolated token, there is no call to introduce some further item *within the scope of the scan* to account for the token's ability to bear a meaning.

The suggestion is that whatever we call conscious content has the status of a Turing token, and the process that infuses it with meaning is exhaustively describable in terms of an unscanned internal state (which in turn can be described in terms of inferential relations to scannable sequences of tokens). Given that the token in itself, or for that matter any mental state considered in a third-person guise, is not a meaning-bearer, and that its meaning must be bestowed on it by virtue of some property or relation it acquires independently of its status as a token or mental state, then that property or relation can be accounted for in one of two possible ways: either through some obscure mental act, some 'act of consciousness', which imposes meaning on the token or state; or else by virtue of sets of inferential relations which the token or state bears to other tokens or states in the thinker's 'cognitive economy'. Because it dispenses with the need to invoke mystery, the machine alternative emerges as the clear winner.

But does it? In the first place, it is phenomenologically false that the conscious (scannable) content of an episode of thinking consists merely in the presence to the mind of a sentence-token. Any sentence-token as it occurs in an actual episode of thinking already bears a meaning. That is not a piece of what cognitive scientists call 'confabulation', i.e. a filling-in of absent information by *ex post facto* rationalization, conscious or unconscious.[35] Further, there is no reason at all to think that its possessing meaning must be the result of some act of bestowing meaning on something already there that initially lacks it. The idea of 'imposing' or 'bestowing' meaning on items which, as contents of consciousness, originally lack meaning has no basis at all in experience; and if the arguments of the previous chapter have any force, there is no theoretical justification for it either: the level of meaning is the one at which we function and there is no compelling reason to regard it as the composite product of the exercise of a set of lower-level capacities. Of course, we find it convenient in certain contexts to discuss aspects of language and psychology independently of their occurrences in actual life, and then it is perfectly appropriate to talk of sentence-tokens abstracted from the meanings they bear in actual episodes of thinking; but there is no justification for taking a homonym, such as 'sentence', or indeed any sentence-token you care to mention (if sentences can be construed as names, then their tokens too are homonyms), constructed especially for discourse at that level, to be a name of some genuine item occurring in actual linguistic or psychological performance, and then requiring something to be added in order to make that performance possible.[36]

If, then, there is indeed any 'mystery' in the notion of intentional experience, it is not the mystery of how intentionality comes to be imposed on items that are not themselves intrinsically intentional. The linguistic or non-linguistic contents of human psychological states are intentional from the start. They are about things other than themselves, and the fact that they are so is part of that content. Any parallel between a Turing machine and a human psychological state would have to be in respect of the relation arising between the single token and the current internal state of the scanning device. For that is where anything describable categorically, rather than just dispositionally, in terms of 'sense' and 'meaning' would have to arise. In the machine, however, there is no locus to which such a categorical description could apply. And that, surely, is where the human psychological state essentially differs. The human psychological state is a locus of meaning, of representations, of understanding – of the 'sense' which according to Frege determines reference (what I am thinking about, or am directing my activity towards or away from) but which equally determines what it is that I am doing (reflecting, pursuing, feeling). In the case of a machine, on the other hand, there is no one location in which the token-in-relation-to-the-internal-state is itself 'represented' or instantiated. It is true, certainly, that the sense which is the content of a current mental state is linked internally with other senses in a network of inferential relations; 'internally' in so far as it would not be the sense it is did it not bear these specific relations, but also in so far as unless there are some such relations there is no sense. And it is also true that the network is not itself represented in the mental state as part of its content. But it is phenomenologically characteristic of an episode of thought that it brings the inferential relations which define a particular thought-content into momentary focus, and there being that focus is then the basis we have for describing consciousness as a locus of meaning.

A defender of the special nature and role of consciousness might, then, aim at something like the following position. Consciousness is a *sui generis* locus or medium which collects organized responses, along with the inferential relations constitutive of such responses, and pulls them out of a purely linear arrangement into a momentary whole. It is a representational medium whose objects reflect the particular relations appropriate to the areas and depths of response activated at a particular time. It is true that our mental states can have the propositional content they do have only because of their 'intricate *relational* features',[37] but it is also true that what it means for a given mental state to have a content is that it represents some state of affairs, and that its doing so is a feature of the conscious content of such a state. Any 'model' of conscious activity that rendered the momentary unity characteristic of conscious response in linear, diachronic terms would delete the very feature that defined the characteristic.

CHAPTER VI

Practice

If human consciousness is intentional, that has to be true not only of reflective thought but also of action. The 'sense' that belongs to a mental state, what the subject/agent 'has in mind', must be a question of there being some description under which the subject/agent perceives or imagines either some object (or state of affairs) or some goal of current physical activity.

This view has been labelled 'cognitivist'. It takes the contents of a human mind to be exclusively thoughts in the Cartesian sense of *cogitationes*, judgments with determinate contents currently in mind. But phenomenology does not bear out this view, as Hubert Dreyfus has shown, drawing on Heidegger's account of what it is like to be an active human being, in criticism of Husserl and others who take the world of perceptual and practical experience to be reducible analytically to the propositional contents of a 'transcendentally reduced' subjectivity; that is, analysable into infinite sets of mental contents, where these are understood to be contents of linguistically expressible thoughts.

On Dreyfus's view, the world we share is one we are embodiedly in and actively about, and the manner in which we are in and about it is not amenable to analysis in terms of conscious thoughts. Against the cognitivists, Dreyfus claims that the model of data-gathering, rule-formulating, and inference-drawing employed in computer technology does not apply to human intelligence or expertise, so the cognitivist claim that human intelligence involves the *unconscious* application of 'programmed' rules is misplaced.

Dreyfus sees in cognitivism (and Husserl) the distorting influence of Descartes. The 'data' the cognitivist employs as elements for rule-manipulation are modelled on Cartesian 'representations'. Dreyfus wants to show that elements of this kind are at best incidental features

101

of human mental life. But there is a latent ambiguity in Dreyfus's programme. On the one hand, the aim is to show how Cartesian representation plays only a secondary and parasitic role in human performance, which implies that consciousness in this 'propositional' sense plays no central role. On the other hand, however, he seems to assume that the considerations he appeals to (the phenomenology of ongoing 'coping') show that we can abandon the first-person point of view as our primary position, and bring it in only in secondary contexts that are 'parasitic' on the third-person viewpoint. But the considerations Dreyfus draws attention to can be used just as persuasively to show that we need a broader concept of consciousness than the Cartesian paradigm suggests, with a correspondingly broader application of the primordially first-person 'stance'. The sceptical point I would raise is that even if what Dreyfus refers to as the 'thickness' of things[1] and our typical ways of handling them are not analytically reducible to mental representations of the things and of our skills with them, the impression given of a securely established vantage-point among things, unmediated by a first-person level of 'understanding', is misleading because based on an unnecessarily narrow concept of consciousness.

The issue is put in focus in Dreyfus's presentation of Heidegger.[2] He presents Heidegger as claiming that consciousness is not even necessary, let alone sufficient, for human activity in general. Human activity in general is here identified as 'everyday coping', which, as against the entertaining of explicit plans and goals, is said in Heideggerian terms to be what 'Dasein's activity' essentially amounts to. Rather than being foundational, as in the Cartesian scheme, the situation in which a subject finds itself in conscious relation to an object is unintelligible except in the prior context of the proficient exercise of human skills. Thus with Heidegger's example of hammering. In normal functioning, the hammer does not stand to the hammerer as an object; it is 'invisible' in the sense that while I am hammering I am unaware of any determinate characteristics of the hammer. Awareness of equipment arises in (three) different degrees, depending on the extent to which smooth functioning is disturbed: (i) *momentary malfunction* brings the hammer into awareness but only to trigger the smooth functioning of some adjustive skill: for example, the hammer slips in my sweaty hand but readjusting my grip is just another exercise of skill requiring no awareness; (ii) *temporary breakdown* requires a shift into the 'subjective mode' as I form beliefs, goals, etc. to 'fix what has failed to function'; and, finally, (iii) *total breakdown*, which, if the operation is to continue, can require us to engage in theoretical explanation, 'a new kind of activity': for example, if the head of the hammer keeps breaking we may 'step back from the specific activity we are engaged in and take a broader look at the general problem of what hammer heads are made of, or perhaps at the even broader problems raised by metallurgy, etc.'. In this way the hammer raises itself to the level of an object of consciousness; the hammerer becomes aware, occurrently cognizant of (not just disposed, when questioned, to affirm) the fact that it is heavy, made of polished wood and metal, and so on.

Although the account is plausible, Dreyfus must surely admit that there are significantly different ways in which a proficient performer can be unaware of any determinate characteristics of a hammer. For example, he may be using a screwdriver, having put the hammer on the bench behind him. Or he may never have seen a hammer, or even heard of such a thing. So clearly some more discriminating formula is needed, something that captures positively the way in which hammers *are* componented into proficient hammering. A comparison might be sought in a corresponding 'invisibility' of hands and legs. When walking or running, one is not normally thinking of these or indeed any parts of the body, and in the case of legs certainly not looking at them. Yet isn't it intuitively plausible to suppose that unless the legs featured somehow in my general awareness of what I was doing, they would not be enabling me to do it? At least it must be admitted that if they do become obtrusive through stumbling, cramp, or a pull on the Achilles tendon, their entry into awareness isn't of that sudden and dramatic kind characteristic of the loss of balance or stabs of pain themselves. That might well be because there is some manner in which we *are* still aware of them even when we are not aware of them in the contemplative, theoretical way which, following Heidegger, Dreyfus takes to be the model of the traditional subject–object schema.

If Dreyfus and Heidegger (following Hegel's lead) are right about this, and subject and object first appear when malfunction causes them to separate out of some undifferentiated matrix of ongoing proficient performance, then the analysis of a non-contemplative consciousness will have to dispense with that venerable schema and find another. However, an alternative would be to see how far a widening of the concept of consciousness permits a correspondingly wider application of the schema. Thus we could assume that in what

Dreyfus calls ongoing proficient performance there is still at least awareness in the sense of occurrent (not merely dispositional) knowledge of what one is doing, for example, hammering a nail rather than tenderizing a steak; an awareness which need not be, and is perhaps unlikely to be, 'predicative': one can certainly be doing this, and knowing one is doing it and not another thing, without making perceptual (or proprioceptive) judgments about the equipment with which one is doing it. In that case, since awareness of one's hammering must be awareness of one's having a hammer in one's hands (and perhaps also of one's hands being part of one's body, and of being embodied, and of one's body being oriented in a certain way in a 'local' space–time continuum), we can also assume that the 'invisible' hammer can be something *of* which the hammerer is somehow, non-contemplatively, not predicatively, and perhaps (though this may be stretching things too far) not even pre-predicatively aware.

In short, Dreyfus's case against awareness ('mental states') employs a contemplative, propositional, or Cartesian model which leaves it open that awareness in some less narrow sense survives his arguments. Moreover, the conclusion for which he argues, that the 'aboutness' characteristic of a person 'going about his or her business' is a non-representational, 'primordial' form of intentionality, seems to call for some wider form of consciousness if the 'aboutness' in question is not to be assimilated entirely with the performances of sophisticated computers. If the kind of performance which is fundamental to human activity contains no element of a first-person perspective, then there is no basis for describing the performance as genuinely intentional, and therefore no reason to oppose Dennett's instrumental analysis. Dreyfus does have an argument which, even from a perspective as solidly third-personal as Dennett's, can distance him from the latter. Dreyfus argues that by applying their computer-compatible model of data-gathering and rule-following to human intelligence, classical cognitivists wrongly conclude that human intelligence requires the *unconscious* application of stored rules to stored data.[3] It is not that conscious processes are involved, but that if one wants to model human intelligence, the models proposed must be able to capture the human ability to adapt continually to new contexts and discriminate huge numbers of special cases,[4] and at least those that are cognitivist cannot. Conceivably, the essentials of human discriminatory power just cannot be modelled in systems which are not conscious. But even if the human ability to deal with ongoing novelty proved beyond the scope of artificial models, the locus of that human ability might still be identified as the brain, the organ of sensorimotor control. If, as 'embodied subjects coming to grips with embodied objects', it is our embrained bodies that do the discriminating, then, since bodies with their brains[5] are parts of public space, might one not still conclude that the first-person view has nothing essential to add?

Granted that ongoing coping (also with changing contexts and new cases) has a physiological basis, and the exercise of skills is in this sense a manifestation of unconscious processes, the discriminations involved must nevertheless be 'realized' in consciousness. The situation with skills is analogous to that of Lockean secondary qualities. Locke called these 'powers [of objects] to produce sensations in us by . . . the bulk, figure, texture, and motion of their insensible parts'.[6] The 'powers' in the case of the discriminations involved in everyday coping are those of the brain transmitted through the sensori*motor* apparatus, and the products activities rather than mere sensations. The activities, of course, are no less conscious for that. But there is one important difference: as was argued in the previous chapter, any present state of the powers would itself be the product in turn of our learning to come to grips with things in everyday experience, so not just the influence of 'insensible parts'. One might reasonably suppose then that, once acquired, the discriminatory power has a necessary secondary-quality component, at least in the sense that actual discriminations require realization at some level above the threshold of what is properly called *sensory* input, i.e. input in a consciously sensory form. Here, of course, we encounter the possibility (supported by evidence for 'blind-sight') that even if necessary for discrimination at the primordial bodily level, sensory input might bypass both the predicative and the attributive (prejudgemental) levels of consciousness. Since there would be little excuse for talking of a first-person viewpoint in respect of what its occupant fails (at the time) to register, this possibility might be taken to show that in this case consciousness is dispensable. But there is no need to take the special case of blind-sight to reveal the dispensability in general of consciously intentional states in the causal explanation of ordinary human performance.

If it is true, as we are proposing, that intentionality is a genuine feature of human mental states but not of any machine states, it would be strange if that fact had nothing to do with the consciousness of the former. That, after all, is the differentia that comes most obviously to mind. On the other hand, if consciousness were indeed inessential to basic human activity, that would seem a strong reason for denying any such essential difference between the principles underlying human and machine performance. The more arguments designed, like Dreyfus's, to show that you can have intentionality without consciousness are successful, the less plausible it becomes to suppose that human mentality affords any anomalies for a comprehensively third-person account of its workings.

But there may be special reasons for withholding the term 'consciousness' without abandoning first-personalism, for instance the association of 'consciousness' with contemplative or attentional states of awareness. Heidegger takes this a step further. According to him the word 'conscious' is too burdened with false Cartesian implications to apply in an analytical description of the kind of intentionality characteristic of what Dreyfus calls ordinary coping. As Olafson puts it:

> Heidegger [concluded] that a concept like that of consciousness could not possibly serve as the instrument of the new ontology of the subject that he was constructing ... because it incorporated the central element in the Cartesian scheme: the detachability in principle of mental states and mental acts from the world that was their object. By virtue of its inner logic, consciousness is the very 'worldless subject' of which *Being and Time* is a running critique.[7]

The origin of the notion of a worldless subject is that of a Cartesian ego whose mental states, even in perception, are never more than mere representations of its objects in an external world. But Heidegger's immediate target is Husserl, whose attempt to analyse the world of experience through successive reductions (the eidetic following upon the transcendental) implied a dissolution of the singular subject and its replacement with a pure field of consciousness which, as Olafson says, 'abstracts altogether from such matters as whether an intentional act is *my* act'.[8] The occupant of this region is a transcendental ego without a world of its own, while the empirical ego and the natural attitude of its active engagement with the world are consigned to a naturalistic psychology. Against this, says Olafson,

Heidegger argues that it is precisely in the natural attitude that 'factual, real consciousness' is given . . . and with it the 'being of the intentional'. . . . It is accordingly in terms of the natural attitude that the task of an analytical description of the being of the intentional must be carried out.[9]

It is the need to provide a description of the intentional from this point of view that is expressed in Dreyfus's insistence that the analysandum is a world we are embodiedly in and actively about. But let us examine briefly the reasons offered for denying that the analysis should include the concept of consciousness. Dreyfus would take these to amount to the following:

1 In everyday coping there is no predicative act, in the sense that no part of what the engaged subject is aware of is some property, or properties, of whatever equipment is being employed in that engagement. Correspondingly, there is no subject aware of itself as engaged in a predicative act or in relation to an object of such predication.

Various questions wait to be asked, but we shall not pursue them. For instance, does the claim include any object, e.g. a nail, towards which the equipment is being directed? What is required for there to be a predicative act? Must it, for example, include the conscious claim that something to which the predicate applies exists independently of the active attention now being directed on it? The main qualification, however, is that the subject–object relation as described does indeed occur, but when the agent shifts into the 'subjective mode' in cases of breakdown. The principal claim is that ordinary activity does not occur in the subjective mode.

The contrary claim would be:

2 What characterizes all human activity, practical as well as theoretical, is the presence of an intentional, representational component, a level of meaning that intercedes between stimulus and response and is essential in the forming of the latter. In other words, all human behaviour is in the subjective mode.

This, we recall, is Searle's position. But consider now a quite different and more radical claim:

3 Even in perceptual judgment itself there is no subject–object relation of a kind which implies that the objects of which the

subject is aware are 'external' to it in a sense which implies that the perceptual basis of the judgment is a mental state forming the final, mental stage of a causal process beginning with events in the real world 'beyond'.

This is the now classical criticism of Cartesian dualism and its derivatives. Whereas (1) says that human activity is basically non-representational, and representational (formed in the subject–object mould) only in its derivative reflective modes, and (2) says that human activity is basically representational in all its modes, (3) says that in none of its modes is human activity representational. That sounds implausible when one considers the representational function of language or mental imagery in intentional activity directed at parts of the world other than those that are immediately perceived. But provisionally we may understand it as a general rejection of the idea that *any* mental activity, active or reflective, can be described in terms of a relation between the mind-and-its-states and the world. Thus interpreted, the claim coincides with Ryle's behaviourism; but as we shall see briefly below in connection with Heidegger's notion of comportment, it is also the form of Heidegger's critique of Cartesian-ism. It opposes primarily the idea that the mind consists of representa-tions out of which the mind's notion of its world is constituted, which 'world' then stands in some relation, not of identity, with the real world which is thus 'external' to it. This is already part of (1) in so far as the world of everyday coping is the real world, the world which when perceived is actually presented to us and not obscured from sensory contact by a 'veil of perception'. But it goes further and says that not even in what (1) allows is our secondary, representational mode of activity is there a relation between mental states and the world of which we have reflective knowledge, or about which we entertain beliefs and desires in the absence of their objects.

As far as our central case of intentionality goes, however, the immediate issue is between (1) and (2). We can pinpoint it by focusing on a particular question. If intentionality is to be a genuine hiatus in any mechanical model of the causal structure of human performance, then there must be a genuine difference between bodily movements that are part of an intentional structure and those that have orthodox causal explanations. The paradigm case for such distinctions is the alleged difference between cases of bodily movement caused by electrically stimulating some part of the motor cortex and cases of normal activity. Let us call cases of the former kind 'Penfield cases', after the neurophysiologist who conducted the first successful experiments of this kind.[10] The question is, first, whether there is any phenomenological difference between Penfield cases and those either of everyday coping or of conscious believings and desirings (in Dreyfus's 'subjective mode'); and, second, whether, if there is such a distinction in first-person experience, it marks a genuine difference in the causal structures.

In Searle's account there is always a phenomenological distinction such that in the non-Penfield case my arm's going up is experienced as going up because of my intention to raise it. In the Penfield case there is presumably (and according to the experimental patients themselves) no such experience of the self's own involvement. To this there may be the following objections:

First, if, as one may presume, there are unconscious intentions, these will not differ in the same way from the Penfield cases. Thus if I raise my arm ostensibly to call the chairman's attention, it may be true that a motivation for my doing that is to call attention to myself; or, to enter the field of psychopathology, my raising my hand in those circumstances may have some neurotic connection with an un-conscious wish to atone for a hidden guilt at having informed on a fellow-pupil at school. In that particular respect, then, my hand's going up has as little connection with my present conscious engagement in things as it would have in a Penfield situation, except perhaps for the fact that in the latter the occurrence could not be explained in the same way as the former, that is by some psycho-analytically retrievable intentional connection.

This need not be a significant objection. Unconscious intentions will have conscious intentions as their vehicles, and at least the latter will follow the general formula according to which the bodily movement is experienced as being caused by the intention to cause it. There is, no doubt, a certain artificiality in this way of talking. When I wish to attract the chairman's attention, it is that which forms the intention-in-action, not that I should raise my arm in order to do that; for the fact that I should do it in that way is normally determined by the circumstances, and the bodily movement becomes in that case a part of the intention, or a means to it, not what enters my mind as what I wish to do. However, one may imagine circumstances where the bodily movement is indeed part of the wish, for example if my arm is heavily bandaged or I am suffering from tennis elbow. As for unconscious motivations in general, they are simply aspects of human performance which do not enter into, and when they do perhaps typically disturb, the normal control patterns available to beings with intentionality as the characteristic form of their modes of behaviour.

Second, surely the fact that intentions-in-action do indeed depend on exercises of skills of performance which are not 'conscious', in the sense that the action in question depends on their being exercised automatically, shows that much human performance – the basic action itself, some may argue – occurs outside the intentional frame. That is true if by this is meant that the intention-in-action does not include details of the means whereby the intended result comes about. My intention to stop the car when I see another approaching the intersection does not include the instruction 'press your right foot on the brake pedal with just so much pressure'; so long as I am a proficient driver all I do is stop the car. But so long as whatever parts or aspects of the performance that fail to rise to the threshold of a conscious intention-in-action (and this may, as Searle also suggests, simply be a matter of degree) are mobilized by the intention-in-action, they can still quite unmisleadingly be referred to the intentional structure which has that particular intention-in-action as its controlling element.

Third, however, there is the objection that not all actions, or activities, do have such controlling elements. This, indeed, is the point that Dreyfus makes, though in addition he claims that the kind of activity in which no such controlling elements are to be found are primary. Dreyfus's claim is that the typical (and basic) form of human performance is one in which we merely find ourselves getting about in various situations at which, through normal development, upbringing, and training, we have become adept. The situations may be of a simpler or more complex kind. A basketball player finds himself responding in infinitely subtle ways to rapidly changing situations; a messenger dodging pedestrians on a busy street does the same. The moral that might be drawn is that the description the agent would give of what he or she is doing comes typically after the event; even that consciously goal-directed behaviour occurs only, as Dreyfus suggests, where there is some failure or inappropriateness of response; so that all of what Searle calls intention-in-action is embedded in some more basic kind of performance which has gone momentarily or totally awry.

The answer is surely that descriptions of what a person does belong to many different levels – within consciousness. The basketball player responds consciously in some sense, but not by means of mental representations, to the subtle changes of circumstance; there is continual sensorimotor discrimination, but at the same time the player can always say, and in any case knows, he is playing basketball – that is the frame in which the responses occur and which also regulates or limits the repertoire of moves, as in playing chess. He not only knows he is playing basketball but also that he is trying to help his team to win, though other more subjective motivations may also be in play. What is true is that there need be no intentional description guiding the particular response. Not every move in basketball is (in Searle's terms) self-referentially caused by the intention-in-action, because there is no one specific intention for it to be caused by. It is also true, however, that the responses are all means to a goal (winning a game of basketball), and so intentional on that account.

At first glance, then, it seems that claim (1) above is false and that claim (2) gives a more adequate account of the nature of human performance from a phenomenological standpoint. But that needs qualification. A possible comment about an account like Searle's is that it must allow a considerable amount of stretch between specific actions (especially those that can be classified as responses to a series of changing circumstances) and goal-descriptions that can plausibly be said to be genuinely experienced by the agents as involved in producing the relevant movements. This was what distinguished intention-in-action from the Penfield cases. There is surely some basis, even here, for the claim that goal-descriptions grow out of actions that are already under way, and that if there is any all-embracing intention-in-action, it is not related to the responses in a way sufficiently close to specify these, and thus be part of what the agent is aware of as a cause of what she or he is doing.

Dreyfus's Heideggerian standpoint gives this notion further impetus. He suggests that the kind of goal-description which sorts an action under some 'stand *Dasein* is taking on the issue of its being'[11] is one that the agent typically arrives at, if at all, *after the event*, or rather *on top of* the event of actual acting in a certain way, or style, or self-constituting manner. Here we have a view of the world as already containing 'meanings' – in the form of learned practices (e.g. turning door-knobs), which Dreyfus opposes to the Husserlian analysis which requires that the mind 'synthesize' visual and other experience before it 'ascribes' a meaning (e.g., of a die, that it is something to throw). There are certain pre-established kinds of activity, and a person's current engagement in any one of these is part of an unreflected, *de facto* resolution of the 'issue of *Dasein*'s being'.[12] Intentions-in-action here, you might say, lie in the roles or parts that are waiting for people, not to choose, but to fall into according to local circumstances, abilities, and opportunities.

The intended theoretical effect of this view is to relieve the mind of creative burdens (bestowing meaning, etc.) ascribed to it in Husserlian phenomenology, and to replace the notion of a mind representing a world to itself with one lacking mentalistic overtones. The Heideggerian notion of 'comportment' (*Verhalten*) is proposed as such a replacement. According to this, no human transaction with the world is to be analysed in terms of the relation of a mental state to that world. That applies not only to practical activity but also to reflection or contemplative knowing. Thus not even perceptual experience itself is to be interpreted in terms of a mind's experiences, if these are understood as mental states. As Dreyfus puts it: 'What Heidegger has to argue is that human beings *experience* things or disclose the world and discover objects in it – and yet this does not entail that they have *experiences*, if this means mental states which are directed towards things'.[13]

Whatever the plausibility of that argument, Dreyfus himself might be accused of distorting the case in the conclusion's favour by conflating two different extremes and losing sight of the typical middle ground of intentionally guided human action. The extremes are cases of absent-mindedness or the kinds of subtle responsiveness typical of such activities as playing basketball and driving cars on the one hand, and on the other the transintentional answers that patterns of a person's activities give to unposed questions about the status of *Dasein* as such or about the identity of a particular instantiation of *Dasein*. What we need is a good look at the middle ground of ordinary human involvement to see what foothold, if any, is to be found there for the subject–object model in respect of the agent's relation to the world.

The Dreyfuses refer to a 'world' as 'an organized body of objects, purposes, skills, and practices on the basis of which human activities have meaning or make sense', as against a 'universe' conceived as '[a] set of interrelated facts'. The Dreyfus 'world' is the cultural background into which a 'whole organism' is 'geared' and its intelligence contexted.[14] So far, there is nothing explicitly first-personal in this conception of a world. But the idea of a world is itself implicitly first-personal. The shared Dreyfusian world is socio-cultural as well as natural, and (to speak non-phenomenologically) it also has a personal overlay; thus it instantiates local and idio-syncratic, even haecceitical, elements (though one may ask whether the latter are nevertheless not universals); consequently it is not shared in some strongly mind-independent sense, and the body it contains and which embodies us in our active engagement is primarily a proprioceptively phenomenal body, a first-personal body – the objective body is to be described in abstract physiological terms which nevertheless, no doubt, borrow from the phenomenal language of phenomenal and proprioceptive experience. The dim awareness of the momentary positions of parts of our bodies which accompanies ongoing activity can be attributive awareness (or less, if there is anything more 'prelinguistic' than that) rather than predicative awareness; that is, an experience upon which perceptual judgment is founded but which itself is not a perceptual judgment. The point would not be to claim the proficiencies in question for the mind *rather* than the body. They would be proficiencies with a bodily 'executive' aspect, but realized in consciousness proprioceptively. Beyond that, however, the form in which they are realized is intentional. At some minimal level of understanding, the coper is *aware* of what it is that her or his 'skill-full' body is proficiently performing,[15] and the description of what that is will be a form of 'action'-description containing reference to some state of affairs, perhaps even the present one, for instance playing basketball, which is related both causally and consciously to the movements of the actual performance.

Let us focus again on Dreyfus's paradigm: finding oneself engaged in infinitely subtle response to constantly and sometimes (as in basketball) rapidly changing circumstances. The description the agent would give of any causally operative intention comes – if it comes at all – after the event, and typically only because of some failure or inappropriateness of response (when 'ordinary coping' breaks down; for example, that particular basketball routine or hammer-swing fails, or the physique needed to maintain it fails, or the hammer breaks). Dreyfus, following Heidegger, maintains that representation in any literal sense occurs only in reflection, dis-engagement, and a refocusing (or first focusing) of attention on to the relevant parts of the world in which one is otherwise actively involved. The argument against Dreyfus was that the ball or the hammer and the movements involving them are there in mind all the same and figure in the contents of a consciousness broadened in accordance with an improved phenomenology of the experience of everyday coping.

But if the notion of representation were similarly broadened, one could say that these elements were included as part of the agent's mental representation. That it cannot, and indeed that there is nothing to include there, is the nerve of the last of the three positions listed above (see p. 107). It denies that any – even reflective – modes of human activity are representational. Dreyfus's argument really has two sides: one is (a) that there is no phenomenological basis for describing human performance in *basically* first-person representational terms (as he claims Husserl does), since (e.g.) in hammering the hammer is not an object for the hammerer; and the other is (b) that the real world is the one in which hammers *are* among the things that are present-at-hand if not always present-to-hand.

What we have, then, is what might be called an 'equipment' realism in which a world of common things, but also practices, pre-exists its individually 'consciously' active natives. The practices are employments 'about' common things, and make use of them, but do not involve mental states with representations of those things (or employments about them) as their contents. So, instead of burdening a putative 'mind' with meaningful states which 'intend' actual and possible common things and states of affairs of the world, we have the world itself 'disclosing' itself, more or less, to the everyday coper. One may think of the coper making do with some kind of presentational – i.e. revelatory, not representational – content. When I move around in an environment, I have presentations which mark out the obstacles I avoid stumbling into – just enough, and in time, to trigger the motor response. It may be, as Searle claims, that there is a specifiable project that the movements can be traced to as their immanent cause. But it is conceivable that there may not be; and even if there is, it is implausible either that every move has its own intention-in-action or that they all come under one highly specified intention-in-action. So if there is a difference here from the Penfield cases, and the difference lies in the fact that the agent has a sense of being the cause of the movements, and that in turn is to be explained by there being an intention somehow in action, which intention includes the condition that the movements be caused by that intention, it seems that the intention or intentions must be largely *ad hoc*, and perhaps even *post facto*, rationalizations. But in this minimally revelatory situation, the

114

degree of awareness may exclude conscious intention-in-action altogether and suffice only to allow monitoring of progress along routine paths for unforeseen obstacles. In that case, some remnant of a Searlean intention-in-action may be traceable to a prior intention that determines the range of unforeseeables one is currently prepared for – in the case of hammering, for instance, hitting your finger but not usually the head of the hammer flying off.

But what about reflective judgment, imaging, explicit beliefs and desires, and the like? Don't we have to postulate mental states at least in these cases, with their representational content? Indeed, yes. However, there are three important qualifications: (1) any reflective judgment is already embedded in a piece of active engagement from which it is a withdrawal, and therefore the contents of such judgments cannot play any 'constitutive' role in the analysis of the world; (2) the contents themselves include constituents which belong not to the category of 'what it would be like to perceive, contemplate, etc.' some thing or state of affairs but to that of 'what it would be like to be doing' this, that, or the other, so that even in their reflective (what Dreyfus calls 'subjective') modes the contents of mental states are not exhaustively representational; and (3) the activity of reflecting is as much a performance governed by a world of pre-existing meaning-structures as any other.

This, then, is the Heideggerian picture of a shared world of things whose primary status is that of tools and in which the most fundamental meanings are pre-established in a system of purposes. But how real is this realism? Hammers are only there for those with the requisite background. The traditional way of talking would be to say that in order to have hammers in your world you need the relevant cultural concepts, so that you can pick out and describe the relevant objects as hammers. Heideggerians would rather say that you need to have acquired the necessary skills. Either way, the shared Dreyfusian world is socio-cultural as well as natural. It is therefore shared only to a certain point and within a certain circle. Some aspects of it may not be shared at all, since it can (and surely typically does) contain idiosyncratic, even haecceitical, elements (are the latter nevertheless universals?). So the realism here is not of a strongly mind-independent kind. Nor is the body with which the Dreyfusian agent is actively 'in' the world of things and equipment and embodiedly 'about' it a purely natural body; it is, for example, a 'hammering', 'door-opening', 'saxophone-playing', 'contract-signing', 'French-speaking' body, and primarily, from the embodied agent's point of view, a proprioceptively phenomenal body, a first-personal body. As with 'things-in-themselves', independently of any relation to human purpose, the objective body is to be described in abstract physiological terms, however much the latter may borrow from the phenomenal language of perceptual and proprioceptive experience.

Locating meaning in the world of practices therefore does not eliminate the first-person perspective. There are two sides to this. First, so long as no particular epistemological or ontological theory is brought to bear on the notion of a 'first person', there is nothing misleading about describing the minimal presentational scene depicted above as first-personal. There need be no 'person' involved, no 'self', or 'subject-pole'; all we need to invoke the notion of a first person here is a state of consciousness as an aspect of embodied activity, enough to allow the embodied activity to be activity of a proprioceptive body, and we have that even in the minimally presentational circumstances outlined above. Second, however, the activities in which the minimally aware agent is embodiedly engaged are ones which only a proprioceptive body in a particular 'world' can engage in. The world we are embodiedly in is a culture-relative world. But what distinguishes one cultural world from another, as indeed what distinguishes one activity from another, is what an embodied agent can be aware of itself as embodiedly doing. The Heideggerian turn which allows Dreyfus to unburden the traditional mind merely transfers the load on to the world which the traditional mind was held to represent. The effect of locating its meanings there is to make that world first-personal. Not just because meanings, however independent of individual minds, must be assumed to belong to the category of the mental. When an inhabitant of a world of pre-established meanings acts, she or he will be 'realizing' those meanings in her or his individual consciousness.

But doesn't this bring us straight back to traditional dualism, with its conception of the mind's representational relation to the real world? On the one hand, we have individual conscious minds, the 'subject-pole', with their 'inner' states, and on the other the 'object-pole', or the 'external' world, and all the traditional epistemological and ontological problems of the relation between them.

In the rest of this chapter I shall outline two opposite approaches to this notion of a subject in relation to its world. One is a third-person approach and the other a first-person approach. Neither is fundamentally dualist, but each has its unresolved problem of the 'other half' and tends to try to resolve it monistically. The two approaches can be distinguished by referring to the concepts of 'world-model' and 'world-version' with which they respectively attempt to explain the first-person aspect we have retrieved from Dreyfus's analysis.

Let us begin with the idea of a world-model. This notion can be used by cognitive scientists in a way that does not imply intrinsic intentionality. According to the Turing machine model, no sentence-token in mind with its semantic content gives us the representational value of the token, because that is part of a deeper system which has the token-with-content as *its* part. This can be a correctable program provisionally 'hard-wired' into the neural system. However, when it comes to perception, cognitive psychologists are willing to let the model take conscious form in the case of perception. Thus vision is, on Marr's account, a computational process beginning with 'two-dimensional retinal images' and ending in a three-dimensional, 'object-centred' representation of the world.[16] So the contents of perception, and of the minimally presentational situation sketched above, are located in a space discontinuous with that of any ideal observer of the computational process, as well as of whatever electromagnetic circumstances in the surrounding medium and other purely physical events causally precede the optical images. From a third-person point of view, this world-model – which must also be the epistemological point of departure for the third person – is unlocatable. But the metaphor of 'inner' comes readily to hand, and the visual experience can be described in terms of 'inner states' of the publicly observable organism.

But can it? It is not literally inside the organism; and if the spatial relation can be employed only metaphorically, the analysis appears to reach a dead end. Third-personalists, from behaviourism on, have extracted their consciousness-denying moral from this and have sought to account for consciousness in other ways, for instance in terms of discriminational capacities chartable within public space – in short, by giving some form of behavioural analysis of conscious states, as also is the case with functionalism.

The behavioural analyses are in order, especially functional analyses, since they acknowledge the causal roles of what they refer to as mental states. But the analyses are deficient in not being able to account for any causal significance in the fact that some mental states are conscious in a first-personal sense. At best they are able to propose models that simulate human powers, but without accounting for any influence that intrinsically intentional states have on those powers and on the general causal structure of human performance. They have nothing to say about the minimally presentational first-person domain.

And yet third-personalists are denizens of that domain. And if they attempt to extend their analyses to cover the domain itself, they end up with a spatio-temporal world-model located somewhere behind their noses but, paradoxically, with their noses located in the model. The predicament is pinpointed but not solved by Gibson's ecological theory of perception, which attempts to put noses back where they belong – in the public world.

According to Gibson,[17] we generally see things as they are. This would appear to ignore all that has been done in the neurobiology of visual perception. Surely, once the causal and computational processes involved in vision are taken into account, perception of X must be taken to be *mediated* by those processes; the visual experience is the result of how the processes 'interpret' the visual stimulus – though, as noted earlier, the kind of view Gibson opposes does not typically take the resulting 'mental representation' to be a conscious image. For Gibson, the proper way to describe the situation is to say that the processes rather facilitate the transmission of visual knowledge of X:[18] '[p]erception of the environment is . . . not mediated by *retinal* pictures, *neural* pictures, or *mental* pictures . . . [but] is the activity of getting information from the ambient array of light.'[19]

There seems, however, to be an unresolved ambiguity in Gibson's position. The position is that light accurately *reflects* objective properties such as shape, textures, edges, and size, in other words properties of a distinctly 'primary' kind in Locke's sense.[20] But at the same time Gibson is talking of objective properties of objects in an *ecological* environment, and ecological objects are the palpable furniture of our everyday world: what we see in all its splendour when, say, the sun shines on it. These are objective properties in some sense other than Locke's primary qualities. For Locke, such properties were aspects of the 'insensible' parts of objects, operating on our sensory mechanisms in the same way – as Locke himself says – as drugs induce reduced sensory activity,[21] and unlike those of such ecological objects as the Niagara Falls. Gibson holds two conflicting views: that the visual system normally allows observers to see objects just as they are, the causal and computational processes serving as transmitters of information rather than producers of an image; and that perceptual experience, what is ordinarily called 'seeing', is the last event in a causal chain, an event in which the information is received in the sensory mode. But obviously it cannot be contained in that mode anywhere further back in the causal sequence. The idea of light's *reflecting* off an object here must be that of something not yet in the sensory mode; but in that case what is the force of saying that light *accurately reflects* objective properties? Subsensory light can transmit sensory information in the sense that knowledge of certain correlations may enable one to infer the sensory-mode equivalent of a certain measurable quantity and structure of subsensory light; but the object in the scientific account is a subsensory one, and the sensory knowledge we have of it is knowledge of what it is for a sensate being to respond to subsensory light in a subsensory environment of (from such a being's point of view) a noumenal reality of abstract 'one knows not whats'. In that case Gibson is still left with a distinction between a subsensory object and a sensate being's sensory reconstruction of that object, a distinction which places him with the mediationists he is out to oppose.

It seems that any step one takes to vindicate a view as close to common-sense realism as Gibson's will lead one in the direction of an 'internalist' position in which ecological objects like the Niagara Falls are, for scientific reasons, mentally presented versions of noumenal originals. The object as *what* we see in an ecological sense, in full phenomenal fig as it were, must be specified in the terms of a language appropriate to the *final* stage in the scientific story's causal sequence. That language is, for obvious ecological or pragmatic reasons, realist. But its realism is in fact inconsistent with the scientific story; it assumes something like divine revelation of 'first things', the sensory incarnation of unperceivable events. One might abandon the scientific story itself as nonsensical, on such grounds as that the terms in which it is formulated get their meaning, and the distinctions they make their point, in a sensory setting, and that to use them to mark a distinction between that setting as a whole and some other non-sensory domain is to empty them of meaning. This would be one way, though I think a precipitate one, of dismantling the representationalist position, since then there would be no intelligible first event in a causal sequence for the final event to portray, or even mediate or 'reproduce' in some non-pictorial way.

None the less, accepting the scientific account does not entail mediationism. Concrete, ecological objects, the ones we explore in the world, can go round and examine from all sides, need not be thought of as containing, in misleadingly sensory form, information about subsensory items; they can be thought of as fulfilments or 'realizations' of the sensory possibilities of conjunctions of physical solids, subsensory light, and sensate systems. Here, there would be no point in talking of 'mediating' the physical solid, since what we get is the realization of a possibility of that solid in such a setting. The setting itself, including as it does the provision of a sensate system, is therefore a part of the source of the information in question. For among a mind-independent thing's possibilities are all the ways it can figure in perceptual, practical, and therefore culturally relative contexts. Nor, then, similarly, is it necessary to talk, as Gibson does, of the so-called mediators as 'facilitating' or 'amplifying' the knowledge we have of something already (for Gibson, 'directly') perceived. What is perceived is perceived by virtue of the presence of a culturally contexted sensate being, and that already involves all that optic nerves and brains can contribute to the end result.

Such a view would be in the spirit of Gibson's ecological approach, but cleared of the taint of naïve realism that surfaces when the alternative, mediationist reading of his informational view is rejected. It allows us to think of perception in a scientific way and at the same time do justice to the idea that in perceiving things we are actually among them. Visual knowledge is knowledge of insensible solids to the extent that we can conceive of the latter, even though they are insensible, as objects with the potential to generate in sensate beings a common perceptual 'core' around which accumulate the fuller specifications proper to ecological things (i.e. things we peep over, step over, look at fondly, find reminiscent of . . . , etc.).

This removes the difficulty of locating the 'world-model' from a third-person perspective. The model is replaced by the publicly shareable world itself. What we have is the environment as it is according to the world-picture, or as the systematic connections based on actual micro-level stimulus conditions make the environment seem. That sounds as though we were back in the third-person perspective from which we began. But the third-person view is now essentially first-personal: what is disclosed to it is disclosed only in the form of a world shared only to the extent that cognitive, cultural, and other conditions permit instantiations of the same first-person universals.

Human life as lived, even by scientific observers, is inherently first-personal. But isn't the third-person perspective nevertheless the proper vantage-point for science? As Nagel points out, the demand for objectivity, understood in one way though still very loosely, is a demand for a description of things that does not depend on vantage-points.[22] One way of shrugging off this dependence is to omit, in specifications of things, anything of merely 'indexical' significance. What we have then is a picture of things without reference to a particular place or time (unless the spatio-temporal reference is included in their description), observer, etc., but still with 'conditions of satisfaction' which could be seen to be fulfilled by any suitably placed observer. Another would be to eliminate everything that depends on its belonging to the first-personal domain. In that case we are seeking to describe a reality that exists in total independence of human or any other modes of cognition. The ambition is intelligible, and in its own terms wholly praiseworthy: it aims to 'depict' in an ideally non-pictorial way the universe in which human life occurs and out of which it arises. Instead of 'worlds' in the Dreyfuses' sense of organized bodies of 'objects, purposes, skills, and practices on the basis of which human activities have meaning or make sense', we are aiming at describing a 'universe' conceived as '[a] set of interrelated facts'.[23] Among these facts one may seek the causes of human life, and also of the general behavioural and cognitive structures of that or any other life. One may seek to answer the question: How are worlds as human beings have them possible? The conventional explanation is evolutionary.

The structures themselves, however, are those from which we are forced to look into any universe of facts. We apprehend that they are *our* structures, if the first-person perspective is given its due. There may be other structures, those of Martians and bats for instance. And a whole realm of possible cognitive 'manners' of apprehending a common, firmly mind-independent world can be separated off as the meta-world of possible 'hows' in respect of a common 'what'. For the exponent of any particular manner, however, its 'how' is incurably local. We are stuck with our own cognitive devices and can only speculate about 'what it would be like' to be an exponent of any other.

One might ask, in that case, with what right we can look upon the results of our best cognitive processes and procedures as the fruits of a *vantage*-point upon a mind-independent universe of facts. Isn't there, from our own 'worldly' point of view, a fundamental epistemological question to be answered before science can even begin? How is this point of view related to the culturally neutral universe of interrelated facts? Have we the epistemological right or even the conceptual means to assume such a universe at all? It seems we are back with Descartes.

There are two opposed ways of looking at this. Through Cartesian eyes, though without the kinds of guarantee Descartes himself sought and assumed, the situation is one in which the sensational and conceptual forms of human cognition appear as filters which distort the true nature of a mind-independent reality. They bring in the mind, in the form of spatial perspective and of theory, and thereby distort the ideal notion of a universe of raw facts-in-themselves. The opposite approach is to see the message in the medium, taking our sensory and theoretical structures to be manners in which the universe itself comes to view. The 'what' emerges in some 'how'; perhaps best of all, at least to date, in the human 'how'. This was Hegel's position. But at least formally it is the phenomenalist position too, or any view for which reality is 'reduced' to the level of the scope of available cognitive resources. The idealist argues from what is, on a first-person basis, inconceivable to the conclusion that all that can be talked about is recoverable on that basis. It is a form of inverted rationalism. Classical rationalism assumes a rational cognitive capacity that connects with the ultimate structure of things; idealism 'reduces' the ultimate structure of things to the domain of possible intentional objects. The move may be the right one, but there are no convincing arguments that show this.

But the issue can be presented in a way that leans less on arguments of the sophisticated kind on which idealism depends, and more on a kind of rational intuition of the kind Descartes tried to describe in terms of what notions were distinctly themselves and clearly not analytically contained in others. The idealist thought is that what first-person perspectives evince are fruitions, realizations, fulfilments of the underlying facts that bring them into being. The fundamental idea is that the universe (not just a world) is *for* consciousness. But sunsets cannot be treated as fulfilments of items in a third-person universe. The glory of the setting sun in an evening sky is an extraordinarily local kind of phenomenon; not just because it happens at a certain time and place but because qualities of experience in general – all secondary and tertiary qualities – apply only to beings capable of experience, and of experience of a given kind or structure. But the electromagnetic radiation that gives us sunsets as we know them is there all the same; so the fact that the sunset is not a realization of the reality of electromagnetic radiation does not lead us to conclude that there is no such radiation. To come to such a conclusion would be to accommodate oneself to a reductive form of idealism.

On the other hand, it makes good sense to say that sunsets, and the whole panoply of lived objective experience, are realizations of those *cognitive* parts of the universe of facts which are our (central and peripheral) nervous systems. If the mind-independent thing is taken to be the neurophysiological system that is my brain, it seems to make sense, even without the backing of idealism, to say that secondary qualities, and all other forms of first-personal qualification of 'worlds', are realizations of the possibilities of mind-independent things. For here the things are such that, in Aristotelian terms, the material has just this kind of 'form' or 'realization'; or, if you like, the existence of first-person experience, of 'worlds', is its 'conditions of satisfaction or fulfilment'. The stuff of our brains is 'meant' to have the form of conscious experience; that is what it is good for. The brain, and the nervous system as a whole, are 'realized' in lived experience.

In whatever way that intuition may be justified or explained, whether on evolutionary or emergentist principles, even dualism (if the continuity of nature is juxtaposed with the thesis that the world is not inherently mental), the intuition itself frees us to treat the contents of our first-personal worlds as aspects at least of those parts of the third-person universe which are capable of this form of fulfilment or realization. We don't have to *reduce* or *eliminate* in favour of what *can* be regarded unproblematically (from a naturalistic evolutionary standpoint) as realizations of a totally mindless reality – namely the generation of excitable cells and their ever more sophisticated arrangement as the 'matter' which has discriminatory behaviour as its 'form'. The form can be variable. Robots have one form, conscious human beings another. The latter are intrinsically intentional; the former are not. Of course, intrinsic intentionality is not a mystical union of disparate things or events in a universe of facts. It is part of what it *is* (of what it is like) to have a world. That is what Heidegger was saying: intentionality is a basic relation in the world of embodied action 'about' things. He called it *Verhalten*, or a relation or attitude or way of being directed to things. But Heidegger's analysis is too defensively anti-Cartesian to bring out the extent to which worlds belong to the category of consciousness and the extent to which consciousness is ultimately particular and momentary. Everything we unreflectingly experience as our local placement in a continuing and shared spatio-temporal universe is the presentational content of a short-lived mental state. We may think of ourselves as enjoying a sequence of vantage-points upon a ready-made vista, open to all. But the sense we have of our 'now' as continuous with a past and with a projectible future, as of our 'here' being placed locally in a wider space of perspectival possibilities, is really just the momentary content of a single state of mind. As Sprigge puts it: 'All that is ever actually experienced is experienced in one of those short stretches of experience which make up a brief segment of the temporal line from the moment of waking till a moment of sleeping.'[24] The object of our intrinsic intentionality is simply *what* we experience or what we know ourselves to be embodiedly about. Mental states (let us think of them in a suitably non-Cartesian way as conscious states of nerves and limbs) 'intend' what can count as objects in specifiable worlds in any 'here and now'. The ability of a mental state to 'refer beyond itself' is not to be understood as an ability actually to reach (or miss, or find empty) some piece of an extensionally disparate reality, but as a consequence of the fact that worlds are universals and in principle (diachronically) repeatable and so also (synchronically) shareable.

Saying that the world is *for* consciousness disinclines us to say that it is *in* consciousness; or that consciousness is *in* us. These spatial metaphors cannot be cashed into possible states of affairs. The fact that one thing is inside another is accessible only to a third-person perspective. Thus we tend to think of another person's mind and mental states as 'inside' her or his visible body,[25] as a 'world-model' located somewhere behind the eyeballs. But the only 'inside' that can be located from that perspective is neurobiological. So the 'mind' and its 'states' acquire the status of myths and are rejected as unscientific. An alternative to the world-model is the world-version. Where the concept of a world-model is representational – a model substitutes for the real thing – a world-version gives you as much of reality as it is possible to acquire. But since world-versions (by definition) vary, how can we form the notion of a universal reality? The answer might be: by abstracting from perspectivity and forming the abstract notion of a universe of interrelated facts. But then we have not included worlds in our inventory of reality. An alternative is to talk of a common core, but that abstracts from the variety which is infinitely more the spice of reality than it is of one individual's life. Further possibilities are Jamesian pluralism and Bradleyan monism. These are higher-order 'world-versions', as are physicalisms and dualisms in all their versions. This is not the place to decide definitively between them; but we have at least argued the case for some higher-order version that can accommodate 'worlds'. In Chapter VIII we shall consider what role consciousness can play in the ways in which those individual instantiations of world-versions which are human subjects enter into each other's worlds.

CHAPTER VII

Control

In a commentary on John Searle, Dennett describes the latter's view that intentionality is something brains can produce but computer programs can't as departing radically from 'the prevailing winds of doctrine'.[1] Whereas Searle believes that the brain's function is to produce first-person intentionality, '[m]ost people in AI (and most functionalists in the philosophy of mind) would say that [the brain's] product is something like *control*'. The brain's role in human performance is to '[govern] right, appropriate, intelligent input–output relations, where these are deemed to be, in the end, relations between sensory inputs and behavioral outputs of some sort'.[2]

There are three strands to separate here. First, granted (what eliminative materialists and Dennett deny) that human organisms do possess (in their case first-person) intentionality, is it correct to claim, as Searle does, that it is caused by the brain? I shall follow Searle in this, assuming that intentionality is a development of natural neural possibility, a kind of state that nerves of sufficient complexity can be in, but argue later that, even if intentionality itself is a product of the nervous system, actual intentional states are not caused by the brain. Second, there is the question whether machine intelligence can ever be genuinely intentional in any way – even third-personally. The winds of doctrine generally whistle 'yes', though here too Dennett is an exception. I shall offer an outline of an argument (other than Dennett's) suggesting that, however successfully robots avoid pitfalls and obstacles, it is fruitless and misleading to describe their performances as genuinely intentional.[3] Third, there is the question with which I shall begin: Why has there to be a choice between treating first-person intentionality as a product of the brain and allowing the brain to be in the business of producing control?

126

Cannot first-person intentionality be an aspect of that business, the way the brain provides control in the case of human beings? For naturalists, who take human capacities in general to be developments of possibilities inherent in nature, that would certainly be a consistent position to hold. Might it not be, then, that besides the ways in which the brain ensures appropriate input–output relations by converting environmental input into appropriate behavioural output at pre-intentional levels, it also converts them, perhaps even more appropriately, by means of a model of the environment in which input and output have the form of conscious beliefs and desires?

There are three main directions from which such a suggestion feels the breeze of current doctrine. One, the eliminativist direction, simply jettisons the notion of intentionality, taking belief, desire, and all the other propositional attitudes to be prescientific notions which fail to grip the principles underlying human mentality. The assumption (belief, desire?) of eliminative materialism is that these will be found in the language of neurobiology. Another direction, psychosemantics, accepts intentionality but aims to explain it in the representational function of *symbols*, rather than mental states, believing it must do so if room is to be made for intentional categories within the physicalist's universe. It goes by way of symbol-processing activities in the brain (or any other functionally equivalent system).[4] A third direction, that of Dennett's 'intentional stance', denies that there can be room in the physicalist's universe for intentional categories and treats intentional explanation instrumentally as a *façon d'expliquer*. Opposed to all of these is Searle's own claim both that mental states are intrinsically intentional and that their being so is compatible with the physicalist view of the world and so stands in no need of further naturalizing.

Common to these positions – including Searle's, as it happens, though unnecessarily, as I shall argue – is the claim that the first-person vantage-point offers no access to the levels where control is assumed in fact to be exercised – except of course in so far as that vantage-point also affords access to a public world in which the nature of the physical control can be revealed to third-person investigation. It may be allowed that awareness of the conscious content of one's own mental states permits one to monitor certain aspects of the exercise of these powers, but the first-person perspective cannot be relied on to provide accurate reports of the complex processes actually at work. Nor, according to one argument, should we expect it to. The brain has been selected for its ability to make appropriate discriminations in the environment, not for any ability to monitor its own discriminational capacities; so while the former may well be mirrored in experience, there is no reason to expect this of the latter.[5]

In one way, of course, that is obvious. If we want to understand the full range of human skills, not just making plans, carrying them out, and justifying them, but also the linguistic and computational skills these depend on, perceptual skills such as judging distance and sheer physical dexterity, or both, as when intercepting objects at speed, then explanations in terms of beliefs and desires will not approach anywhere near what is required. If I want to know why my legs move appropriately when I am crossing the road, why my sentences generally arrive in good grammatical shape, and what it is that enables me to remember my name and how to get home, then the explanations will not be found in what I have in mind. Yet on the common-sense view, knowing my beliefs, desires, etc. is exactly what provides the justifications I can give for doing what I do, just as it provides others with explanations of what I do. It is a view in which the conscious agent is itself assumed to be the locus of whatever control is being manifested in the exercise of choice. In a sense, then, one could allow with the naturalist that it is the brain which is exercising control, but add that it is doing so at a level above that at which it is appropriate to refer to neuronal processes. With people, the brain controls movement through the propositional attitudes. One might say in this vein that the evolution of the brain has given rise to people, and in their case the brain's control is exercised by the beliefs and desires out of which they act.

However, the view seems to be beset with problems. Both the kind of control (exercising choice) involved in explaining behaviour and the theoretical autonomy enjoyed by the explanations savour of dualism. If we are to avoid that, then granted that intentional states such as beliefs and desires are states of nerves, as Quine put it, any kind of control exercised at the level of propositional attitudes must be subject to the kinds of explanation appropriate to physical science. Apart from the threat of dualism, then, there is the question of whether physical science has room for explanations in terms of what an organism has in its mind when what is there is something (an intentional object) other than the organism itself, or at least some state of it other than the one which is its having whatever it is in mind.

A promising approach seems to be via the notion of mental representation. Beliefs and desires are also representations. They are about other things. But then, cannot the same be said of states of organisms, or even of organisms themselves, at least their behaviour? If a lobster were taken from its habitat and its receptors wired to a program reproducing sequences of stimuli corresponding to topographies that lobsters are used to, its movements could 'represent' those topographies. It would be as though the lobster had some form of cognitive map of the hypothetical terrain.[6] In a more general way, it might be said to have a map, or a map bank, of all possible lobster environments, though with *terra incognita* at the edges for when it gets caught in a creel or plunged alive into boiling water.

If you begin in this way, or as low down on the evolutionary scale as you can, you may find all you need to explain what later emerges in the form of beliefs and desires. The behaviour of believers and desirers can then be said to 'map' their environments in the same way. So when looking for the basic explanations of what it is we are doing when we are engaged in what we call the propositional attitudes, we should look to the internal cognitive economy that produces the behaviour in question. Even if we assume that some mental states are irreducibly intentional in a sense that fits ill with physicalist ontology, we may still say that it is not their intrinsic intentionality to which we should attach basic explanatory value. Rather, we can take it that an internal economy of representational states (its basic elements symbols or neural networks) provides the structure and the causation sufficient to explain the behaviour. The semantic values of the behaviour can then simply be read off by observers whose linguistic competence enables them to fill in the denotational gaps; that is, by watching an organism cope with its environment. In fact, if the internal economy is treated as a symbol-processing system, its outputs can be treated as theorems generated mechanically in a formal system, and then the 'aboutness' specifications of its states can be arrived at by giving the theorems appropriate interpretations.[7] The third-person scenario already provides a world of inputs, adaptational processing, and outputs; consequently the 'semantics' can be superimposed as a kind of transparent, i.e. ontologically innocent and theoretically redundant, overlay on a computationally and/or neurally generated syntax. The representations themselves need possess no denotational content in order to perform their explanatory role.

Although the notion of mental or 'inner' representation here does not imply intrinsic intentionality, it stands – though in the current state of functional theory still somewhat empty-handedly – for elements holistically related to one another in that 'cognitive economy' of causally structured states which enables a system or organism to convert environmental input into appropriate behavioural output. Thus mental representations are postulated as causal factors in the generation of appropriate, intelligent response. In general, the term 'mental representation' seems to be thought fitting here because the presence of a cognitive economy mediating input and response indicates the organism's ability to take account of things which are not sensorily present to it. But clearly, even where the organism is sensate, the notion has nothing directly to do with consciousness; systems, organisms, humans produce their own 'representational' programmes in formalizable physiological processes without the essential collaboration of first-person intentionality.

There is much to be said for the view that the term 'mental representation' here, as functionalists and others well squared off to the winds of doctrine use it, has itself only a functional role in the theorizing in which it is used. By this I mean that just as a functionalist analysis renders consciousness redundant, so the term used to achieve that end, namely 'representation', may here be replaced by others that perform the same explanatory function but do so more economically.

What kinds of distinction provide excuses for introducing a concept of mental representation in the way outlined? One such is the distinction between organisms supposedly in direct causal interaction with their environments and those whose interactions with their environments appear to be indirect. As paradigmatic cases of the former, we may think of organisms which must actually collide with obstructions before moving away from them. Thus when the single-celled paramecium bumps into something, it reverses the power beat of its cilia, backs away from the obstacle, and swims off in another direction.[8] It looks as though its activity is entirely *ad hoc*, and that might lead us to infer that it lacks a cognitive map of its environment. The fact that it doesn't keep on bumping into the obstacle might even be explained by classical dynamics; after all, billiard balls don't consecutively hit the same cushion either. But paramecia are organisms, and it is more natural to explain their responses biochemically, by tropisms. There is no real foothold here for the notion of a cognitive map, though in the interests of laying the basis of belief and desire as far down in the evolutionary scale as possible, it might be suggested that they do have very elementary, possibly only very short-lived, and *ad hoc* representations of the relevant parts of their environments – after all, they seem to display some minimal grasp of the local geography, enough to make them back away and not keep on bumping into the same obstacle.

If a purely biochemical explanation seems the more economical option here, what about organisms which systematically avoid obstacles before colliding with them? To us it might look as if they were actually perceiving parts of the world outside them, 'referring' to their cognitive maps, and changing course accordingly. But what would be the difference between a biochemical reaction to actual contact with an obstacle and a change of course due, say, to electromagnetic contact with an obstacle 'from a distance'? Or some more extended biochemical contact? The 'distance' might simply be an observer's illusion due to an inability to discern the actual micro-level (electromagnetic, biochemical, or whatever) causes invisibly linking the organism with its environment. In fact, there may be an even greater illusion. The very distinction between an organism and its environment is a flexible one and to a large extent arbitrary. The microprocesses can be indifferently interpreted as extensions of the organism or of the environment. What we have is simply a series of events leading from some arbitrarily selected entrance to an arbitrarily selected exit. To the natures of some of these events we have either visual or scientific ('mediated') access, and somewhere in the centre the events cluster very tightly, including some with causal antecedents based in previous environmental encounters. The term 'mental representation' functions merely to express the fact that somewhere in its temporal centre the series acquires antecedents additional to those provided by the present environment. The idea of an organism is, then, simply that of a life-supported neuroncomplex capable of responses linked to the past of the system itself or of its species.

'Representation' in this sense can be applied to anything capable of making appropriate responses, from even the paramecium, if need be, up through crustaceans, and on to robots. The distinction between direct and indirect patterns of response appears to have no empirical justification and to be applied simply by various rules of thumb. Normally the responses of paramecia and fuel gauges are regarded as direct, while the input–output relations of mammals and robots are 'mediated' by representations. Perhaps, intuitively, the distinction is one that could be expressed by saying that there is mediation if the organism or system can be said in some sense to 'field' its environmental inputs and respond to them through the intermediary of a regulative mechanism which discriminates between inputs and produces outputs congenial to the organism's 'interests', i.e. its continued integrity. That makes it look as though we have three things, and not just two, or even one – an arbitrarily divisible series (or a process arbitrarily divisible into a series of events).

If the idea of an inner representation employed by cognitive scientists has only metaphorical significance, then using it is to be in a position analogous to adopting Dennett's 'intentional stance'. That stance is applied to systems thought to be incapable of a 'real' semantics of the kind implicit in the idea of intrinsic intentionality. Here, explaining the behaviour of a system in terms of inner representations when it is incapable of 'real' representation is a matter of adopting a 'representational stance'.

This has to be understood precisely. What those who adopt the representational stance assume is that organisms and machines can be understood in representational categories independently of their having or lacking a first-person point of view. Even mere sentience plays no essential role in the kind of explanation given. It is here that we pick up the second of our three threads: the question whether machine intelligence can ever be genuinely intentional. I propose that if there is a core concept of representation that is logically tied to the concept of consciousness, and such a concept plays a theoretical role in explaining the behaviour of conscious beings, that will be a reason for saying that not even the 'cleverest' robot has intentional states. That is, if the question is: Is the program's internal representation of the world genuinely intentional?, then the answer is no, because in describing the events forming its physical realization it is neither necessary nor plausible to refer to any characteristically representational activity. The point is not the triviality that machines do not possess first-person intentionality; it is the claim that the presence of awareness in an organism betokens something functionally special, and that what is special about it plays an essential role in the explanation of belief, desire, and the propositional attitudes in general. The claim relies on the assumption that, contrary to the typical physicalist programme, the place to look for the origins of the kind of control that human brains exercise is not the tropism or its more discriminating sequels, but something constituting a hiatus in the input–output series and has the status of a genuine explanatory node.

What might that be? Awareness? Hardly, since the notion is wide enough to include visual or other responses which lead to motor responses directly or serve as parts of automatic feedback mechanisms. Something more is needed. Ability to communicate? The reason for that proposal is that to explain communicative behaviour we seem to have to postulate a third term in the shape of the message. But consider the example sometimes invoked to support the belief in the possession by organisms of 'cognitive maps', namely the 'communicative' behaviour of bees. When one honey-bee finds food it does a dance in front of others, which then are able to locate the food. The temptation is to say that the behaviour is the bee's motor response to an internal symbolic representation, and that the other bees acquire their own tokens of that representation, which then produce in them their own food-finding behaviour. But there seems no theoretical compulsion to introduce an internal symbolic factor in the explanation of this complex behaviour. The dance is a set of motions caused by the bee's recent proximity to food and (one guesses) its present proximity to other bees, which then produces in the latter an effect corresponding to the former cause, that is, proximity to food. That there are symbols and processes of interpreting involved is an arbitrary supposition based apparently on nothing more than the traditional rationalism still pervading most cognitive science.

Gillett has proposed problem-solving. There are cases of the ability to solve sorting and other problems where representations do seem to be a necessary, or at least rational, part of the explanation. Take the double-alternation task performed by a monkey. The task contains two options – e.g. a circle and a square – and consists in choosing the circle twice, then the square twice, and so on. As Gillett describes it:

> It is clear that the monkey must represent not only the shapes but also the temporal pattern of their presentation in order to succeed. . . . [T]he correct response can only be made if the subject takes account *not only* of his present orientation *but also* of the place in the sequence occupied by the present stimulus and learns differentially to exhibit or inhibit its response to the same stimulus at different times. In other words, a double alternation requires that we explain behaviour by appeal to a representation of the sequence or temporal pattern of events.[9]

The substantive, 'representation', must of course be treated with caution here, not being taken straightaway to imply some imaging capacity, but simply as reserving a space for whatever more perspicuous form of words expresses the kind of activity thought to be required here. In describing the monkey's performance we should probably say something on the lines that it is an ability to grasp that, when one immediately previous occurrence of a stimulus situation (the circle and the square) has correlated with a circle choice, *this* stimulus situation correlates with the same choice but the next time it occurs it correlates with a choice of the square. This suggests that the ability required is a grasp of the present token of the stimulus situation's being *this* token rather than either that previous one or the expected future one.

That might presume too much awareness on the part of the monkey. Perhaps it need have no particular expectations for the future; the monkey is prepared to choose the circle once more before choosing the square *if* the same stimulus situation occurs next, though it has no tendency to believe that it will. Nor, of course, should it be presumed that where it does, or even if it must, have such expectations, that these involve mental events of 'representing' the expected situations. The mental fact of the matter may simply have to be described as one in which the monkey, at this juncture, is 'prepared' to choose the circle just once more before choosing the square.

However, an organism might conceivably be 'prepared' in this way with no consciousness at all of being so; indeed we ourselves are obviously prepared for many things without occurrent consciousness of our being so. It seems evident, too, that a robot could be programmed to produce the same double-alternation behaviour as the monkey, in which case there would be no call to refer to any characteristically representational activity. However, one could not claim in any literal sense that the robot's behaviour constituted a solution to the double-alternation problem. That is because the task is to give a certain patterned response to particular stimulus situations. But there is no stimulus–response relation for the robot: a programmer or observer can identify the two terms and the relation from their own point of view and apply it by analogy to the robot's performance, but there is no stimulus *for* the robot. In fact there is nothing at all *for* the robot, since the ideal of anything being present to it makes no literal sense. Nor is there any foothold for the thought that it *inhibits* a square response in favour of a circle response; all that strictly happens in the case of the robot is that two distinct causal chains occur in a double-alternation pattern due to the effect of a superimposed causal-link selection, either triggered by the experimenter or incorporated as an automatic patterning device in the machine. If any stage in the causal chain is described in terms of 'stimulus–response' (as in principle all or none of them might be), then what happens is simply that the stimulus situations themselves change, i.e. are not tokens of the same situation-type: the circle or its machine equivalent enters into the chain twice and then the square takes over. Any inhibiting has to be done by the programmer, in the triggering or the programming, and the double-alternation task is solved by her and not by the robot.

What the introduction of the notion of a representation implies here, then, is a grasp of the present situation in relation to situations past and future, which in the case in question you might say is a virtual grasp of the present stimulus situation as a member of a temporal (though not necessarily consecutive) sequence of further tokens of the same type. It is this that enables the monkey to comply with a task that calls for responding to a stimulus situation in a way that exceeds strict stimulus–response correlations. The ability seems in no obvious way essentially to involve a capacity to form mental images. Nor, of course, does 'representation' in this explanatory context imply the traditional epistemological notion of an 'inner' mental picture presented as 'given' to a cognitivistically conceived subject and in some questionable relation to the 'outside' world. Whatever else is involved, the capacity in question is initially simply an ability to respond to what is presented to a conscious organism in its present orientation in a way that involves its 'taking account' of what is not presented to it in that orientation, such taking account implying some kind of virtual presence nevertheless, in its way of consciously responding. As Gillett puts it, the general rule is that '[w]hen the patterns of information utilization . . . required to explain the configuration of a broad range of behaviour are unified only on the basis that they signal the presence of x, then we must invoke a representation of x as an element in the mental ascriptions we make to the organism'.[10]

In the previous quotation Gillett talks of the agent's ('subject's') taking account 'not only of his present orientation but also of the place in the sequence occupied by the present stimulus'. On a cognitivist reading, 'taking account' of anything at all, and thus also of the present orientation in itself without further addition, might be taken already to imply the exercise of an ability to distinguish that orientation from others, simply as being what it is. In that case the conditions for representation appear to be satisfied from the start. But the notion is ambiguous and even tropisms may be construed in the language of 'taking account of', so the question is rather in what form we are to think of the reference to the further addition as being made. The monkey's skill might conceivably be explained in a purely mechanistic way in terms of word–shape association and abstraction. But let us suppose that its behaviour here is more economically understood as due to an ability to perceive its actual present orientation as being in a temporal sequence that extends beyond the stimulus resources of that orientation. Beyond being representational in this as yet minimal sense, is any further specification of this ability available?

Some might claim that it is a conceptual ability on the grounds that concepts are essentially interdefinable and to be able to 'take account of x' is necessarily to be able to distinguish x here and now from anything other than x. But it isn't clear that anything in the notion of representation in the sense introduced here requires us to call a representational capacity conceptual. On the other hand, the term 'concept' itself hasn't yet really settled into any stable conceptual niche and we might find a use for the idea of languageless creatures as capable of rudimentary conceptual thought. It has sometimes been supposed that mental images can serve as primitive surrogates for concepts, and it may be that in the monkey's case the stimulus pattern can extend beyond the resources of the sensorily available environment, and in the required way, simply through an imaging ability. But that would have to be understood as something other or more than just a centrally excited image-supplement to the input supplied by the optic nerves. Otherwise the organism would be unable to discriminate between what is presented and what only represented, and the lack of fit between the actual surroundings and what presents itself as a version of those surroundings would surely produce inappropriate behaviour and prove highly unadaptive. Whereas if the organism can indeed make that distinction, as when it can take account of the temporal place in a sequence occupied by a present stimulus, some discriminative capacity of a modal character seems to be required enabling the organism to envision what is only a possible stimulus situation in the light of the actual stimulus situation and vice versa.

Lurking here are the seeds of the topics of the previous two chapters. Doesn't the ability just mentioned also require the sense of a continuing identity on the part of the subject for whom an actual stimulus situation can be related 'in thought' to some other possible stimulus situation? The relation itself can be conceived in terms of a spatio-temporal distance between an actual and an 'ideal' state, a distance which the sensorimotor system is activated to reduce. This may as yet include no thought in the sense of judgment, if that is taken to imply an ability to withhold sensorimotor 'assent' from any particular conjunction of actual and ideal stimulus situation.[11] But if we add that component and also an ability to vary the extra-stimulatory content, from base, as it were, i.e. to select the non-presentational ingredient, a 'conjectural' component let us say, and further, a capacity to represent such representations in a linguistic form, we seem to arrive by fairly easy stages at a rough specification of the human-specific repertoire. The only item missing seems to be the human organism's capacity to represent *itself* as a continuing node within a 'practical' space of representable possibilities, though further analysis may show that some combination of the above elements already amounts to that capacity. Here, at any rate, we have what looks like an outline of what it is to react *in thought* to an item in the environment. Whether or not such a reaction should be considered conceptual, it is evident at least that language is not a requirement; there is no need to appeal to linguistic representation in explaining the monkey's ability to place a present stimulus in a sequence of possible stimuli.

On the other hand, once the linguistic ability is in place, it will be possible to do that too, and then also to represent the former ability linguistically, or – let us at least assume that this is the same – conceptually, as for instance a relationship between a subject and its objects. In general, there is a clear adaptational advantage in the power of conceptual thought; it enables an organism to act with maximum flexibility in relation to its environment. Not only can organisms thus equipped pick out features common to several situations and pattern their activity in ways in which behavioural output is not related to specific stimuli,[12] the flexibility is such that the organism can also ignore present stimuli altogether and carry on a process of thought in total independence of the environment.

Recently, it has been suggested that as empirical psychology progresses the theoretical utility of the concept of consciousness diminishes; indeed it is claimed that as the various areas with which the concept of consciousness has been associated undergo scrutiny, the very concept itself begins to fall apart, so that the chances of there being any coherent concept or concepts for science to exploit are slender at best. In the light of the case for the adaptational advantages of (particularly conceptual) consciousness, that is a remarkable suggestion. It is one thing to claim that consciousness will become a more differentiated concept as the levels and aspects of conscious experience are brought into view, quite another to envisage its total scientific eclipse. What, then, is the reasoning behind the suggestion?

A parallel has been drawn with the case of temperature.[13] The representation of temperature in gases by mean molecular kinetic energy is often cited as a paradigm of successful theoretical reduction. Since, in other media, temperature has to be represented in other ways, for instance in vacua by radiation frequencies, thermo-dynamics seems bound to proceed on the assumption that there can be no unitary concept of temperature. Similarly, so it is alleged, with consciousness. Given the immense diversity of conscious phenomena, there is little likelihood of closer inspection's revealing some funda-mental feature which all of them share. Further, for any distinguishable subclass of the states we call 'being conscious' or 'being aware', the fact that it is a state of consciousness or awareness need by no means be essential to whatever organizing principle experimental psychology eventually finds it useful to define in connection with that state. Take the stock example of pain. There may be good scientific reasons for taking the *kind* to which the explanatory factor found for a prima-facie class of felt pains belongs to embrace explanations also of parallel phenomena that are *not* typically felt. But because of their shared functional characteristics these may nevertheless deserve to be classed along with felt pains, perhaps even *as* pains, and – who knows? – perhaps even as the central cases, in a general taxonomy. What is envisaged is the possibility that noticed pains might not form a *de facto* 'natural' kind, as would allegedly be required were they to enter into some discoverable functional regularity. In other words, the fact (whatever it amounts to in itself) that one knows what it is like to have a pain – to be feeling or noticing pain – may well have no independent explanatory role. We should be prepared, as Patricia Churchland maintains, to see the brain as 'a battery of monitoring systems . . . where consciousness may be but one amongst others, or where these systems cross-classify what we now think of as conscious states'.[14] In addition, findings such as Penfield's on hypnotic states and those of Weiskrantz on blind-sight, together with the results of commissurotomy, show that the very phenomena centrally associated with the traditional notion of consciousness fail to find a place within the only phenomenological 'theory' of consciousness we have; that is, of states of a self-intimating medium. All in all, there seems little to prevent the concept from simply disappearing from psychological discourse altogether, just as phenomenal heat no longer plays any part in thermodynamics.[15]

Armed with this analogy, the eliminative materialist, far from finding the conclusion paradoxical, sees in the collapse of the traditional consciousness a promising new prospect. With the traditional belief in the centrality and unity of the concept out of the way, we are free to build an understanding of human functioning afresh. Taking as their explananda certain subclasses of the broad class of states called 'being conscious' or 'being aware', the theorists can now look for neurobiological explanations suitable for each case. The task of arriving at a theory will be that of finding the mechanisms, for example, neural networks, which have the relevant phenomena as their effects. It will then be neurologically based distinctions which in the end afford us the 'new and better large-scale concepts'.[16]

There are some initial points to note about this programme. One is that eliminative materialists, unlike behaviourists, cannot be accused of 'feigning anaesthesia'. Even though the phenomena dealt with in, say, optics are to be understood in terms of electromagnetic radiation, the reduction is theoretical.[17] So no qualia need be eliminated as such. That may seem a minimal virtue of the position to a defender of the first-person vantage-point. But for the eliminative materialist it hints at work undone. Commitment even to a general theory of consciousness as 'mere qualia' carries with it an obligation to incorporate that (no doubt not very useful) theoretical term within the general materialist framework, and, as we noted earlier, it is unlikely that the obligation can be fulfilled. However, eliminative materialists effectively avoid that task by treating the 'qualitative aspect' exclusively as (provisional) explanandum.[18] There is no room in the programme for a conscious content that, in virtue of its being conscious, can be appealed to as an explanans; that is, as a cause and explanation of human performance. The principles of that performance are neurobiological. This also means that, from the eliminative materialist's point of view, there is no urgency attached to the problem of finding a workable explanandum. It is not as though some important aspect of the human control repertoire might prove too slippery to succumb to reductive analysis. If there should be anything to explain there, it won't be anything that can be used to explain anything else. And if something of the old concept does survive, that will only be because successful reduction through neurobiological explanation happens to leave original phenomenal distinctions intact. Whether they do so or not is a matter of indifference, however, since, should consciousness go the way of phlogiston and the angels, nothing significant will be felt to have been left unexplained.[19]

How can that be plausible? There are, I suggest, three reasons which together might mislead one into thinking it so. The first is uncontroversial and can be labelled the thesis of 'micro-necessity'. Whether or not it is also the seat of consciousness, the brain is at least the seat of organized response. If the internal mental economy that converts environmental input into behavioural output is realized in anything it is realized in the brain. The brain is necessary for controlled response. But what about the inputs and the outputs themselves? In describing these it is not enough to refer to the brain and nervous system. They are macrophysiological and contain essential reference to such things as size of tooth, set of jaw, limbic configuration, and so on. The molar human performance, then, is not recoverable at the micro-level. That we should not expect it to be so is supported by an argument appealing to the aetiology of human (or, in general, animal) powers. If these are the result of behavioural adaptation, there must be some functional relationship between whatever brain states are involved in movements of the relevant macrophysiological properties and the features of the environment which have made them adaptive. As prey in an environment of predators it pays to have long legs. This is not only a matter of the aetiology of human capacities; if they are capacities generated by environmental success, the presumption is also that in their current exercise they are to be described as ways of succeeding in the environment. Since an important part of that success must be accounted for by the organism's powers of discrimination (not just being able to bite or flee, but to recognize what to pursue and what to flee from), some of these capacities will be best identified as capacities to pick out things in the environment and others as capacities to cope with whatever is found there.

The second reason is therefore the false belief in what can be called 'micro-sufficiency'. It is thought that whatever the causal origins of powers currently possessed by brains, the powers themselves are those of the brain here and now; they should therefore be available in principle to an exclusively neurobiological investigation. As noted, functionalists hold a similar position with regard to the semantic content of mental states: the states themselves result from computational processes on syntactic elements within the organism which can be described independently of the content-giving relationship of the organism to its current environment. In both cases it is held that because the processes of the internal cognitive economy comprise a two-way term in a causal relation, an effect of the environment and a cause of it, and such terms are logically independent of each other, the fact that the other term makes essential reference to the transactions of the organism with its environment has no implications for the way in which the processes themselves have to be characterized. Against this, there is at least an initial plausibility in the view that a capacity, the explanation of the origin of which (let us say) essentially includes reference to macrophysiology (tooth size, length of leg, etc.), is a capacity which can only be identified in terms of the macrophysiological properties in question. But since these properties are properties of the organism which can only be fully characterized in terms of the organism's relationship to its environment, the neurobiological account of the circuitry that has the exercise of the capacity as its effect will have to be supplemented by descriptions and factors that exceed the neuroscientist's stock-in-trade. In brief, neurobiology can begin only when the macro-events whose neurobiological micro-causes it is looking for have first been identified as macro-effects also of macro-causes.

The third reason is a version of what might be called the fallacy of 'analytical realism', or the error of construing the analytical components of a concept as causal factors in the production of the corresponding phenomenon. It is only a 'version' because the analysis here is functional, not conceptual; the analysanda are not to be found in the connotations of words in their conventional use, but in phenomena identified as tools for the cross-classification of higher-level phenomena of which they are taken to be constituents. Thus the phenomena of consciousness may be arranged initially in a broadly hierarchical categorization, with sensation at the bottom, attention or awareness in the middle, and articulation at the top. There can be

141

sensation without attention, but not vice versa, and there can be attention without articulation, but (let us grant) not vice versa.[20] Articulation requires not just sensation (the ability to discriminate different shapes and sounds) and attention, of course, but also the ability to see phonological structure, to recognize grammatical structure in strings of phonemes, and to read definite meanings into the structures. There are other factors too, for instance short-term and long-term memory, image-substitution for receptor-stimulation, and so on. The fallacy is to treat the hierarchical arrangement as a causal structure in which higher-level 'functions' are *defined* simply as the *effects* of combinations of more basic 'functions', which are then defined in turn as combinations of yet more basic functions, until some basic (though in respect of fundamental physical theory itself still compound) level of events described in the taxonomy of, in this case, neurobiology is reached.

Take the ability to recognize grammatical structure. In evolutionary terms it is natural to think of this as an acquired trait which builds upon earlier capacities, such as the ability to use symbols or signs. 'Building upon' the earlier capacities here implies actually superseding them, while the abilities built upon will in turn have been erected upon and have superseded such lower-grade abilities as the ability to distinguish aspects of the visible environment. But there is no question of higher-level abilities superseding lower-level ones if the former are no more than 'analytical' products of the latter. If the psychophysical organism is something whose evolution consists in the acquisition of new superstructural levels which actually take over control from the previous top levels, the analytical procedure is seriously misguided. The elemental operations it aims to uncover will belong to the distant past and the analysis miss the level of operations at which the brain currently supports top-level performance. Of course, accounts at levels below the current top will be relevant in cases of impairment of such performance, but in general it will be a mistake to take the analytical parts of some current complex performance to correspond to genuinely autonomous capacities working in concert to produce that performance.

A realistic approach for the materialist, according to Patricia Churchland, is 'to search for the neurobiological mechanism which results in an organism being conscious . . . hopeful that, in the long run, neuroscientific techniques will reveal the inner secret of what seems terribly mysterious about consciousness'.[21] Certainly, if the third-person perspective of physical science were adequate to the task of explaining human mentality, then any facts of consciousness – including those that we may want to call facts about what conscious states produce – would have to be facts about what produces conscious states. But if, as is implicit in our argument, conscious states produce something significant by virtue of some feature of those states that is not captured in the definition of them as mere products of brain states, then the third-person perspective generates rather than reduces mystery. To accommodate that possibility, some totally different kind of causal factor would have to be introduced, thus forcing the theorist back into dualism. In fact, even in describing the task of the materialist as that of locating the neural mechanisms which produce consciousness, there is the still untouched mystery of the product itself. For instance, there seems no way in which the first-person phenomenon of consciousness, even at the minimal level of sensation, can be satisfactorily explained in terms of third-person accounts of how receptor-stimulation occurs.

There are two antithetical positions here. Both acknowledge that the full range of human performance extends beyond the limits of first-person intentionality, so that mechanisms like receptor-stimulation, accessible only from a third-person perspective, have to be taken into account. They also agree that first-person intentionality and its contents must be brain-based and cannot be something totally different in kind from these mechanisms. The difference is where they think the uniformity lies. According to the one view, it consists in their being the topic of a special science: neurobiology (or any science of functionally equivalent systems). But that leaves the phenomenon of consciousness entirely out in the cold. According to the other, uniformity is to be found in the range of phenomena to which consciousness belongs: namely, modes of discrimination. It belongs then with tropisms and other correctional devices accessible from a third-person perspective. But the general category spans the transition from those preconscious modes to the kind of control that organisms exercise over their environments when they are able to form conscious *re*-presentations of it. There is still the mystery of the transition; and we still seem at a loss what to say when asked to put into words whatever it is we know when we know what it is to be conscious. But at least we have a framework in which to discuss the causal roles of whatever it is we know; and we don't have to face the fantasy that neuroscience may one day put the right words into our mouths.

That consciousness might go the way of phlogiston and the angels seems absurd if one considers the causal potentialities of specifically conscious states; and contrary to physicalist protestations, there appears to be no good reason to suppose that an adequate psychology could be 'indifferent to consciousness'.[22] In the next chapter we shall examine claims about the sociological implications of the capacity to form representations of our worlds and of ourselves in those worlds; if Humphrey is right, consciousness affords a mutual modelling capacity which supports social life. It gives us, in the form of self-images, a tool for social interaction based on analogical reasoning.[23] The more the search for the principles of a scientific psychology departs from the level of first-person intentionality, and the greater the trust in a psychology which is ideally indifferent to that surface phenomenon, the more mysterious becomes the fact that conscious states exist at all. The fact of consciousness, however we describe it and whatever heterogeneity the concept reveals under analysis, cries out for an account of the functions which have given conscious beings a reproductive advantage. Even those who argue that a computer program can duplicate all the control powers of the human brain must concede this. For that argument merely says that the control has been achieved without consciousness, and we are left wondering what evolutionary advantages attach to conscious mental states if nature could have done as well without. Of course, the mistake of those who claim we can remain indifferent to consciousness is not that the levels below the surface are unimportant for psychology. The error is to suppose that no genuinely explanatory principles are discoverable at the conscious level, while it would be precisely in accordance with evolutionary theory to assume that the acquisition by a physical system of a higher-order property such as consciousness implies some structural modification which leads you to look for the principles of the consequent improved adaptational performance.

It is important to see what such a modification implies. At the beginning of this chapter I noted that there are two matters on which I disagree with Searle: first, over whether the brain causes particular intentional states; and second, over whether the first-person vantage-point offers access to the levels of control currently exercised by the nervous system. In concluding the chapter, let me indicate the reasons for denying that the brain causes intentional states and for allowing that the vantage-point does offer such access.

First, then, the matter of the causation of intentional states. What the evolutionary perspective suggests is that conscious states are developments of natural powers of discrimination, so in a sense they are the outcome of the mechanisms underlying those powers. But on Searle's view every particular intentional state is itself the effect of microphysiological processes in the brain. One consequence is the illusoriness of any sense a subject may have of engaging in voluntary, free, intentional action; but that is a topic we shall postpone. What is important here is the implication that control lies below the intentional surface.

According to Searle, conscious mental states are both '*realized in* the structure of the brain' and '*caused by* the operations of the brain'.[24] They are 'realized' in the brain structure in the sense that to describe something as a conscious mental state is to describe (some aspect or part of) the structure of the brain itself, not something over and above the structure to which the structure has somehow given birth; it is just that we are describing the structure at a higher level of description than that of neurophysiology. They are 'caused' by the operations of the brain in the sense that if one effects some change in the operations, a given conscious mental state, or in some cases the state of being conscious itself, will not occur. By analogy, liquidity is a property of a certain molecular structure and so realized in that structure, which differs, for example, from that in which ice is realized; and yet it is caused by the molecular behaviour, since if we altered it in a certain way we would get ice or steam, as the case may be.[25] The causation here is 'bottom-up' causation simply because the surface features in question correlate with differences at the micro-level.

Searle's 'bottom levels' are characterized broadly as neurophysiological, and he is content to refer collectively to these bottom levels and those for surface features generally as the 'basic microlevels' of physics.[26] But there is a hierarchy of levels in physics. Microphysics is concerned with subatomic and subnuclear phenomena and with the constitution and behaviour of atomic particles quite generally. Its laws do not include those of the behaviour of whatever specific body of matter a given particle happens to be part of. Again, submolecular properties are of interest to physics but not, say, to chemistry, which assumes that the molecules of any element or compound are of the same size and mass, these being the 'bottom level' below which further divisions do not correlate with distinct chemical identities and so fall beneath the purview of chemical laws. Thus the level of structure which maps (relevant) surface changes may be relatively high. While it is of course true that the structures below that level continue to have a constituent role to play in so far as they sustain the structural level whose changes *are* reflected at the surface, in terms of what causes surface phenomena we may well want to say that these are not caused by the merely constituent levels in the same way, or sense, as that in which they are caused by the relatively higher structural level.

More pertinent, however, is the relation between the laws governing the behaviour of a molecule, say, in some wider, mechanical or dynamical context. Take a molecule located on the rim of a wheel in motion or at the periphery of a cyclone.[27] Clearly there is a constitutive role played by the laws of microphysics, since the fact that they apply is essential to there being the context in question. But in what sense can it be said that the relevant microphysical laws enter in any way into a causal explanation of the actual behaviour of the molecule in its context? Is it not rather the case that, given the microstructural explanation of why the corresponding surface phenomenon is wooden or liquid, as well as the subatomic and subnuclear presuppositions of there being the relevant micro-structures, what causes *that* molecule to be behaving contextually as it does is the applicability of certain mechanical or meteorological laws? Thus liquidity, to take Searle's example, depends on there being a subnuclear and subatomic level supporting the molecular structure specific to that surface property. Of course, if you remove the bottom level here you remove the structure, and this might seem to justify talking of the latter as an effect of the former, and conversely of the former as a cause of the latter. But it is not *the* cause of the latter in the sense of causing the structure specific to liquidity as opposed to, say, ice or steam. And it is, as Searle says, the fact that you are able to produce some specific modification of the surface when you alter the microstructure that makes the relation between the two 'clearly causal'.[28] However, once you specify a context or set of boundary conditions in which the surface quality occurs, whether a bucket of water, moisture in a cloud, a drop about to enter the ocean, or an eddy in a stream, another level of causal influence with its own principles comes into play. Take the behaviour of a molecule in an eddy.[29] Here the context is at least that of a *body* of fluid, and that already means that the molecule is subject to forces other than those affecting, say, liquid particles. But in addition we have to reckon with the forces specific to movement of bodies of water at certain velocities and in given topographical circumstances. Thus it seems undeniable that the behaviour of any actual molecule is largely determined by a complex of systemic influences 'from above' in the sense that the laws of molecular motion cannot of themselves account for the actual movements of a molecule when it is part of some ordered structure whose very identity such laws leave open.

We note that in an obvious sense top-down causation is readily admitted in Searle's account. Intentions-in-action genuinely cause their conditions of satisfaction, and if my intention is to 'release . . . the neurotransmitter acetylcholine at the axon end-plates of my motorneurons', I can do that simply by deciding to raise my arm and doing so.[30] But this is causation 'over a passage of time', and the question of where the controlling power actually lies is answered by having to say that the decision itself and the intention-in-action are predetermined by the micro-levels that support them. Although the above argument suggests that the latter relation is not as comprehensively bottom-up as Searle assumes, the relation Searle refers to as 'bottom-up' remains nevertheless intact. It is not altogether clear to me why Searle takes the micro–macro correlations between molecular properties and the surface features to be causal, or, if causal, why specifically in the micro–macro direction. But whatever the best analysis of these correlations, the correlations themselves are not affected by contextual influences. On the contrary, that they remain intact is among the boundary conditions of whatever ordering, organizing, or operating principles fill out the laws governing the motions of the parts of the context-given whole. The top-down factor in the explanation is simply that it is these principles that enable us to predict when and where, and with what consequences, a given token of a molecular type with its surface correlate will occur. The parallel in the neural case would be that whatever the contextual influences at work at the surface here, it is they that govern the placement in time and space of a given neural event together with its conscious correlate.

Many conscious states, for example thirst, drowsiness, or pain, may seem too irremediably bottom-up for the analogy to apply. But this misses the point. What any laws of a dynamics of conscious mental states would systematically state are the behavioural dispositions of brain cells contexted in some analogue of, say, a body of water subject in turn to the kind of factors that take account of eddies, rapids, undercurrents, sluicing, pollution, or any other relevant 'vicissitudes' of the transport of a given body of water. Indeed the case of water transport could prove a particularly apt analogy. The mental surface forms a 'stream' (of consciousness) whose 'course' and to a considerable degree 'contents' are fixed not just by a sustaining infrastructure but by an unfolding environmental topography. According to this picture, all surface-preserving bottom-up relations are maintained, but the microstructural levels relevant for sustaining the surface properties in question (the succession of conscious mental states) are subject to forces which apply only because there are indeed these surface features. That is, for instance, the biochemical conditions of thirst acquire a new set of determinants, and acquire dispositions correspondingly, by going into a 'body' of conscious states which are subject in turn to factors analogous to those brought to bear on a body of fluid by a given topography. Certainly, thirst, drowsiness, and pain are 'due to' their underlying chemical and neural origins, but particular activations of their chemistry and neurophysiology, even in the case of such clearly physically dependent mental states as these, are typically owing to whatever forces and factors apply at the level of a putative mental dynamics (plans, projects, decisions, prevailing prejudices, susceptibilities, to mention just a small selection out of any plausibly adequate list).

Second, this answers our question whether the first-person vantage-point offers access to the levels where control is being exercised. If conscious states belong to a level at which control is not exercised by forces working *upon* surface phenomena, whether from below or above, then accounts of these forces will be in terms of the dispositions of such phenomena themselves. This is not to turn our backs on neurobiology or to deny that the forces are realized in physiological processes. But you will not be able to provide an account of the relevant dynamics by investigating the brain, and they are only partly realized there. Indeed you will not know what to look for in the brain without prior access to the forces at work 'from above', i.e. from a first-person point of view. The strong way with first-person intentionality, we saw, was to jettison the notion, along with the ways in which we find it natural to describe our inner lives. The assumption that the flux and content of lived experience sorts into beliefs, motives, desires, fears, etc. which are the causes and explanations of our actions has no privileged status. It has the status only of a provisional theory based on the 'primitive psychological taxonomy of ordinary language' and can expect replacement by a 'more penetrating taxonomy of states drawn from a completed neuroscience'.[31]

We have seen reasons for believing that, to avoid having to admit to having given only a partial picture of the facts, a completed neuroscience will have to include (first-person) intentional categories in its taxonomy. Admittedly, ordinary language isn't in the business of (explicit) taxonomizing, and our ways of talking about our own mental activity can be very sloppy, but the human mind's own operations can be self-intimating for all that. The knowledge may be faulty and the mistakes due to faulty articulation or plain inadvertence. If we take judging, desiring, fearing, etc. to be modes of consciousness, then why should it not be, as Sprigge says, that 'to ask about the character of these modes is to seek to articulate clearly what one already implicitly knows'?[32] In the case of sensate organisms, if distinctions in first-hand experience did not mirror the brain's powers of environmental discrimination, there would have been no reproductive advantage in the organism's being sensate; similarly with intentionality and the distinctions we can make in experience between believing, being motivated, desiring, and fearing, etc. From an evolutionary perspective, there are clear advantages in knowing your own mind. And if, because we are, as Locke says, 'usually employed and diverted in looking abroad',[33] our taxonomies of that employment tend initially to be inaccurate, the same could be said of an introspective device which, when they do look 'inside', allows the employers' theories of intentional behaviour to coincide better with their employments.

We asked earlier whether there is an intentional form of control in which consciousness – implying the presence of a first-person point of view, or the occurrence of episodes of knowing what it is like to be conscious – plays an essential part. Let us assume now that the answer to that is affirmative. We also said that this could be examined independently of the question whether the control manifested in conscious human behaviour is freely exercised in some sense relevant to the free-will issue. There is a certain aspect of that issue, however, upon which the conclusion can throw some light.

People not involved in Penfield situations typically have a sense of personal involvement in their own actions. If the arguments of the previous chapter are accepted, that could be explained by the fact that, simply by virtue of belonging *qua* conscious being to the level where the major determinants of human performance belong, they are 'where the action is'. But the sense of personal involvement surely amounts to more. If the action were merely the operation of forces of attraction and repulsion in the intentional mode, there need be no more sense of being personally involved in the outcomes of those than if the operative dynamics were subconscious. On the other hand, from our discussion above we have the kernel of a relative notion of freedom as unimpeded or successful coping. If part of the conscious content of an ongoing activity were that it is a case of smooth functioning, so far without malfunction or breakdown, that in itself would be a sense of freedom. Of course, there need be no such content; the very thought may even tend to invite malfunction or breakdown. But past experience of these may very well confer on the marginally conscious content of smooth functioning a sense of its being smooth in a sense that has some essential connection with what is meant in general by 'freedom'.

Since the freedom here is relative it does not amount to libertarian freedom, for libertarian freedom is an absolute freedom. In our terms that implies an ability on the part of the organism to dispose freely over its own control possibilities in a way which means that in exercising the ability there is no control over which it does not dispose. Critics of indeterministic accounts of free will, from Hume on, have pointed out that the responsibility for our choices which proponents of free will aim to capture implies that they are in some sense determined. However, there seems no *a priori* reason why the distinction we make in consciousness in marking off an event as due to the special kind of engagement on our part that makes us regard it as an accountable action of ours, cannot be *experienced* in some way other than that of libertarian freedom. For example, the sense we have of an action's being ours might be described – and be described more accurately – in terms of some conscious effort, say, to improve on or compensate for past below-par performance, without that implying a past misuse of a capacity for free choice. This is a future-oriented rather than a past-oriented notion of accountability; it compares a less attractive life-history projected on the basis of past performance with a more attractive one incorporating a change in overall performance, the comparison – with its cost–benefit quotient – then being 'factored into' the circumstances which cause whatever changes occur in future performance patterns.

What is more, and what less, attractive in this regard can be construed as what the agent considers as being in her or his best interest. And consciously conforming with some goal or ideal identified by the agent as being in her or his best interest will afford a sense of freedom analogous to that of unimpeded coping, except that the performance is now consciously controlled by a higher-level determinant which (so long as it remains in effect) excludes 'malfunctions' and 'breakdowns' of the self. The primary sense of an interest's being 'mine' is that in which having an interest is to have desires and projects that one is at least attributively aware of having. An interest of mine in this sense need not be one I have chosen or personally underwritten. It may have a natural basis and I simply find myself inhabiting this scheme of comparisons. On the other hand, standards of comparison are more liable to have socio-cultural origins, and one may think of them in the way Dreyfus, following Heidegger, proposes: namely, as 'meanings' already waiting to be instantiated prereflectively as implicit stands that *Dasein* is taking on the issue of its being. Whether or not this is the right way to think of it, in terms of the determinants of actual human behaviour, it is surely important to include the fact that human agents are able to give some account of the 'import' they find themselves attaching to things,[34] and from which it is possible for them to sketch, predicatively, an inventory of their current patterns of preference and choice. For it is a feature of intentional control systems that they are able to take a stand on their own inventories. Their patterns of preference and choice may be adjusted in line with higher-order preferences which embody ideals in which they believe they have identified their 'true' interests – though again their 'identifying' them may simply be another case of prereflective instantiation of currently available 'meanings'. Even if there is no higher preference than that to which existing patterns conform, there is this ability to take a stand on these one way or the other, and thus a capacity for self-determination, though itself no less relative a form of freedom than those of unimpeded coping and conscious and successful alignment with a first-order preference.

The notion of 'self' is as highly ambiguous in this context as that of determination. Much of the traditional burden of the concept is borne by various versions of an ideal formed at the level of higher-level preferences. These include concepts of a substantial soul and especially forms of dualism which portray selfhood as the victory of asceticism over desire or inclination. Philosophers of a physicalist bent often assume that because such conceptions are superstructural, and so dispensable, there is no need for their accounts of human behaviour to include a concept of *consciousness* of a self. But, as a long tradition of authors (Fichte, Hegel, Kierkegaard, Heidegger, Sartre, Taylor, Tugendhat, Dreyfus, and others) has realized, it is structural to human consciousness that ongoing purposive activity can become the topic of higher-order purposes of theoretical and normative appraisal on the part of the agent; and, whatever one's conclusions about the particular results of such appraisals (and about the irrationality of the thought-process they often involve), the self-relatedness which makes them possible is an undeniable feature of the 'control powers' which underlie human performance.

CHAPTER VIII

Others

Certain things follow from our freedom to treat the contents of conscious mental states as realizations of neural and limbic conditions. The most central have to do with the social and the moral world, or in general the world of communicative behaviour, and it is with a discussion of the implications for this that we shall conclude this examination.

If consciousness is granted the kind of status we have outlined, one question that arises concerns its place within a general evolutionary framework. Freed from the constraints of physicalism, however, we can tackle this question head-on. We shall assume to begin with that consciousness has something like the status we have tried to ascribe to it. It is perfectly natural, then, to ask what specific role or roles consciousness plays in the kind of life those endowed with it find themselves living. One way of characterizing that life would be to say that it is social in form. That is a third-personal characterization; it says that conscious organisms live in some form of interaction with one another. That might be true of ants and bees as much as humans. But in their case we are far from inclined to assign consciousness any vital role in the respective interactional processes – so little so, perhaps, that on the basis of the usual connotations of the term we may even be disinclined to say that their behaviour involves any form of 'interaction' at all. As far as we ourselves are concerned, however, the form of social life we live is one to which we have some access from our own first-person points of view. And from that point of view, if we follow the conclusions of the previous chapter, one thing that characterizes our form of life is the presence there of value. If that is what characterizes us as being *actively* about things, then the notion of value here may be extended into the domain in which we initially find it natural to describe the form of *our* social life as *inter*actional.

In an evolutionary perspective, value is often presented as if it were there from the start. The notion of 'value' is explained in terms of survival. The term 'survival' itself is normative; evolution is described as a 'fight' for survival, and the processes involved in it are spoken of as 'serving' the interests of life, or of whatever species survive. But the normative component here is supplied by the theorist. Whatever value inheres in the survival of an organism, and by derivation in the means to that end, is tied ontologically to the existence of sensory states.[1] As Sprigge says, '[w]e would not mean anything in calling something good in itself if we did not mean that it possessed some specific quality of the same broad genus to which pleasures and pains . . . belong'.[2] If neural complexity realized itself only in environmentally adaptive behaviour, without the causal influence of consciousness, values would not exist. Nor would interests, or rights. Dennett, interested as he himself is in resurrecting the vocabulary of the human repertoire in a third-person world, denies this. He asks why, if the ability of something so zombie-like as the 'lowly lobster' to take 'self-regarding steps to prolong its own survival' can earn it some modest consideration in the allotment of good and evil, the deserts of the heterophenomenologically proficient zombie should not be even greater: 'Why wouldn't a zombie be a member in good standing of the class of things with *interests*, with desires to be satisfied, projects to complete, harms to be protected against?'[3]

The first response is to reject the implication that the lobster has such interests, even on a modest scale, simply in view of its alleged ability to 'take self-regarding steps'. If the ability to take self-regarding steps is assignable to robots or conceivable consciousless alternatives to *Homo sentiens et sapiens*, then the kind of regard for self that occurs here implies no desideratum, no normative hole to be filled. In a 'soulless' world (to echo Vendler) there is no inherent value in the prolonging of life in the face of environmental threat, for in such a world there is nothing that can count as the *preference* for life over death. Evolution in itself is no more than a selection process and, normatively speaking, whether surviving is better than going under is as arbitrary as whether large objects caught in a sieve are to be preferred to the smaller ones that 'disappear' through it. If we are to talk of the lobster's self-regarding steps in terms of their promoting the lobster's 'interests', and of these as accordingly deserving our respect, then one of two factors must be added: either the lobster looks upon itself as worth keeping (in which case it can claim or be given membership of the kingdom of ends), or it is capable of pain and pleasure (in which case its mental states can count in some hedonic calculus). Both factors presuppose consciousness. Without it, our regard for the lobster – as for the zombie – as a locus of value would have to rely on its having acquired that value by being, say, part of God's creation; but then its value would be one it had even if it lacked an ability to take self-regarding steps.

The second response is to say that, even if the lobster does have sensory powers and they are adaptational, survival-promoting sensory powers don't yet earn it membership in the 'class of things with interests' ('desires to be satisfied, projects to complete, harms to be protected against'). Although someone else may act *in* my interest by promoting my survival and well-being, even where these are not conscious aims of my own, the primary sense of an interest's being 'mine' is that in which having an interest is to have desires, projects, and fears which one is at least attributively aware of having. That being so, the inclusion here of the notion of self-knowledge, which we may feel reasonably justified in not attributing to the lobster, provides a basis for distinguishing between steps (of the organism itself or anything else) that protect an organism's integrity and those taken by the organism with 'regard' to its own protection or betterment. Let us henceforth assume that the latter alone evinces an ability to take self-regarding steps.

In what does that ability consist? Or, to put it in a way that gives room for the question of its evolution, what is it that the lobster lacks? In Chapter VII we noted a distinction between genuinely representational behaviour and behaviour which can be described as representational only because, for descriptive and perhaps predictive purposes, it is convenient, though also to some extent metaphorically appropriate, to do so. What characterized genuinely representational behaviour was the ability of an organism to have in mind situations other than those presentationally available, to have them in mind *as* other than presentationally available, and – at least in those practical situations where the ability must be thought to acquire its adaptational function – to have them in mind as connected in a temporal sequence with what *is* presentationally available. This might, not altogether equivalently perhaps, be described as the ability to take account of what is presentationally available in the light of something that is not there, where – and this seems an essential requirement if the non-presentational component is not to function simply as an extension of the presentation – there is a capacity to envision the present as though the absent factor were not involved.

By this path we arrived at a distinction between its being like something to be an organism, where quale-tative features play a part in a direct interaction with its environment, and its being like something *for the organism itself* to be in some way or other. Given the latter, it becomes possible for the organism to take account of *itself* as being in a certain way in the light of some other version of itself, for instance a better version, where the scale of value may be thought of as provided in the first instance by attachments of pain or pleasure quanta to the respective versions. From the capacity to be in pain and to envision a version of the same 'subject' in a situation giving less pain, one arrives, by no obviously unaccounted-for step, at the capacity to act in ways likely to bring about a replacement of the painful version with the less painful one.

This gives us a picture of the eponymous 'self-regarder' which seems to fit well within the evolutionary framework. We have an organism equipped to move *itself* from less to more propitious circumstances. Given that much, there seems to be no difficulty in also assigning to the organism a capacity to address itself to its own functioning, thereby speeding up the process of evolution by making it unnecessary for better abilities or updated versions of what is or is not propitious to be left to random mutation. All that is involved here is a redirection of focus, from 'looking abroad' to its own advantage to looking 'within' in order to adjust either the means or the ends, or both, in terms of which advantages are sought. Thus the organism can be the editor of its own desires and of its established longer-term goals, as well as its own taskmaster in acquiring greater proficiency in appropriating advantageous states.

But clearly there are other morals for the evolutionist to draw from the ability to take self-regarding steps. The capacity which allows you to think of yourself in a better situation and to take appropriate steps for achieving it is, in itself, also the capacity to think of yourself vicariously, or in imagination, as being in the better situation, and equally to think of yourself vicariously as being in that situation thinking vicariously of yourself in your present situation. But then, of course, you are also able to think away the initial continuity between occupancy of a present situation and occupancy of another situation, and thereby arrive at the conception of the occupant of the imagined or present situation as another self-regarding subject. What we have here, then, is an ability to draw upon knowledge of our own intentional activity in our understanding of the intentional activity of other self-regarders: not just an ability to move from actual to ideal situations but also to grasp others as engaged in similar movements. In arguing the adaptational advantages of this ability, Nicholas Humphrey says that 'reflexive' consciousness, 'by giving each individual a picture of the "psychological structure" which underlies his own behaviour . . . provides him with a framework for interpreting the behaviour of others like himself'.[4] On Humphrey's view, self-consciousness is 'the most peculiar and sophisticated development in the evolution of the human mind'.[5] Its function is 'to hold society together' by enabling those thus equipped to solve the problems of their social way of life. This requires more than cognitive ability; that is, more than the ability to identify things or situations relevant to the current state of play. It must also be possible to plan and innovate against states of play in constant flux, to make rapid rule-of-thumb calculations about others' reactions, and to weigh costs of self-denial in terms of loss of self-advancement against whatever long-term personal benefits may be felt to accrue from preserving the integrity of the group.[6]

What was added to the minds of 'certain social animals' in this 'revolutionary advance', says Humphrey, was 'a new set of heuristic principles . . . devised to cope with the pressing need to model a special section of reality – the reality comprised by the behaviour of other kindred animals'.[7] That sounds as if the added capacity were a continuation of the evolutionary ascent. But it is appropriate to ask (1) whether this revolutionary advance is indeed also an evolutionary advance. That is, can both its origin and survival be attributed to the classical mechanism of chance variation and natural selection? This is not altogether unconnected with another question which immediately comes to mind: (2) can the 'do-it-yourself' introspective psychology from which such analogically based calculations are derived afford insight into the actual workings of the human mind?

Here is the link between those two questions. If the answer to (1) is negative, as I shall argue, then the illusion of a teleological process produced by evolutionary mechanisms can only be preserved either – and implausibly – by the widespread, conscious, and successful application of ideals of rationality or, the best remaining alternative – by social mechanisms which the sustained appearance of organic growth indicates are intuited in the main correctly by successful social actors – thus answering (2) affirmatively. Another possibility, the plausibility of which it has been the general drift of this book to undermine, is that the actual workings of the human mind will in the end be unravelled from the third-personal stance of physical science, whether in a fully developed neuroscience or by a successful modelling of human performance in abstract functional terms. However, although there are strong reasons for taking this not to be a genuine possibility, this alternative is interesting because it is based on a kind of thinking which seems very unlikely to be explainable on evolutionary principles. Of which more in a moment.

Let us look at our first question. Can reflexive consciousness in an organism be understood as the acquisition of a new set of heuristic principles 'devised' by evolutionary mechanisms to cope with the pressing need to model 'other minds'? The existence of social animals is linked in evolutionary theory with the phenomenon of neoteny, or what amounts to the premature birth of animals capable of properly social existence. It is hypothesized, on some evidence, that pre-hominid men had brains much larger and better developed than ours at birth, with the result that a vast proportion of childbirths ended fatally both for mother and for offspring.[8] However, premature birth, initially an impending catastrophe for the species, created a situation in which, spared the need to protect themselves, offspring were provided with a period in which, in the first instance by imitation, to assimilate state-of-the-art survival expertise from devoted adepts. Thus was imminent disaster turned by nature's inexhaustible inventiveness into an additional means of reproductive success.

But is that not too superficial a proposal? What neoteny brought about was the need for a family-based way of life, and also for the social apparatus required to protect that way of life (for the devising of which that way of life no doubt created exceptionally favourable conditions). True, it improved the reproductive potential of the species threatened in the way mentioned, but some other solution – a solution other than that which gave rise to *Homo sapiens* – might well have guaranteed the hominid strain a more stable future. The problem with random mutation is that worse solutions can upstage better ones which then lose their turn. In any case, the immediate significance of the hypothesis is not that neoteny improved the reproductive success of a threatened species but that it created a totally new set of survival problems. And it is here that Humphrey's account begins. Psychological skills based initially on reflexive self-knowledge allow animals forced to live social lives to solve the special problems which that life entails. Such skills are a 'biologically adaptive trait', and in the course of evolution 'the best psychologists have proved to be the best survivors'.[9]

What that amounts to saying is that reflexive consciousness enables the individual to survive in a community of 'psychologists'. Given that there are others who also have 'the power and inclination to use a privileged picture of [their own selves] as a model of what it is like to be another person',[10] an organism will need its skills in this domain to avoid being exploited, and thus a competition of psychological excellence is set in motion. One consequence, which we shall return to, is that the 'folk psychology' of any place or period will represent the current state of a finely polished art whose best exponents will occupy conspicuous *social* positions. But that the further consequence should be the existence of a well-ordered society, and that the polished art should include the art of such ordering, is not something one can similarly explain by straightforward appeal to evolution.

Nor, we should note, does Humphrey attempt to account for the evolutionary origin of reflexive consciousness itself. It is merely assumed that somehow, in the space provided by neoteny, a capacity for reflection upon the inner life begins to be exercised.[11] Presumably the organism can now 'take five' from its incessant 'looking abroad' and turn its gaze inwards. But then the capacity is simply taken for granted as something lying dormant in the species until the accident of premature birth provides the opportunity for its exercise. The case is similar to that where attempted functionalist theories of human consciousness just assume some primitive form of consciousness and then postulate that at some stage in evolution it acquires functions mirroring those of controlled activity and long-range intentional control.[12]

But, granted there might have been another solution for the survival of the hominid strain, just consider the solution we are. If, as Humphrey claims, 'the chief role of creative intellect is to hold society together',[13] that could only be understood in evolutionary terms if we could think (i) of reflexive consciousness as 'devised' solely to generate useful insight into the workings of human psychology, and (ii) of the organism as a device for converting that knowledge automatically into social behaviour. But reflexive consciousness has other strings to its bow, among them capacities the exercise of which can lead to inhibitions and distortions of such knowledge, though also more constructively to criticism of it. At least that is how it seems from our self-conscious point of view. As O'Hear points out, the fact that the idea of self-consciousness is itself that of being conscious of having an experience implies 'a notion of *experience* . . . which in turn implies a contrast between how things are experienced by me and how they *are*'.[14] Thus, if a reflexively conscious social agent can be said to be one for whom there is 'something that it is like to be' that social agent, then in this case that something must include being 'something that it is like to *know*' (in an as yet epistemologically innocent sense of that word) what it is like to be that thing. One result of the neotenous interlude between congenitally premature birth and social adulthood is the ability to raise the question of whether what it takes itself to know in this respect is truly knowledge. For reflexive knowledge includes, or brings with it, the capacity for disinterested inquiry.[15] And assuming, as we all do from this vantage-point, that the results of such inquiry can be applied to our social as well as to our scientific practices, in the form of ideals or goals about how we think things should be instead of how we think they are, it seems to follow that our social behaviour cannot be an automatic response to creative intellect. If society holds together, and if it is our creative intellect that holds it together, that is because the intellect creates goals which social agents have set themselves and each other and which they have in some measure attained.

Granted that, by and large, society is indeed held together, and that what holds it together is not just knowledge but knowledge which people apply, the question is, How do they apply it? The intellectualist answer (implied by Humphrey's terminology), which is surely false, is that it is applied consciously and strategically with social cohesion written into the intentions of social actors. That will seem plausible only to someone with very few psychological skills and fortunate still to be among the survivors. Institutions form perhaps the most significant source of social cohesion. But institutions are products and to that extent expressions of more basic facts that go into their production. Among these more basic facts we need to look for the sources of communicative interaction.

There seem to be two main such sources: sheer interactional expertise, getting along in interactional contexts, and the power of natural sympathies. Take the first. According to Humphrey, the 'picture' of the psychological structure that social animals glean from their own case and apply to the behaviour of 'kindred animals' isn't a coherent theory of any kind, but a 'plain man's guide' put together pragmatically with no philosophical scruples and in disregard of scientific respectability.[16] As Humphrey presents it, this is the familiar 'folk-psychological' picture of a 'conscious spirit which wills, feels, wants etc.'[17] The picture is to be thought of fundamentally only as a tool, a method for interpreting the behaviour of kindred animals; and if philosophical scruple and criteria of scientific respectability are given due weight, as a representation of reality the picture quickly acquires the status of myth. Yet, according to Humphrey, 'natural selection has ensured that the description which reflexive consciousness gives of inner experience is anything but a meaningless fantasy'.[18] There is obviously something to that. If the picture has worked that well, surely it must be because the subjects in interaction have the structure the picture represents them as having? But there are other possibilities: for instance, the success may be due to the picture's being shared, rather than to its being true. The structure may be basically empty, and successful social interaction dependent only on the frame's containing a shared 'myth' as a common reference for mutual interpretation. Moreover, since we are self-conscious creatures, are we able to take it without further ado that what works is true? Isn't it just that distinction which being the self-conscious solution to the problems of hominid survival allows us to make? And should we not therefore put the plain man's picture in parentheses and look for the truth about human structure elsewhere, for instance in functional models or brain science?

On the other hand, being that solution to the problem of hominid survival may also incline us to construct scruples and requirements which make us miss the point. We may be too ready to reject the plain man's picture just because the ideal picture we are able to create of an objective, one-dimensional truth has no place for the kinds of things the picture contains. That at least is what the third-person vantage-point of physical science leads us to conclude. But if the first-person vantage-point is first allowed, and agency of a first-personal nature is added, the picture of a unitary 'I' acting in the light of its moods, desires, beliefs, and perceptions does acquire credibility. But suppose we therefore concede Humphrey's claim for the partial truth of the folk-psychological picture. In granting the picture a certain degree of veridicality it is easy to focus on the catalogue description of it at the expense of its working content; that is, on the traditional terms of (rational) psychology and not on the skills that go into everyday coping, awareness, wariness, readiness to respond to contextually determined ranges of new opportunities or interruptions. The psychological skills we find ourselves equipped with do not sort into neat categories; and the intelligence they manifest is of a kind quite other than that of those who make it their business to describe them. If, as Humphrey maintains, man's intellect is 'suited primarily to thinking about people and their institutions', it is not in the way of the political or social philosopher. The scientific study of social interaction no doubt compares quite badly with the 'knowledge' implicit in the psychological skills of even the least articulate human beings. And the moral to be drawn from the fact that, as Humphrey himself says, much of the best literature on the subject so far available 'is in fact genuinely "literature"',[19] is that what the social actor knows best is not how to assign bookish concepts from the official folk-psychological taxonomy, such as 'thought', 'belief', 'desire', 'fear', etc., or how to deploy the ideal types of game theory, but how to apply infinitely variable patterns of action and reaction to the behaviour of other social actors. However, even if the knowledge of 'psychological structure' which a social animal has to rely on is not in any literal sense in the form of a simple or coherent 'picture', it is still first-personal, and the superior social interactor is the one who is better able to deploy psychological insights derived from his or her own case in given social situations. And even if, compared with the creative articulations of Aesop, Dryden, Dickens, and Proust, the official taxonomy belongs to the world of the comic strip, there seems every reason to suppose that it articulates a framework of standing assumptions on which the intricate details of social interaction depend, and to grant it the role Humphrey claims for it in the life of social animals.

Without self-consciousness, then, there would be no communicative interaction and the foundations of social life would collapse. But there is another aspect of social life which, though perhaps not foundational in the same way, is also linked to the ability to know what it is to be a psychological being, namely sympathy. There are clear, if at first only associational, links between sympathy and morality, and this gives us the opportunity to raise, in conclusion, the question of the place of consciousness in moral thought.

Let us note first of all that sympathy is made possible by the very same facts that explain social interaction. Being able to apply your knowledge of what it is like to be yourself in order to predict, and respond in turn to, the responses of other 'kindred animals' also exposes you to the possibility of being 'affected' by what, on the basis of your own experience, you suppose it is like to be them. And the same reflective capacity which allows you to think of yourself as the same self in a better situation, also allows you to think of others in situations calling for the same remedial steps as you would try to take in your own case. That is, the ability to have 'this is what it is like to be worse off' in respect of 'that is what it would be like to be better off' can be exercised in respect of others and the goal of *their* being better off.[20]

There are two ways of understanding sympathy: one from the evolutionist's point of view and the other from what we might call the moralist's point of view. According to the first, sympathy is a natural development of social life and can take the form, say, of turn-taking and the acceptance of certain limits on allowable actions. Humphrey himself instances these as marks of sympathy, which he describes as a 'tendency on the part of one social partner to identify himself with the other and so to make the other's goals to some extent his own'.[21] But that overdescribes the examples. Seen in a certain light, taking turns at some task which requires constant attention, refraining from singing while the other rests, and so on, are simply co-operative forms of the pursuit of coincident self-interest. They are cases in which concerted action is needed to achieve some goal which the agents share only distributively, i.e. in a merely statistical sense. That is clearly a very important aspect of social cohesion, and perhaps it is all the glue that is needed. But the idea or ideal of genuine sympathy involves the actual appropriation of another's goal as an end in itself. Perhaps something like approximating to that does often occur in co-operative enterprises, but the two are inherently different. The one is self-regarding, the other is other-regarding.

There is a certain ambiguity in the term 'other-regarding'. To have regard for others may be no more than a conventional form of deference. As one learns through experience to avoid bumping into obstacles, so one learns to be careful not to injure others' feelings or treat them with undue disrespect. But in a moral sense to have regard for others is to have regard for their 'selves' in some much stronger sense. One way in which this may be understood, in terms which fit well with the current discussion, is epistemological. One person can have regard for another by having – though necessarily only vicariously – a perception of the reality which is the other person. If the 'heuristic principles' allegedly acquired by the organism in its achieving reflexive consciousness allow it to interpret that 'special section of reality . . . comprised by the behaviour of other kindred animals' and thus permit interaction with that section of reality, they also allow the organism to conceive of, or imagine, individual subsections of that reality, to dwell on what it is like to be those subsections. Sympathy is then a response to that 'regard *of*' the other in the form of regard in the more normal sense *for* the other, the concern being now spontaneous and not a matter of mere convention or deference. And, as in the case of effective social interaction, one's 'skills' in this respect will depend on the extent of one's own knowledge of 'what it is like' to be in circumstances calling for concern.[22]

Is sympathy 'natural', and the response genuinely 'spontaneous'? In the hypothesized case, yes. But there are grounds for supposing actions of an 'other-regarding' or selfless nature to be based more often on inherited or self-chosen norms, or on deviously concealed forms of self-regard and even misconceived attempts to *find* an identity in that of others. Furthermore, in modern societies concern is largely institutionalized. Some people regard morality itself as an institution; that is, as a means of social cohesion operating through historically variable norms, such as those that cultivate loyalty or those that cultivate a sense of individual responsibility. But the word 'moral' is itself normative, and I suggest that we see *its* functional role more clearly if we connect it with the question of the naturalness of sympathy.

There is such a thing as natural concern or sympathy. The simplest way to conceive of it is in terms of suffering, in some suitably wide sense. Concern is then a response to the recognition of suffering in others. But, given the extent of that special section of reality comprised by the behaviour of other kindred animals, it is a very local response. Here too there is an evolutionist's and a moralist's way of looking at the matter. From a naturalistic, evolutionary point of view, local concern is the product of the neotenous interlude, with its introduction of the need for parental protection and upbringing. Seen in this light, concern for the 'near and dear' is a naturally local relationship, though through processes of identification it can extend beyond the original limits to include (e.g. in time of war) compatriots. But from a moralist's point of view any such extension is still unsatisfactorily partial. That is because the moralist analyses the original situation in a special way, a way typical of the universalist standards that self-conscious beings are able to set themselves. What the moralist sees, and sees correctly, in the original situation of natural concern is the recognition of a small part of the other-personal aspect of that special section of reality comprised by the behaviour of kindred animals. 'Other-personal' may put it too strongly for the initial mother–infant relation, but even there it can be allowed that there is a recognition of the existence of a shared personal reality. Already, then, we have the form of a relationship which can be conceived in separation from the 'accidents' of its natural instantiations. The form can then be applied universally and confinements of it to specific natural relationships and their extensions judged to be instances of partiality and preference.

Morality is an 'ideal' in a standard normative sense of that word. It specifies some form of goal. In this, however, it is really no different from science. But while scientific objectivity can seem a natural requirement, the ideal of morality appears to offer no foothold on our sense of reality. The reason is clear enough. Usually we think of scientific results as measuring up to a palpable reality which exists outside us. The furniture is already there, so to speak, and we can test our science by seeing whether the map it gives us enables us to get around without bumping into things. Morality, by contrast, seems to pronounce its ideals in a vacuum; there are no facts of the matter to test and therefore it issues its commands in a void. Indeed, ethical language has been pronounced basically fictitious on the grounds that it irrationally assumes the existence of objective values.[23] However, this way of contrasting science and morality misses points they significantly share. In the first place, scientific investigation is an attempted fulfilment of the injunction to find truth by separating truth from error; and, as Feyerabend and others have convincingly argued, the notion assumed by this distinction of there being a settled state of the furniture of nature is an ideological assumption and corresponds to no *scientifically* determinable fact of the matter.[24] Second, the moralist's approval of concern beyond the call of nature, if one may so put it, is based on appreciation of the fact that there really is a world of 'kindred animals', a world comprised not just by their behaviour but by their 'being what it is like to be them'.

Ordinary experience is 'sensitive' to a vast range of aspects of life. Central, one may suppose, is sensitivity to bodily trauma in the form of pain. If moral prescriptions differ from ordinary, 'natural' sensitivity to aspects of the world we live in, it seems plausible to maintain that it is by being expressions of a higher-order sensitivity based on scruples possible only for beings capable of disinterested inquiry. Disinterested inquiry is not inquiry without sensitivity, but inquiry with an appreciation of the selectivity of individual points of view. Disinterested inquiry is itself sensitive to the partiality of a 'science' which accepts as true only what it finds useful or convenient to believe. And in the case of moral prescription, it is sensitive to the partiality of a 'concern for others' which disregards others (including future others) in general. Where science prescribes: Seek what is true independently of what you find it useful or convenient to believe, morality prescribes: Show concern also to those with whom it is not natural to do so. The prescription is cognitivist: it takes account of what is only partially, because only partly, accounted for in *natural* sentiment, namely concern for those in the immediate circle. Morality is concern for, and concern with concern for, the whole of that part of reality comprising the behaviour of kindred animals, beyond the small sub-part in which one's natural feelings of attachment ('sympathies') lie, however much these may temper one's 'selfishness as a social animal' by making one identify *naturally* with the other 'so as to make the other's goals to some extent [your] own'.

We asked what role or roles consciousness plays in the lives that those endowed with it find themselves living. We have identified foundational roles for 'reflexive' consciousness in two spheres, social interaction and morality. There are two final points to clarify: (1) what one might also have said about morality; (2) what physicalist science is able to say on these points.

First, then, it has to be admitted that moral thinking need not be analysed in the way outlined. That way is, indeed, itself a prescription about how 'best', 'most appropriately', 'with least commitment to non-naturalistic assumption', etc., to apply the normative word 'morality'. But the standard (not uncontroversially distinguished) deontological and teleological alternatives apply principles which remove the moral agent from the relationship of immediate concern which our question about the relation of consciousness to morality has led us to focus upon. To put it crudely, the deontologist requires that you remove yourself from the push-and-pull of inclination and treat every morally relevant situation as one in which your regard is not for any particular other but for an ideal of impartial considerateness; while the consequentialist asks you to justify your concern as a sort of payment into a communal bank account, making your regard for the other's welfare conditional on your inability at the moment to pay more by directing your regard elsewhere. Both approaches adopt a rule which intervenes between the moral agent and the moral subject and has the effect of desensitizing the ordinary experience on which 'other-regarding' actions are based.[25] They make disinterest a feature of the relation, instead of a rule that enjoins the proliferation of that relation. On the view outlined, our primary obligations are, on the contrary, not to principles but to particular persons whose needs we are in the best position to understand and satisfy. Morality can be in this sense inherently situational, as I have argued elsewhere.[26] Of course, it is possible to formulate principles, rules, or goals common to all or most types of moral intention: principles specifying certain kinds of suffering, for instance, which one is *generally* but not always bound to seek to alleviate, and principles specifying the spirit in which one seeks to alleviate them, e.g. unselfishly, honestly, in a sense of fellowship, mutual trust, co-operation, and so on. But it is unclear what purpose formulating the principles will serve. The former are too abstract to specify the moral course in the particular event, and the latter are mainly ways of describing an initially moral frame of mind. They might be used to point out to people who don't have that frame of mind what it would mean ('be like') to have it; or to remind those who profess to have it what the requirements are when they seem to be slipping. They might even stand as basic moral commands. But they should not be written into moral handbooks, for then the situational aspect which is primary will either be ignored or, if not ignored, give rise to spurious conflicts between the general rule (e.g. Do not kill) and the moral requirements (Kill in this case in order to alleviate intolerable suffering). In fact the only rule required for a situational morality based on our regard for others is: Keep looking.

Finally, what are the consequences of all this for a physicalist view of things? A ready answer would be that the physicalist universe cannot encompass values, just because values belong to the phenomenological domain. But physicalists deny this; they treat that domain as a product of subphenomenological processing which, when top-down identities have been established, gives us the facts of normative behaviour. Sheridan has argued that at least in the case of the moral subject, that is, something deserving moral consideration, the behaviour is not recoverable at the subphenomenological level.

According to Sheridan, however, moral agency is compatible with physicalism. A robot can think, and freedom in an indeterminist sense is not needed – that is, we have compatibilism as a genuine, freedom-allowing alternative. But physicalism cannot account for anything's being a moral 'subject', that is, a being with moral rights. Sheridan concludes that the concept of a moral agent must be evaluative, or prescriptive, while the question of whether something or someone is a moral subject is a question of fact.[27] According to our own account both concepts are natural and prescriptive, and in the same way.

Consider first his argument for saying that the concept of a moral subject is descriptive. To qualify for moral consideration, something has to be capable of happiness and unhappiness. Take the familiar example of pain. 'Pain is not really pain if it is not like anything to feel it', and without the phenomenological capacity to suffer, one could not be a moral subject,[28] that is 'a single logical subject to whom suffering and other effects of actions can be assigned'.[29] But physicalist analyses cannot capture 'the idea of a (phenomenologically) suffering subject'.[30] Yet the claim that there is something it is like to suffer pain is a factual claim (and verifiable at least in one's own case). I at least am a moral subject. But whether I am a moral agent is another matter. Indeed the world might be such that there were only moral subjects, moral deservers, but with no moral agents; that is to say, no one in a position to give moral subjects their due in the way required of properly moral action. Moral agency requires 'a capacity to reason or think', and 'a capacity for free (or voluntary) actions for which one is accountable'. Sheridan grants that '[u]nlike sentience (in the phenomenological sense) the sapient features of mentality seem receptive to computer-simulation and programming', this in spite of the fact that whatever thinking computers are capable of is not, as Frege noted that ours is, 'saturated with feeling'.[31] Since 'it may not be like anything to be a thing that thinks', it is not entirely implausible that we are 'physical realizations' of blindly co-operating sub-personal agencies.[32] Second, as for accountability, 'soft determinism is a viable and defensible compromise with mechanism', and even if non-libertarian freedom is rejected we might still make some sense of a minimal form of moral reasoning bound by cast-iron mechanistic principles.[33]

Against this we could say that if an additional condition of moral agency is the agent's ability to apply his or her own experience of suffering analogically to others in recognizable causal situations, then the moral agent is expelled from the physicalist universe for the very same reasons that the moral subject is expelled. The agent must also be or have been a phenomenological sufferer. But other points can be made too. What is it to be a *moral* subject? In Sheridan's account all that is needed is (let us call it) a phenomenological capacity; according to this even a lobster qualifies. But in the world of human experience, where morality can be said to be an aspect of that experience, being a moral subject might be something particular that it is like to experience moral relationships. In other words, there may be grounds for saying that there is, for us, something it is like to be a moral subject. In that case, and because these are a special type of interactional relationship, it might be thought that what it is like to be a moral subject includes what it is like to be owed an accountably given moral service. In that case to be a moral subject would presuppose the belief that moral agents can indeed, perhaps that they do, exist – perhaps even that one knows a few. Further, although thinking may be a broad enough concept for a computer, for which we can still safely assume there is nothing it is like to think, to be some genuine kind of thinker, it doesn't follow that what goes on in human thinking can be something too sub-personal for there to be anything it is like to think. Or rather, if it is true that there is nothing in particular that it is like for human beings to think, the more likely explanation is that the concept is broad enough to cover such a wide range of conscious performance that no particular phenomenological speci-fication will cover all cases. Thinking is so many things, saturated not only with feeling but also with value. It might even be the case that human thinking without a moral component is *un*thinkable. So we should be sceptical, I believe, of the claim that there can still be some point in (merely mechanical) 'moral' reasoning without the moral agent.[34]

As for Sheridan's proposal that the Kantian conception of 'person' as a prescriptive notion be reserved for moral agency,[35] I think that is false. Although what we can describe in nature includes the realities of kindred animals and it is certainly true, therefore, to say that their happinesses and unhappinesses are matters of natural fact, these facts are not moral until they are conceived in the light of an ideal of impartial other-regarding as facts to be taken into practical consideration. Such ideals, as I suggested earlier, are possible only for self-conscious beings capable of distinguishing themselves from other things and by projection also other selves; more particularly, capable of envisaging an 'objective' reality that is not just for them but also for those others. In this sense moral agency and moral considerability are both prescriptive notions. But, as in science, the prescription boils down in essentials to the injunction to take account of what is there.

CHAPTER IX

Agenda

So there are clear grounds for rejecting current dismissals, explicit or by neglect, of the importance of the concept of consciousness. Self-conscious action and thought play vital roles in the kind of life characteristic of humans. Indeed they are constitutive of such life. Consciousness and the first-person point of view are concepts crucial for grasping human performance; but also ineliminable ingredients in any analysis of cognition itself, of what it is for an intelligent being to be situated in a world over which it exercises some species-appropriate degree of mastery. In both respects the previous chapters may be seen as an extended comment on Rorty's (admittedly programmatic) proposal to the effect that 'consciousness' be treated merely as a word for referring to some pragmatically chosen space–time region (e.g. brain–behaviour relations), and that there is no reason why we shouldn't redraw the boundaries in ways that let the first-person view of consciousness drop out altogether.

Rorty's remarks are prompted by the perplexity and frustration felt by many at the apparent impossibility of putting what he calls the 'inside' character of consciousness into what our opening motto called 'satisfactory scientific terms'.[1] The problem is that the terms into which it would have to be put, on any current view of what counts as scientific, have an exclusively 'outside' character. If the concept of consciousness is to survive it will have to be emptied of anything in the 'inside' metaphor that cannot be given a literal translation in words belonging to a scientific vocabulary. Part of this programme involves trivializing, and perhaps in the end even abandoning, the notion of a first-person perspective as anything of more than formal significance, if that. The burden of our argument has been to bring the first-person point of view firmly to the fore and to suggest that the fundamental role traditionally assigned to it is deserved, though by

171

no means yet properly understood, and that in the conversation of mankind the puzzles it presents for science should certainly be kept on the agenda.

A significant and insidious feature of discussions which aim to make consciousness less of a problem for physicalism is the tendency to give anything that might count as irreducibly 'inner' a preliminary kick upstairs into the realm of 'metaphysics'. The move is made easier by linking the first-person viewpoint to Descartes and substance-dualism. As the unlocatable 'epistemological subject' it drops out of consideration in favour of readily accessible regions of space–time, and we are then prepared for such (now less surprising) discoveries as that if particles don't have 'insides' (particles of course lack internal structure) then persons don't either.[2] From the first-person point of view, however, what from a third-person vantage-point seems to have to be 'inner' in relation to what that vantage-point makes available can be as empirical as you could wish, and there are several ways in which one may talk of an 'inner' aspect without inviting the charge that the notion is just a 'refuge for our metaphysical hopes'.[3] It is of course relevant to remark that in the traditional sense of the term physicalism itself is a paradigmatic 'metaphysical' view, to the effect that all events can be given full explanations of the kind para-digmatically provided by physics.[4]

Paradoxically, it is physicalist metaphysics, with its commitment to looking exclusively 'abroad', that leaves empty rooms asking to be haunted by the dualist's ghosts. It seems fair to say that, in general, the third-person perspective, made absolute, generates at least as much mystery as it dissolves. This may be seen from Rorty's comments on his own test case, his 'living' physicalists, the Anti-podeans, who manage to act and talk much like us Descartes-programmed Terrans but with no conception of what they do or say being a matter of being in or having mental states. Their conceptual apparatus is that of neurology. And

> the success of Antipodean neurology, not only in the explana-tion and control of behavior but in supplying the vocabulary for the Antipodean self-image, shows that none of the other Terran theories about 'the relation between mind and body' can even get a look-in. For parallelism and epiphenomenalism can only be differentiated on some non-Humean view of causation – some view according to which there is a causal mechanism to be discovered which will show which way causal lines run. But

nobody, not even the most diehard Cartesian, imagines that when a molecule-by-molecule account of the neurons is before us (as, *ex hypothesi*, it is before the Antipodeans) there will still be a place to look for further causal mechanisms. (What would 'looking' amount to?)[5]

For Rorty, that parenthetical question is evidently rhetorical: 'looking' could only be searching for gremlins or ghosts working away in the interstices of molecular space. But it is a better one than he intends and it can be given a defensible answer. For consider. Literally to follow some neural event molecule by molecule, one's (microscopically amplified) eyes would have to be fixed in a frame whose own molar movements were not given as part of the molecular vista but which would certainly have to be included in an explanation of what was going on. To revert to our earlier analogy, the molecules in the rim of a rolling wheel might be filmed by a camera attached to a microscope on the rim itself, but the camera would only be able to capture the movement of the wheel as a whole by also picking up additional, non-microscopic information about the passing landscape, information which would then provide a basis for locating the relevant laws of the wheel's motion. Of course, the wheel analogy is defective. The molecules at the rim only sustain the wheel's structure, whether the wheel is rolling or not, as the molecules in my knee-joints sustain my body when I walk or just stand; they do not contribute to an explanation of the fact that the wheel is rolling. But the general point is the same. To explain my movements the molecular processes in my brain must actually *exhibit* the relevant higher-order principles, and it is only when we are able to identify these – only when we can look in *this* way – that we can tell what the molecular events actually are. Otherwise we will have no idea of what to look for in the brain, and our molecular narratives will be pointless ramblings.

It was argued in Chapter VII that the higher-order principles can include intentional concepts at the conscious level. If that is the case, then adoption of an exclusively third-person perspective commits one to a denial of the information needed to grasp what one observes from that perspective – unless, of course, the interpreter exploits his own knowledge of those principles in explaining observed human behaviour, but in that case it would be misleading to say that the third-person perspective was adopted exclusively, since here it presupposes the first-hand knowledge the interpreter has of his own higher-order performance. Note also that, if the argument is accepted, non-Humean causation seems not such a bad idea after all: if the relevant factors and principles are directly experienced, the agent *qua* conscious being knows itself as an important part of an actual mechanism and should even have some fairly good idea of the direction in which the causal lines are running. In suitable circumstances the first-person point of view will, on this account, be where the action is, and when it isn't the subject will be aware of that fact as often as not. If, then, the first-person point of view can itself supply the higher-order principles according to which molecular activity is to be grasped, there is no temptation to look for gremlins working away in the cracks.

That mental processes have a hierarchical structure seems to be a point on which most parties are agreed. So-called Structural Functionalists, however, see higher-level processes as products of lower-level processes. 'Top'-level performance is conceived, explicitly in Lycan's recent exemplary version, on the lines of an organization or institution, where the overall operation is the result of a complex interaction of distinct but mutually blind departments.[6] The most satisfactory account of overall intelligence is one that is given at a level of operation of minimal intelligence and rationality, and in general mental states are to be (type)-identified with processes at a suborganizational level where all that is left of the traditional notion of consciousness is some idea of the mechanical 'scanning' of one level by a next-higher level. Even a state near the top of the hierarchy, such as believing that something is the case or aiming to make it the case, need not be conscious if it is conceivable that Tinfoil Man can exemplify all the appropriate causal relations.[7] Naturally, that there is a quality of experience is a fact no functionalist can plausibly deny, but it is an article of functionalist faith that the qualitative, sentient aspect plays no essential part where it counts, namely at the explanatory levels of least intelligence and rationality. And if actual human consciousness does play any role, then it is one for which some functional equivalent can be found in the case of Tinfoil Man, a scanning role for instance, where sensitivity to the qualitative aspect of things in the environment, or in the psychological processes themselves, substitutes in the brain-based organism for some mechanical, non-sentient alternative. Most important for the functionalist, however, the actual top levels, the levels of sapience as opposed to sentience, are not themselves *conscious* scanning operations, nor operations dependent on *being* scanned by some shadow operation at the same (or would it have to be some even higher?) level. Overall control is based democratically in the grassroots of unwittingly cooperative idiocy.

The problem for functionalism is to justify these claims without overtaxing the credulity of the lay experiencer. What has to be shown is that the qualitative aspects play *no* essential part, that is to say, no part that cannot be played by some suitably sophisticated machinery. It goes without saying, though the examples in the genre nevertheless suggest it needs increasingly to be said, that the lay experiencer is not to be duped in this regard by a tendency to focus on words, the words with which conscious events and states (e.g. words such as 'event' and 'state') are described, rather than on lived experience itself and the practices that go into its being lived, a tendency which is reinforced by a special feature – it might be called the current mythology – of functionalist theories, namely the assumption that mentality, in a sense significant for grasping the nature of the human mind, is already established prior to consciousness. According to this myth not only may organizations, whether biological or mechanical, display mentality even if they are not conscious, but also organisms such as ourselves which *are* conscious are mental independently of that fact. The problem of consciousness is then that of identifying the 'level' at which mental processes 'become' conscious, and of explaining the peculiar origin and role or roles of that characteristic. Jackendoff has labelled this the 'mind–mind' problem, the problem of the relation between the computational mind and the phenomenological mind, though that way of putting it suggests misleadingly that two independent mental structures are involved, whereas the question as posed is rather how to explain the phenomenological aspect as an accessory to a mind already constituted in all essentials.[8] Jackendoff's own proposal is that consciousness encompasses a middle range of mental processes, between on the one hand those, say, that produce the *grammatical* structure of the sentences expressing our thoughts, and on the other those comprising the *conceptual* structures in which our thoughts move. The proposal is based on the assumption that the processes which occur 'outside' consciousness can significantly be called 'mental', as well as on what is evidently a traditionally introspective account on how to establish what goes on 'inside' consciousness. Thus in the case of linguistic awareness we are aware of certain 'units of phonological structure' (the speech stream is experienced as segmented at least into words, and phonological units are responsible for 'the rhythm, stress pattern, and intonation of inner speech') but, on the one hand, not of units of syntax ('nouns, verbs, prepositional phrases, and so on') nor, on the other, of conceptual structure (which is 'by definition language neutral' and so beyond the reach of the natural language of our actual inner speech).[9]

Two closely related questions emerge from this as main items on the agenda on mind: What is to count as mentality? and, What is to count as the content of consciousness? Let us take these in turn.

In addition to general agreement on the hierarchical structure of mental processing, it is also fairly widely accepted that what makes a state, event, or process mental is its being in some (though never very clearly defined) sense 'representational'. Within the computational theory, where the notion is introduced on the basis of the ability of computers to process symbols mechanically, and thus of course also unconsciously, the term 'representation' is clearly metaphorical. In any literal sense representations are, in at least some aspect, intrinsically intentional: for some conscious subject they refer to something other than themselves. Against those who hold that a metaphorical sense of the term suffices for mentality, the principal claim of this book has been that only intentional concepts within the domain of conscious performance properly count as mental. The mind is best grasped as the domain of *conscious* states, events, and processes. If the claim were generally accepted, then of course the mind–mind problem by any name would vanish, since if the claim is true then the mind simply *is* the phenomenological mind.

Still, anyone who holds this must admit that there are states we feel impelled to call mental that are not conscious. The obvious example is attribution of beliefs: I can be truly said to believe that Oslo was once called Christiania without consciously entertaining the belief at the time when someone truly affirms it of me. Another example is the postulation of causal processes underlying actual entertainings or avowals of, say, our beliefs. One may feel that unless conscious representation has its physical counterpart the mental (as what has representational structure) will have to be conceived in Cartesian terms as in some way totally distinct from the physical, and concede therefore that, to that extent, the architecture of the underlying physiology (be it brain or whatever) will have to be representational.

So there are unconscious representational (mental) states after all? Well, yes, but here one may wish to distinguish, as Searle does, between two kinds of unconscious processes: those, on the one hand, that function in the *production* of mental states and which as such do not count as representational, and those, on the other, which can in principle be *brought to* consciousness, such as the belief just mentioned, and which can then qualify as representational. Since the notion of representation, and in these terms of mentality too, applies only in the latter case, it will be possible to say with Searle that any notion of unconscious *mental* processes must be parasitic on that of a conscious state.[10] If one wanted to go further and expunge all vestiges of unconsciousness from the mind's representational function (or of the mental from what is not conscious), one could insist that presently holding, but not consciously entertaining, a belief requires no more than certain physiological states of a kind capable of *producing* representational occasions (entertainings, avowings, etc.), but are not themselves representational. In that case Searle's two kinds of unconscious state collapse into the second kind. And it is of course an implication of an account like Searle's, which treats the physiological states underlying occurrent entertainments of belief, etc. as causing the intentional structures they exemplify, that the physiology itself cannot then be regarded as itself mirroring the intentional structure of states like belief, etc. Otherwise there would be an infinite regress in which the intentionality mirrored in the physiology had to be produced by a further physiological state mirroring *its* intentionality, and so on.

But doesn't pressing the case for the phenomenological mind in this way sound suspiciously Cartesian? This impression may be modified by drawing attention to how strangely affected the nature and plausibility of a concept of an exclusively phenomenological mind seems to be by whether a third-person or a first-person point of view is adopted. From a third-person point of view we see brain, body, and behaviour as comprehensively physical magnitudes – something of which one could in principle give an equally comprehensive molecule-by-molecule account – and then whatever this phenomenological mind is becomes some elusive extra hovering over the physical performance laid out before us, in space, with all its component processes and particles. From a first-person perspective, however, we *are* in some quite concrete sense the mind, which now embraces our own actual bodily performance in all its phenomenal range. And if we allow the perspective to extend beyond artificially confined moments of inactive sentience, such as lying back looking at the ceiling, and to take in the activity of lived experience in all its corporeal range, then the mind as representational (or whatever other word better covers the structure of what is generally referred to as the intentionality of human behaviour) is not an elusive extra at all but bound up in the bodily activity itself, and with everything else that can count as that activity's being engaged in consciously (in the wide sense advocated earlier). As for whatever unconscious processes 'produce' (or whatever other word better covers the nature of the causal dependences) this infinitely complex and variegated phenomenological domain, there is a sense in which they do mirror its representational structure, since because the principles involved are higher-order principles, they affect the total physical operation, including the relative motion and rest of every constituent molecule.

We know that Searle himself resists this view. Although he regards consciousness as a 'causally emergent feature of the behavior of neurons', in the sense that it cannot 'be deduced or calculated from the sheer physical structure of the neurons without some additional account of the causal relations between them', he denies that consciousness can itself 'cause things which couldn't be explained by the causal behavior of the neurons'.[11] So although Searle regards descriptions of mental states as higher-order descriptions of the brain itself, and thereby accepts some hierarchical account, his physicalism nevertheless leads him, like the functionalists, to regard intentional thought or experience as exclusively a product of the lower, micro-levels. Our own argument, outlined in Chapter VII, was that macro-phenomena bring with them their own levels of explanation.

If a vindication of that claim requires that the phenomenological mind be given more weight than current theories accord it, the same can be said of the second of the two issues we noted above. Closer attention to the phenomenology of our 'reflexively' conscious engagement in the world can release us from a narrow Cartesian account of consciousness and open the way to a more generous conception of the *content* of consciousness than the criterion of introspectibility provides. It may, of course, also turn out that the phenomenological case for this more generous conception undermines the thesis that consciousness and representation are correlative notions, since the descriptive resources of the latter term may themselves in the end prove too narrow, or too tendentious.[12] But if representation were indeed a flexible enough notion, both it and the notion of the content of consciousness could be extended to refer to the conceptual structures in terms of which a conscious agent's environment is articulated, and by means of which the human organism enjoys what, in contrast to other organisms, is its extraordinarily flexible (in most cases personally idiosyncratic and often quite tenuous) relationship with its immediate environment. No doubt we are not introspectively aware of conceptual structures as such and they reveal themselves only through their unfolding in performance. So if we become aware of them it is not by means of an 'inner light', but in the development of stretches of our own or others' verbal and active behaviour. That, however, is not behaviourism, not at least in any sense that implies the adequacy of a purely third-person point of view. The generous concept of consciousness allows us to include as specifications of the 'inside'-character of consciousness not just the sensational content of first-hand experience, but also the projective and retrojective background scenarios of on-going performance, together with the selective focus that determines the specific preparednesses which belong essentially to any transaction that a self-conscious being has with its environment.

Giving the phenomenological mind a monopoly of the mental is one way of collapsing Jackendoff's mind–mind problem. The situation envisioned by Rorty is another: it aims at dismantling the phenomenological mind by showing that there are no 'inside' features out of which to build it. Our argument has been that this is not a genuine option. But that, as the remarks above about unconscious and conscious states in some kind of relation emphasize, still leaves us with a third issue: the traditional mind–body question. And since we aren't going along with Rorty's Antipodean answer to it (redrawing the distinction in just one of the domains), it may appear that we have no option but to grapple endlessly with the familiar (i.e. non-Antipodean) attempts to answer it. But shouldn't these attempts at answers simply be rejected, as Rorty suggests, along with the inner-eye view they responded to? That would be too hasty. It isn't clear that the inner-eye model isn't really just a provisional metaphor for relationships still awaiting their adequate literal description. Of course, if we are to follow Rorty's proposal, the metaphors should simply be replaced, if at all, by specifications of certain space–time regions. But whether *adequate* literal descriptions will ever be provided for the relationships depends on the range of questions we are willing to ask, as well as on what is going to count as literal and what metaphorical. Both conditions turn at least to some extent on what is taken to be intelligible empirically. For those for whom 'empirical' means 'observational', the questions we want answered about consciousness must be resolved *within* space–time, in terms say of brain–behaviour relations and without the embarrassment of epistemological subjects or minds and their states. But then it follows that the mind–body question can no longer be asked in a way that allows answers to clarify and define relations *between* minds and space–time. True, asking them in that way is widely regarded as itself deeply mistaken, the unfortunate product of the inner-eye model which puts space–time exclusively on the object-side, so that all we can get out of the epistemological subject are puzzlingly spaceless states of itself. Accordingly, why don't we just regard minds as aspects *of*, or ingredients *in*, space–time, without then having to raise further questions about relationships between space–time as such and some mysteriously unlocatable entities called 'minds'? After all, in a post-Heideggerian climate space–time regions can be populated with things, people, and the projects out of which we and our minds are made, our 'minds' then being our relations to (observings of, conversings with, and engagings in) items in these pleasingly concrete categories. This merger of mind with the constituent activities of a 'world' may seem to dispense with the need to refer to minds at all as entities in relation to the world, and by implication in some way separate from it. But several factors tell against dropping it.

One is, of course, the long-recognized dependence upon sensory processing by our own organisms of the surface or phenomenological characteristics which form the content of our everyday experience of space–time. To think of the world of objects and events 'out there', in the way we experience them, as composed of items much as we recognize them and lined up outside our current perceptual horizons waiting to enter and then leave them, is an indefensible thought; as indefensible as it is for migraine patients to think of their headaches throbbing away just round the corner and ready to enter consciousness. Whatever pitfalls await the unwary in the analysis of secondary qualities, this feature does raise the question of the relation of surface- to non-surface properties, and with it one very significant context in which answering mind–body questions can be seen to be a matter of clarifying and defining relations *between* mind on the one hand, here conceived as the general category of phenomena, and space–time regions on the other.

Another factor is the mind-dependence concealed in the kind of 'equipment realism' we find in Heidegger. Since it is only by incorporating culturally local ranges of projects that the items comprising 'worlds' present their specific 'use-values',[13] we find ourselves impelled to talk here of 'world-identities', and of there being a 'project-perspectivity' in the very notion of a world. Questions then arise not only about the relation of worlds thus identified to each other but also about their relation to what, in his recent probing discussion of this topic, O'Hear refers to as 'an absolute conception of the world, not tied down to our or any other specific manner of perceiving it'.[14] There is a hint of *déjà vu* here. Doesn't the second of these questions sound suspiciously like the old one of how 'subjective' content represents an 'objective' world? Though we now assume we have what we used to call the 'external' world in our grasp, its incorrigible perspectivity makes us wonder how it can be related to anything objective if an objective reality has to be a reality ideally abstracted from all perspective. The general framework here even invites the thought that 'worlds' themselves have an 'inside' character of the kind traditionally accorded to mental states. They stand to one another as subjects of consciousness traditionally stand to one another, each inscrutable to the other, but also all of them inscrutable to the notional (or perhaps, more circumspectly, the notionally notional) observer of the view from nowhere. Taken in a Heideggerian direction, then, Rorty's proposal falls foul of perspectivity, while taken in an Antipodean direction, or even beyond to the abstract realm of fundamental physics, it raises the question of the very status of that 'absolute conception' of the world within which terms like 'consciousness' and 'mind' are supposed now to find a new lease of life without implying anything 'inner'.

Not, of course, that one cannot try to find room for perspectivity in a world-picture which offers no foothold to the 'inside' character of consciousness, or perhaps even succeed. Thus one might postulate on the one hand a realm of common objects, shared in some sense also phenomenologically, though perhaps not necessarily in the same sense modes, by all cognitive beings, Martians included, perhaps even bats, and on the other hand the ways, styles, or psychological modes of the engagement of such beings with these objects. We might be able to distinguish in this way between the stable, common 'what' and a variable, subjective 'how', the 'how' then being treated not phenomenologically and from a first-person point of view, but observationally, so that the ways, styles, or modes are identified, say, behaviourally (functionally) or neurologically. The 'what' and the 'how' need not then command their own separate territories, the one outside and the other inside.[15]

However, this would fly in the face of experience; the picture offered would not be empirical. If we begin with our own experience with things, we appreciate that our responses to them, our feelings and attitudes with regard to them, are aspects of the experiences themselves, of what I suspect we are inclined to call our 'inner' states even without the help or interference of Descartes. Why should we be so inclined? It might have to do with a certain inaccessibility, and the metaphor be based on such literal uses we have in the public world for 'inner recesses', cupboards, and the like; the idea would be that our own inner states do not come readily to light in the public medium of language. But the metaphor might also be a social one, that the feelings and attitudes I myself have in regard to the things I share with others, and in regard also to activities that I share with them, are not open to those others in the same way as the activities themselves are, or of course the objects. In contrast to the shared world of things and activities, then, I see my own feelings and attitudes as states that can only be made public indirectly, by awakening similar states in others.[16] By adopting the point of view of others, then, I can look upon these states as 'internal' to me, and the states they can only make known indirectly to me as 'internal' to them.

If we first let ourselves think in this way, then the idea of the 'inside' character of consciousness may be given a much wider currency. It is an unusual thought, but one that is very hard to deny once it has taken hold, that everything we experience – objects, other people, processes, all things – in the only way in which we are familiar with it belongs in the general category of streams of consciousness. When we 'look abroad' we see others' bodies disclosed to us in this general, abstract category of the phenomenal, and at least in a first-personal sense the category of the phenomenal coincides incontrovertibly with that of the mental. But if those bodies are, as Vendler puts it, 'deserving' in the sense that we feel justified in ascribing first-person content to them, there is little we can do to describe the fact that we cannot see such streams but to say, for example, that they occur 'inside' those bodies. On the particle model, of course, the notion of 'inside' here is metaphorical and we have a mystery, a mystery as great as the mind–body question itself and indeed one aspect of it. But from a first-person point of view, however mysterious this 'inside' feature may be, the mystery cannot take the form of not grasping what it is like in general to be an embodied consciousness consciously engaged in this or that, because that is something we do indeed know in our own case. The mystery can take that form only if we prescind from such knowledge and pretend that all we know occurs in regions of a unified, public space–time. What is genuinely mysterious is how something made of particles, and which can be looked into with suitable tools and instruments, can have an inside not at all accessible to such tools and instruments, how it can have an inside in a sense quite different from that in which having an inside is also something it shares, if not with particles properly so-called, then at least with things composed of particles. But this inside which it shares with things composed of particles can also generate a mystery. From our own first-person point of view, others' streams of consciousness are 'outside' our own streams just as much as they are 'inside' their bodies. But that is not all that is outside. There are also all those (but then just what?) aspects of their bodies and brains and of the 'world' around them (but then how to describe it?) *not* disclosed to us in the general abstract category of the phenomenal, and which a scientific conception of reality abstracting from all perspectivity tries to bring, in yet another and this time radically mystery-bearing metaphor, 'to light'. The mind–body problem has recently been described as that of how 'technicolour phenomenology' arises from the 'soggy grey matter' of the brain.[17] But in terms of the more properly elusive notion of what the absolute 'inside' of a brain is, or of its ultimate construction out of things that don't have insides even in the normal spatial sense (i.e. particles), a more basic way of stating the problem would take us beyond the brain's sogginess and greyness and ask how what we know when we know what it is to be conscious can be related to something we can never know what it would be like to be conscious of.

The deep truth of solipsism is the pervasiveness but also initial narrowness of consciousness. Not 'thinness' but narrowness, for as Sprigge points out there is no need to think of consciousness as some elusive ethereal stuff floating over the observable world. Rather,

> one's consciousness, or whole of experience, includes the most grossly physical aspects of one's being, and of the world around one's body, as it and they are for oneself, and is far from some stream of mere thoughts. . . . The self side may consist merely in thinking, saying or writing things or it may consist in strenuous physical doings, in playing tennis, in washing a car, and buying

someone a drink, in fighting, or in making love. In these cases both the activity and that on which it is directed are at once contents of consciousness and real portions of the physical world of daily life.[18]

But it is still only *one's* consciousness that includes these real portions of the physical world as its contents. That is a very narrow start and there is no cheap way out of this basic structural separation of selves by saying, for example, that everything you could identify as 'content' on the inside corresponds to or represents some observable state of affairs in a world common to all lookings-abroad. That is a vulgar third-personalism which the empirical facts of the matter (facts of experience) do not support; it ignores the engagement that is constitutive of experience. That may work for large parts of nature, including the brain if attention is confined to a fairly general selection of its environmental tasks. It can also work for co-operative or collective activities where we focus on or manipulate the same objects in ways which actually require us not to bring to them particular qualities of our own experiencing. But if 'content' is given its due in the way we have urged, and consciousness with it, then these are special cases and do not provide the basis for a concept of consciousness based on brain–behaviour relationships or any other exclusively third-person alternative. The same applies to attempts positively to discount the role of subjective mental states in theories of meaning which appeal to the now much-publicized public nature of language. Once what might be called the 'vertical holism' of actual segments of streams of consciousness is properly allowed for, so that content is no longer artificially restricted to knowledge of the truth-conditions of the sentences of a language but allows for the modes, manners, styles, and qualities of the 'inner' states that form the 'hidden' context of what any truly radical interpreter should be trying to determine, it is impossible to base a theory of meaning on a third-person, evidential approach alone. Theories of meaning are constructed to specify the semantic knowledge needed for mastery of a given language, and that knowledge must of course be shareable and to a large extent also already shared with others, at any rate with regard to whatever things and activities are also shared. But there is much that is not shared, and much that is shared but expressed in ways not captured by whatever knowledge the subject displays of the truth-conditions of the sentences in her or his language. We are not immediately accessible to one another in this way, and the notion of a common world of shared content abstracts from the manner and quality of our first-personal engagements. A useful and even necessary abstraction no doubt, but an abstraction none the less.

Similarly with the claim that I know what it is like to be conscious. Knowing it from my own case does not enable me to know what it is like for you to be conscious just now or even in general, though I can guess, and no doubt in either especially banal or especially close circumstances sometimes get quite near. What I succeed in nearing or fail to get near to is indeed a reality. It is the reality I referred to in concluding the previous chapter, and it would be unfortunate both socially and morally if that reality failed to get on the agenda of the future conversation of mankind simply because third-personal preoccupations deprived us of the sense and eventually the means of that reference.

Notes

I The Problem

1 W. V. Quine, *Quiddities: An Intermittently Philosophical Dictionary*, Cambridge, Mass.: Harvard University Press/Belknap Press, 1987, pp. 132–3.

2 The idea that what is essential to a conscious being is that there is 'something it is like to be' it (a human being, a dog, a bat, or a spider) is due to Timothy Sprigge's 'Final causes', *Proceedings of the Aristotelian Society* suppl. vol. 45 (1971), and was later taken up by Thomas Nagel in 'What is it like to be a bat?', *Philosophical Review* 83 (1974), reprinted in Nagel, *Mortal Questions*, Cambridge: Cambridge University Press, 1979, ch. 12. It is unclear that the formula identifies conscious states as such, since one might want to say there was something it was like to be a stone, e.g. grey, detached, and not all that heavy. The point is to call attention to the fact, already recognized in one's own case, that there is experience and that it has a quality which probably differs considerably between different species of conscious being.

3 Immanuel Kant, *Critique of Pure Reason*, trans. Norman Kemp Smith, London: Macmillan, 1933, e.g. B 410, 411, p.371.

4 William James, *Essays in Radical Empiricism*, New York: Longmans Green & Co., 1912, pp. 26–7.

5 Daniel C. Dennett, *The Intentional Stance*, Cambridge, Mass./London: MIT Press/Bradford Books, 1987, p. 5.

6 Cf. Daniel C. Dennett, 'Toward a cognitive theory of consciousness', in *Brainstorms: Philosophical Essays on Mind and Psychology*, Brighton: Harvester Press, 1985, pp. 149-73; William G. Lycan, *Consciousness*, Cambridge, Mass./London: MIT Press/Bradford Books, 1987, ch. 4.

7 For germane remarks on attempts to analyse consciousness by 'looking elsewhere', see Ted Honderich, *A Theory of Determinism: The Mind, Neuroscience, and Life-hopes*, Oxford: Clarendon Press, 1988, pp. 71ff.

8 Quine, op. cit., p. 133.

9 Thomas Nagel, *The View from Nowhere*, Oxford/New York: Oxford University Press, 1986, p. 51.

10 For a recent essay in this area see John F. Post, *The Faces of Existence: An Essay in Non-reductive Metaphysics*, Ithaca, NY: Cornell University Press, 1987.

11 Cf. T. L. S. Sprigge, *Theories of Existence: A Sequence of Essays on Fundamental Positions in Philosophy*, Harmondsworth: Penguin Books, 1985, p. 46.

12 Daniel C. Dennett's Jacobsen Lecture, 'The evolution of consciousness', University of London, 13 May, 1988. Mimeo. pp. 28–32.

13 Cf. P. N. Johnson-Laird, *Mental Models: Towards a Cognitive Science of Language Inference, and Consciousness*, Cambridge: Cambridge University Press, 1987, pp. 470–7, on the 'recursive embedding of models' and 'self-reflective automata'.

14 Those functionalists like Lycan (cf. op. cit., pp. 123ff.) who envisage the possibility of conscious robots that are also sentient and have inner lives have still to account for the possibility that sentient experience can be a state of nerves. To do that they must either deny that experience is necessarily part of a point of view, or that there are no such things as points of view, or that points of view can be integrated into the physicalist's universe. Though they invariably are physicalists, functionalists, of course, need not be.

15 See, e.g., Daniel C. Dennett, 'Toward a cognitive theory of consciousness' (1978), in Dennett, *Brainstorms: Philosophical Essays on Mind and Psychology*, Brighton: Harvester Press, 1985, pp. 149–73; also his 'How to study human consciousness empirically or Nothing comes to mind', *Synthese* 53 (1982), pp. 159–80, and 'The evolution of consciousness'.

16 Colin McGinn, 'Can we solve the mind–body problem?', *Mind* 98 (1989), p. 352.

17 Richard Rorty, *Philosophy and the Mirror of Nature*, Princeton, NJ: Princeton University Press, 1979, pp. 70ff.; cf. Rorty's 'Comments on Dennett', *Synthese* 53 (1982), pp. 181–7.

II The History

1 Thomas Reid, *An Inquiry into the Human Mind*, ed. with intro. by Thomas Duggan, Chicago: University of Chicago Press, 1970, p. 12.

2 See Chapter VI.

3 John Locke, *An Essay Concerning Human Understanding* (1690), abridged and ed. John W. Yolton, London: Dent/New York: Dutton, 1976, p. 42.

4 ibid., p. 34. Original emphases removed.

5 ibid., emphasis removed.

6 ibid., p. 42.

7 ibid., p. 35.

8 For a use of 'consciousness' in the context of a 'moral sense', see Francis Hutcheson, *Illustrations on the Moral Sense*, ed. Bernard Peach, Cambridge, Mass.: Harvard University Press/Belknap Press, 1971, p. 116 in conjunction with pp. 163–4.

9 G. Ryle, *The Concept of Mind*, London: Hutchinson's University Library, 1949, p. 159.

10 ibid. In explaining why Heidegger chose to abandon the concept of consciousness, Frederick A. Olafson (*Heidegger and the Philosophy of*

Mind, New Haven: Yale University Press, 1987, pp. 14 and 262 n. 20) seeks assistance in the etymology of both the English word 'consciousness' and the German *Bewußtsein*. 'Both these words either derive from or are formed on the model of the Latin word *conscius*, which has the meaning "knowing with . . ." [see *Bewußtsein* in *Historisches Wörterbuch der Philosophie*, Basel/Stuttgart: Schwabe, 1971, I, p. 888]. The original context for this word appears to have been legal, so that "knowing with" is knowing with someone else in a sense that involves complicity. There are also Latin uses of *conscius* in which this element of duality – one person knowing *with* another – has apparently been internalized. Someone may thus be described as *conscius sibi*; and the reflexive construction indicates a relationship in which that person stands to himself. Typically, this is a matter of knowing something about oneself, such as one's own guilt or innocence – that is, something that one may be able to know only about oneself. This is true of the earliest English uses of the word as well. Such a concept is evidently designed to signify, not an awareness that we may have of any object whatever, but rather a special reflexive awareness that we have of ourselves. When the word "conscious" and its nominalization, "consciousness," came into general philosophical use, they were, in effect, preformed to express the kind of internal knowledge that the mind has of itself and of its own acts and states. Although a number of philosophers have continued to use this concept while disassociating it from its original connotations, it is by no means clear that they have been successful.' In connection with the implication of 'complicity' one may note Shakespeare's use of 'conscience' (see Sonnet 151) to connote 'carnal' knowledge.

11   See Kathleen V. Wilkes, 'Is consciousness important?', *British Journal for the Philosophy of Sciences* 35 (1984), p. 242.

12   In the *Orestes* of Euripides, Orestes replies to Menelaus, who asks what ails him, 'Consciousness [*hi synesis*] – being conscious of what dreadful thing I have done [*hoti synoida dein' eirgasmenos*]'. (I owe this reference to Marianne McDonald.) The primary sense of *synesis* is that of a joining, or meeting, together, from which is derived its sense as the faculty of apprehension, judgment, understanding, or intelligence (cf. putting two and two together). Here it is guilt that is apprehended, and Liddell and Scott's *Greek-English Lexicon* gives the word as a synonym for *syneidesis*, from *syneido*, whose connotations are the same as those of *conscius*, and include 'sharing in the knowledge', 'cognizant of', 'privy to'. But apparently it can also mean 'conscious of oneself as knowing'. In that case it is somewhat misleading of Wilkes (see above) to claim that in spite of having a 'rich, flexible and sophisticated psychological vocabulary', the Greeks 'managed quite splendidly without anything approximating to our notion of "consciousness" '. It is interesting, in view of the etymology of *synesis*, to contrast the claim sometimes made that what is necessary and sufficient for consciousness is that at least two things (e.g. one and one if not two and two) are 'put together' with the claim that all consciousness is of difference; that is, that the necessary

minimum for 'constituting' consciousness is not two objects conjoined but that 'a thing [be] seen to be what it is in contrast with what it is not' (J. S. Mill, *Collected Works* IX, London: Routledge & Kegan Paul, 1979, p. 4).

13 Locke, op. cit., p. 36. Reid makes the same point in advocating the 'way of reflection' as the 'only way in which we can form just and accurate notions of [the] operations of the mind': 'But this ... reflection is so difficult to man, surrounded on all hands by external objects, which constantly solicit his attention, that it has been very little practised, even by philosophers' (*An Inquiry into the Human Mind*, p. 252).

14 Ryle, op. cit., pp. 156–8.

15 ibid., pp. 15–16.

16 ibid., p. 199. Cf. my *Mental Images – A Defence*, London: Allen & Unwin, 1971, pp. 28–9.

17 J. L. Austin, *Sense and Sensibilia*, Oxford: Clarendon Press, 1962, p. 3. Cf. 'A plea for excuses', *Philosophical Papers*, Oxford: Clarendon Press, 1961, p. 130: '[O]ur common stock of words embodies all the distinctions men have found worth drawing. . . . '

18 See Edmund Husserl, *Ideas*, trans. W. R. Boyce-Gibson, New York: Crowell Collier and Macmillan, 1962, Sections 30–2.

19 The transition was facilitated by Aristotle's use of the notion of 'substance' (*ousia*) to convey both the particularity of concrete objects (primary substance), like Socrates or this horse, and what it is (secondary substance) that makes the former what they are, i.e. Socrates rather than a horse and vice versa.

20 Ryle, op. cit., p. 159.

21 ibid.

22 See Martin Heidegger, *History of the Concept of Time: Prolegomena*, trans. Theodore Kisiel, Bloomington: Indiana University Press, 1985, pp. 121–2. As we shall see later, Heidegger criticizes the subject–object schema in which he alleges Husserl reconstructs the world of experience in terms of an '*inspectio sui*, as an inner inspection of itself as the ego of intentionality, that is, the ego taken as subject of *cogitationes*' (p. 122). Cf. Olafson's comments in his excellent account of Heidegger, op. cit., pp. 23–4.

23 See Søren Kierkegaard, *The Sickness Unto Death*, trans. Alastair Hannay, Harmondsworth: Penguin Books, 1989.

24 Quoted in J. W. N. Sullivan, *The Limitations of Science*, New York: Viking Press, 1933, p. 130. It seems that according to Descartes, however, removing the animal would make no difference, since on his view of the soul, animals are soulless machines, unless sensation is not exclusive to souls.

25 See E. A. Burtt, *The Metaphysical Foundations of Modern Science*, Garden City, NY: Doubleday Anchor Books, 1955, p. 104. The author is here discussing Newton.

26 See Ryle, op. cit., ch. 7.

27 Locke, op. cit., p. 34, emphasis altered.

28 Gottfried W. Leibniz, *New Essays Concerning Human Understanding*

(written 1704, published 1765), II, i, 19. The *Essays* are a critique of Locke's *Essay*.

29 Locke, op. cit., p. 42.

30 See William Lyons, *The Disappearance of Introspection*, Cambridge, Mass./London: MIT Press/Bradford Books, 1986.

31 Reid, op. cit., Bk I, ch. 2. See Charles Landesman's article on 'Consciousness' in *The Encyclopedia of Philosophy*, London: Collier-Macmillan, 1967, II, pp. 192–3.

32 Thus Sydney Shoemaker: 'It is a distinguishing characteristic of first-person-experience statements . . . that it is simply their *being* true, and not the observation that they are true, or the possession of evidence that they are true, that entitles one to assert them' (*Self-knowledge and Self-identity*, Ithaca, NY: Cornell University Press, 1963, p. 122).

33 See Jean-Paul Sartre, *L'Imagination*, Paris: Presses Universitaires de France, 1956, p. 126: 'la seule façon d'exister pour une conscience c'est d'avoir conscience qu'elle existe.' This is stronger than Locke's claim that whenever we think we are conscious of doing so (op. cit., p. 42); Sartre maintains that whenever we think, we are aware of being conscious that we think, though because he rejects the notion of a substantial self engaged in its mental operations, it would be more accurate to say that in Sartre's account consciousness is aware of itself as thinking.

34 op. cit., p. 34.

35 See Jean-Paul Sartre, *The Transcendence of the Ego: An Existentialist Theory of Consciousness*, trans. Forrest Williams and Robert Kirkpatrick, New York: Noonday Press, 1957, pp. 40–1.

36 See Timothy L. S. Sprigge, 'The importance of subjectivity: an inaugural lecture', *Inquiry* 25 (1982), p. 153. If we take judging, desiring, fearing, etc. to be modes of consciousness, then, Sprigge says, 'to ask about the character of these modes is to seek to articulate clearly what one already implicitly knows'.

37 G. E. Moore, 'The subject-matter of psychology', *Proceedings of the Aristotelian Society* (1909–10), extracts reprinted in G. N. A. Vesey (ed.), *Body and Mind: Readings in Philosophy*, London: Allen & Unwin, 1964, p. 238.

38 ibid., p. 237.

39 ibid., p. 240.

40 David Hume, *A Treatise of Human Nature*, Everyman's Library, London: Dent, 1977, Bk I, p. 239: 'I never can catch *myself* at any time without a perception, and never can observe anything but the perception. When my perceptions are removed for any time, as by sound sleep, so long am I insensible of *myself*, and may truly be said not to exist.' Hume denies that 'perceptions' might inhere in a material or immaterial substance on the grounds that 'we do not so much as understand the meaning of the question' (p. 223).

41 Immanuel Kant, *Critique of Pure Reason*, trans. Norman Kemp Smith, London: Macmillan, 1933, B 131–2, pp. 152–3.

42 ibid., A 107, p. 136.

43 ibid., A 398, p. 362.

44 ibid., A 108, p. 136.
45 ibid., A 382, p. 353; B 404, p. 330.
46 Edmund Husserl, *Cartesian Meditations: An Introduction to Phenomenology*, trans. Dorion Cairns, The Hague: Martinus Nijhoff, 1970, pp. 24 and 25.
47 ibid., p. 26.
48 ibid., p. 21.
49 Kant, op. cit., e.g. B 105, p. 113.
50 G. W. F. Hegel, *Phenomenology of Spirit*, trans. A. V. Miller, Oxford: Clarendon Press, 1979, e.g. Sections 21 and 36, pp. 11 and 21.
51 G. W. F. Hegel, *Philosophy of Right*, trans. T. M. Knox, Oxford: Oxford University Press, 1967, Section 144, p. 105.
52 ibid., Section 163, p. 112.
53 ibid., Section 270, pp. 164–5.
54 Hegel, *Phenomenology of Spirit*, Section 25, p. 14.
55 ibid., Sections 22 and 25–37, pp. 12 and 14–21, *et passim*.
56 G. W. F. Hegel, *Sämtliche Werke*, ed. H. Glockner, Stuttgart: Fromann, 1927–30, X, pp. 204 and 255.
57 See esp. Søren Kierkegaard, *The Sickness Unto Death*, trans. Alastair Hannay, Harmondsworth: Penguin Books, 1989.
58 Martin Heidegger, *Being and Time*, trans. John Macquarrie and Edward Robinson, New York: Harper & Row, 1962, p. 32.
59 Jean-Paul Sartre, *Being and Nothingness: An Essay in Phenomenological Ontology*, trans. Hazel Barnes, New York: Philosophical Library, 1956, pp. 47–70.
60 Jean-Paul Sartre, *The Transcendence of the Ego*, p. 42.
61 ibid., p. 36.
62 William James, *The Principles of Psychology*, London: Constable, 1950, I, p. 336.
63 William James, *Essays in Radical Empiricism*, London: Longmans Green and Co., 1912, e.g. pp. 48–50.
64 William James, 'Does "consciousness" exist?', *Journal of Philosophy, Psychology and Scientific Methods* 1 (1904), reprinted in *Essays in Radical Empiricism*, p. 3.
65 ibid.
66 James, *Essays*, pp. 94–5.
67 James, *Principles*, I, p. 401.
68 ibid., pp. 340–1.
69 James, *Essays*, chs 1 and 2; cf. Bertrand Russell, *The Analysis of Mind*, London: Allen & Unwin, 1921.
70 James, *Essays*, p. 13.
71 James, *Essays*, p. 25. Original italicized.
72 James, *Principles*, I, p. 338. See Graham Bird, *William James*, London: Routledge & Kegan Paul, 1986, pp. 77ff.
73 Sartre, *The Transcendence of the Ego*.
74 I owe this way of putting it to Andrew Feenberg.
75 As Peter Caws suggests in his *Sartre*, London: Routledge & Kegan Paul, 1979, p. 59.

76   See Johann Gottlieb Fichte, *Grundlage der gesamten Wissenschaftslehre* (1794) in *Gesamtausgabe der Bayerischen Akademie der Wissenschaften*, ed. R. Lauth and H. Jacob, Stuttgart: Fromann, 1965, I, 4.

III   Quality of Experience

1   John Haugeland, 'Semantic engines: an introduction to mind design', in John Haugeland (ed.), *Mind Design: Philosophy, Psychology, Artificial Intelligence*, Cambridge, Mass./London: MIT Press/Bradford Books, 1981, pp. 32–4. Cf. Owen J. Flanagan Jr's useful introduction, *The Science of the Mind*, Cambridge, Mass./London: MIT Press/Bradford Books, 1984, p. 238.

2   Cf. J. Levine, '*The Nature of Psychological Explanation* by Robert Cummins: a critical notice', *Philosophical Review* 96 (1987), pp. 249–74.

3   ibid., p. 265.

4   Cf. William James, *The Principles of Psychology*, London: Constable, 1950, II, pp. 154 and 156.

5   See Ned Block, 'Are absent qualia impossible?', *Philosophical Review* 89 (1980), p. 257.

6   Ned Block, 'Troubles with functionalism', in Ned Block (ed.), *Readings in Philosophy of Psychology* I, London: Methuen, 1980, pp. 276–8.

7   Ludwig Wittgenstein, *Philosophical Investigations*, trans. G. E. M. Anscombe, Oxford: Basil Blackwell, 1958, Pt. I, Section 580. Cf. P. F. Strawson, *Individuals: An Essay in Descriptive Metaphysics*, London: Methuen, 1959, p. 106.

8   T. L. S. Sprigge, *The Vindication of Absolute Idealism*, Edinburgh: Edinburgh University Press, 1983, p. 99.

9   See Jerry A. Fodor, *The Language of Thought*, Hassocks: Harvester Press, 1976, p. 201.

10   Paul M. Churchland, *Matter and Consciousness: A Contemporary Introduction to the Philosophy of Mind*, Cambridge, Mass./London: MIT Press/Bradford Books, rev. edn. 1988, p. 39.

11   T. L. S. Sprigge, *Theories of Existence: A Sequence of Essays on Fundamental Positions in Philosophy*, Harmondsworth: Penguin Books, 1985, p. 45.

12   See David M. Armstrong, *A Materialist Theory of the Mind*, London: Routledge & Kegan Paul, 1968; J. J. C. Smart, 'Sensations and brain processes', *Philosophical Review* 68 (1959), pp. 141–56; U. T. Place, 'Is consciousness a brain process?', *British Journal of Psychology* 47 (1956), pp. 44–50.

13   Paul M. Churchland, 'Reduction, qualia, and the direct introspection of brain states', *Journal of Philosophy* 82 (1985), p. 16.

14   Etienne Bonnot de Condillac, *Traité des sensations* (Paris, 1754; re-edited 1778), *Œuvres philosophiques*, ed. Georges Le Roy, Paris: Presses Universitaires de France, 1947–51, I, pp. 224ff. Cf. James's discussion in *The Works of William James: Manuscript Essays and Notes*, Cambridge, Mass.: Harvard University Press, 1988, pp. 266ff.

15   ibid. Cf. also the chapter on sensation in *Principles* II, pp. 3ff.

16 Frank Jackson, 'Epiphenomenal qualia', *Philosophical Quarterly* 32 (1982), p. 130.

17 The law consists of the two following principles: (1) if a group of things have all their properties in common, or belong to exactly the same classes, they are identical in the sense of being really only one thing; (2) if a group of things are really one thing described in different ways, they have all their properties in common.

18 Churchland, 'Reduction, qualia, and the direct introspection of brain states', p. 23.

19 ibid., p.23.

20 ibid., p. 24.

21 ibid., p. 6.

22 Geoffrey Madell, *Mind and Materialism*, Edinburgh: Edinburgh University Press, 1988, pp. 81ff. Cf. Madell's 'Neurophilosophy: a principled sceptic's response', *Inquiry* 29 (1986), p. 155.

23 ibid., p. 82.

24 See Nathan Stemmer, 'Physicalism and the argument from knowledge', *Australasian Journal of Philosophy* 67 (1989), pp.84–92.

25 Gregory McCulloch, 'What it is like', *Philosophical Quarterly* 38 (1988), pp. 3, 13, and 15. 'Physicalism misses something. One can and should grant that it is all right in its own place, but there are other places too, and *what it is like* is to be found in one of them' (p. 19).

26 George Graham and G. Lynn Stephens, 'Are qualia a pain in the neck for functionalists?', *American Philosophical Quarterly* 22 (1985), p. 73.

27 ibid., p. 77.

28 What sort of theory would be responsible for 'telling us the nature' of pains Graham and Stephens leave open (ibid., p. 80). That pain qualia are not psychological entities is argued as follows: while the unreflective belief that pain is in, e.g., the toe deserves a hearing, arguments for pains being in the mind based on (a) privacy, (b) phantom limbs, and (c) *esse est percipi* are inconclusive: (a) because pain qualia like shape qualia do not require special direct knowledge (the knowledge is shared, and the fact that blind people are incapable of perceiving light does not mean light is a 'feature of the inner world' [ibid., p. 75], and perception can be private without the pain qualia being so); (b) because the phantom limb pain will not be believed to be in a phantom limb but in, say, the stump – without legs a person cannot feel pain in the legs but only think he does, but this is consistent with the feeling occurring in his body and his being mistaken about its exact location; also the phantom-limb phenomenon is compatible with the hypothesis that pain qualia are locatable (ibid., p. 77); (c) though pains are part of cognitive and motivational complexes, so that no pain can occur without the cognition and belief essential to its being pain, nevertheless pain qualia are not cognitive-state-dependent, for (i) the same quale as produced by burns can occur as pleasant in one case and as painful in another (their descriptions are by association), and (ii) a pain quale (but not being in pain) can be instantiated without being the focus of any cognitive state (ibid., p. 78), as ordinary usage suggests (I didn't perceive the pain in my ankle until after the game) – also the

Cognitive State Sufficiency Argument does not compel, for it is false that anything (e.g. a tree) for which cognitions are sufficient is psychological, and (according to the Absent Qualia objection to functionalism) it is not true that certain cognitions are sufficient for pain qualia.

29   John Dewey, *Human Nature and Conduct*, New York: Modern Library, 1930, p. 179; *Experience and Nature*, New York: Dover Publications, 1958, p. 303. I owe these references to Anthony O'Hear, 'Evolution, knowledge, and self-consciousness', *Inquiry* 32 (1989), pp. 142–3.

30   As argued, e.g., in Sydney Shoemaker, 'Functionalism and qualia', *Philosophical Studies* 27 (1975), pp. 291–315; 'Phenomenal similarity', *Critica* 7 (1975), pp. 3–37; 'Absent qualia are impossible – a reply to Block', *Philosophical Review* 90 (1981), pp. 581–99; Lawrence Davis, 'Functionalism and absent qualia', *Philosophical Studies* 41 (1982), pp. 231–49; William G. Lycan, 'Form, function, and feel', *Journal of Philosophy* 77 (1981), pp. 24–50; *Consciousness*, Cambridge, Mass./London: MIT Press/Bradford Books, 1987.

31   See Daniel C. Dennett, *Brainstorms: Philosophical Essays on Mind and Psychology*, Brighton: Harvester Press, 1985, e.g. pp. 171–2.

32   ibid., p. 165; cf. Madell, op. cit., p. 79.

33   Dennett, op. cit., p. 228.

IV   Subjects

1   Franz Brentano, *Psychology from an Empirical Standpoint* (1874), ed. Oskar Straus and Linda L. McAlister, London: Routledge & Kegan Paul, 1973, pp. 79–80.

2   ibid., p. 79.

3   In G. N. A. Vesey (ed.), *Body and Mind: Readings in Philosophy*, London: Allen & Unwin, 1964, p. 238. Cf. pp. 27–8 above.

4   See, e.g., Alasdair MacIntyre, *Whose Justice? Which Rationality?*, London: Duckworth, 1988.

5   See, e.g., Jacques-Alain Miller (ed.), *The Seminar of Jacques Lacan* Bk II: *The Ego in Freud's Theory and in the Technique of Psychoanalysis 1954–1955*, trans. Sylvana Tomaselli, Cambridge: Cambridge University Press, 1988.

6   Part of what Moore wanted to show echoes the position discussed at the end of the previous chapter: namely that even a colour, such as red, is not 'mental'. Moore claimed that the most fundamental sense of 'mental' was that in which what is called mental is an 'act of consciousness'.

7   See Vesey, op. cit., p. 238

8   This way of putting it borrows from Ted Honderich, *A Theory of Determinism: Mind, Neuroscience, and Life-hopes*, Oxford: Clarendon Press, 1988, pp. 80–2.

9   Vesey, op. cit., p. 237.

10   ibid., p. 239.

11   Zeno Vendler, *The Matter of Minds*, Oxford: Clarendon Press, 1984, pp. 117, 96; cf. ch. 2.

12   ibid., p. 41; cf. p. 93.

13 ibid., pp. 117, 111.
14 Immanuel Kant, *The Critique of Pure Reason*, trans. Norman Kemp Smith, London: Macmillan, 1933, A 354–5, pp. 337–8, and A 382, p. 353.
15 Vendler, op. cit., p. 109.
16 ibid., p. 227.
17 The procedure whereby the subjective 'I' establishes its connection with this particular instance of the 'sentient beings of the universe' has a strongly Kantian flavour: '[M]y identity is a matter of access: I am this man, I am Z.V. [this thing that is called Z.V. taught logic at Cornell, sits at this desk writing these lines] because it is his experiences to which I have a privileged access . . . because what I am feeling and perceiving now is what Z.V. ought to feel and perceive at this moment. . . . when I feel cold now, it is Z.V. who feels cold, sitting in a cold room . . . ' Similarly, in perception, 'what is needed is a scheme determined by or associated with the concept [e.g. of a lamp], which enables the imagination to evoke a picture into which the actual perceptions can be integrated . . . [to] see a lamp . . . is to be aware of an appearance which the imagination represents as belonging to a lamp'. In short: 'One becomes aware of oneself by fitting one's current experience into the pattern projected by the imagination – now along the subjective path – as pertaining to a particular body' (ibid., pp. 92–4).
18 The point can also be argued at a more fundamental level, e.g. in terms of the referentiality of experience, or thought, to the experiencing subject (cf. R. M. Chisholm, *The First Person*, Hassocks: Harvester Press, 1981, and C. McGinn, *The Subjective View: Secondary Qualities and Indexical Thoughts*, Oxford: Clarendon Press, 1983, ch. 5.
19 Vendler, op. cit., p. 88 fn.
20 Cf. ibid., p. 97.
21 ibid., p. 134.
22 For relevant comment on an earlier presentation of Vendler's view see J. L. Mackie, 'The transcendental "I" ', in J. L. Mackie, *Selected Papers* II: *Persons and Values*, Oxford: Clarendon Press, 1985, pp. 15–27.
23 T. L. S. Sprigge, *The Rational Foundations of Ethics*, The Problems of Philosophy: Their Past and Present, London: Routledge & Kegan Paul, 1988, pp. 249–52. Cf. Sprigge's, 'The self and its world in Bradley and Husserl', in Anthony Manser and Guy Stock (eds), *The Philosophy of F. H. Bradley*, Oxford: Clarendon Press, 1984; and 'Personal and impersonal identity', *Mind* 97 (1988), p. 44.
24 Sprigge, 'Personal and impersonal identity', p. 44.
25 Cf. Sprigge, *The Rational Foundations of Ethics*, p. 250.
26 The regress can also be expressed in Moore's terms of *acts* of consciousness. For a given act of consciousness to be conscious of itself, there must be another act of consciousness with the original act as its object. But that act, too, must be a conscious act, and so there will be an act of being conscious of it, and so on infinitely. See G. Ryle, *The Concept of Mind*, London: Hutchinson's University Library, 1949, pp. 162–3 and 195–6.

27 Brentano, op. cit., ch. 2.
28 See p. 26 above.
29 Ryle, op. cit., p. 161; cf. pp. 195ff.
30 Reinhardt Grossmann, *Phenomenology and Existentialism: An Introduction*, London: Routledge & Kegan Paul, 1984, p. 53.
31 According to James, the 'original paragon and prototype of all conceived times . . . the short duration of which we are immediately and incessantly sensible' (*The Principles of Psychology*, London: Constable, 1950, I, p. 631, emphasis removed.
32 See T. L. S. Sprigge, 'Intrinsic connectedness', *Proceedings of the Aristotelian Society* 88 (1987–8), pp. 129–45.
33 See Chapter II, pp. 32–3.
34 See G. R. Gillett, 'The generality constraint and conscious thought', *Analysis* 47 (1987), pp. 20–1. The following comments are due to this article. Gillett maintains: 'In as much as the thinker is able to conceive of the same feature as common to a number of situations and the same object as the potential instance of a range of predicative judgements, so there must be [that] flexible "aspect seeing" attentional control and selectivity of response [which] is just what it is to be conscious.' This may be compared, or contrasted, with Humphrey's view that organisms lacking the ability to reflect on their own subjective feelings are not conscious – they are not social beings and so do not need consciousness, any more than magnets do (see below, Chapter VIII, note 11, p. 203).
35 There are claims made for states of 'pure' consciousness.
36 Ludwig Wittgenstein, *Notebooks 1914–1916*, 2nd edn., Oxford: Basil Blackwell, pp. 80e and 82e.
37 Brentano, op. cit., pp. 155, 163.
38 Thomas Nagel, *Mortal Questions*, Cambridge: Cambridge University Press, 1979, pp. 156–64.
39 ibid., p. 163.
40 Cf. Wittgenstein, op. cit., p. 82e.
41 For a more detailed discussion see G. R. Gillett, 'Brain bisection and personal identity', *Mind* 95 (1986), pp. 224–9.
42 Nagel, op. cit., pp. 152–3.
43 Gillett, op. cit., pp. 226–7.
44 ibid., p. 226.
45 Nagel, op. cit., p. 160.
46 See Gillett, op. cit., pp. 225 and 227, and Nagel, op. cit., p. 160.

V Objects

1 Donald Davidson, 'Mental events' (1970), reprinted in D. Davidson, *Essays on Actions and Events*, Oxford: Clarendon Press, 1980.
2 See Jaegwon Kim, 'Psychophysical laws', in Ernest LePore and Brian McLaughlin (eds), *Actions and Events: Perspectives on the Philosophy of Donald Davidson*, Oxford: Basil Blackwell, 1986, pp. 369–86.
3 See Daniel C. Dennett, *The Intentional Stance*, Cambridge, Mass./London: MIT Press/Bradford Books, 1987, p. 26. Cf. Geoffrey Madell,

'Physicalism and the content of thought', *Inquiry* 32 (1989), p. 119.

4 Madell, op. cit., p. 112.

5 See Ted Honderich, *A Theory of Determinism: The Mind, Neuroscience, and Life-hopes*, Oxford: Clarendon Press, 1988, pp. 110 and 165ff.

6 See Jaegwon Kim, 'Honderich on mental events and psychoneural laws', *Inquiry* 32 (1989), pp. 46–7.

7 One problem with identity theories is that any evidence they can be based on is consistent with constant correlation. On the other hand, so long as the mental and physical domains follow different constitutive principles there will be no possibility of establishing such correlations. Or, to be more precise, so long as the 'laws' of the actual diachronic and synchronic relations that apply to each of the domains do not themselves specify identical sequences of events, any actual correlations between types of mental event and types of physical event will be accidental.

8 Franz Brentano, *Psychology from an Empirical Standpoint* (1874), ed. Oskar Kraus and Linda L. McAlister, London: Routledge & Kegan Paul, 1973, p. 97. Brentano writes: 'Every mental phenomenon is characterized by what the Scholastics of the Middle Ages called the intentional (or mental) inexistence of an object, and what we might call, though not wholly unambiguously, reference to a content, direction toward an object (which is not to be understood here as meaning a thing), or immanent objectivity. Every mental phenomenon includes something as object within itself, although they do not all do so in the same way. In presentation something is presented, in judgement something is affirmed or denied, in love loved, in hate hated, in desire desired and so on' (p. 88).

9 See John Haugeland, 'Semantic engines: an introduction to mind design', in John Haugeland (ed.), *Mind Design: Philosophy, Psychology, Artificial Intelligence*, Cambridge, Mass./London: MIT Press/Bradford Books, 1981, pp.1–34.

10 John R. Searle, 'Minds, brains, and programs', *The Behavioral and Brain Sciences* 3 (1980), p. 451.

11 John R. Searle, 'Indeterminacy, empiricism, and the first person', *Journal of Philosophy* 84 (1987), p. 123.

12 ibid., p. 145.

13 W. V. Quine, *Word and Object*, Cambridge, Mass.: MIT Press/New York: Wiley, 1960, ch. 2; Donald Davidson, 'The inscrutability of reference' (1979), reprinted in *Inquiries into Truth and Interpretation*, Oxford: Clarendon Press, 1984, pp. 227–41. Quine's famous thesis of the indeterminacy of translation is based on the insight that languages contain theories of the world, i.e. specific categorizations of things, and claims that these theories cannot be mirrored in any finite ranges of linguistic behaviour. The sheerly linguistic evidence at the translator's disposal therefore underdetermines the language-use of the target speaker.

14 Cf. Searle, 'Indeterminacy, empiricism, and the first person', pp. 136, 139, 143.

15 In Davidson, Searle notes, the issue between first- and third-personalism
    is obscured to the advantage of the latter by the claim that the things I
    can mean are themselves restricted to what can be determined by an
    external observer (ibid., p. 143).
16 John R. Searle, 'What is an intentional state?', *Mind* 88 (1979), p. 76.
17 John R. Searle, *Intentionality: An Essay in the Philosophy of Mind*,
    Cambridge: Cambridge University Press, 1983, p. 1.
18 See ibid., pp. 66, 69, and ch. 5 *passim*.
19 ibid., p. 146.
20 ibid., p. 145.
21 ibid., p. 147.
22 Richard E. Aquila, Critical notice of Searle's *Intentionality*, *Journal of
    Philosophy and Phenomenological Research* 46 (1985), p. 165.
23 Searle, *Intentionality*, p. 154
24 John R. Searle, 'Intentionality and the use of language', in A. Margalit
    (ed.), *Meaning and Use*, Dordrecht: D. Reidel, 1979, p. 196, cf. p. 182.
25 Gottlob Frege, *Translations from the Philosophical Writings of Gottlob
    Frege*, ed. and trans. P. Geach and M. Black, 3rd edn., Oxford: Basil
    Blackwell, 1980, p. 61.
26 Cf. A. J. Ayer, *The Foundations of Empirical Knowledge*, London:
    Macmillan, 1940, ch. 1, sect. 3.
27 See A. R. White, 'Seeing what is not there', *Proceedings of the
    Aristotelian Society* 70 (1969–70), p. 62.
28 Cf. K. W. Rankin, 'The role of imagination, rule-operations, and
    atmosphere in Wittgenstein's language-games', *Inquiry* 10 (1967),
    p. 288: '[W]hen we see a cluster of fruit hanging from a bough we tend to
    experience it directly as pluckable, as edible, and even as *to be* plucked
    and *to be* eaten.'
29 Cf. Donald Davidson, 'Toward a unified theory of meaning and action',
    Grazer Philosophische Studien 11 (1980), p. 5.
30 Cf. Frege, op. cit., p. 59.
31 Gottlob Frege, *Posthumous Writings*, ed. H. Hermes, F. Kambartel,
    and F. Kaulbach, trans. P. Long and R. White, Oxford: Basil Blackwell,
    1979, p. 259.
32 See Ludwig Wittgenstein, *Remarks on the Philosophy of Psychology* II,
    ed. G. H. von Wright and Heikki Nyman, trans. C. G. Luckhardt and
    M. A. W. Aue, Oxford: Basil Blackwell, 1980, sect. 45.
33 Something like this argument is offered by the Churchlands' claim that
    content divides into 'calibrational' and 'translational' aspects, both
    ascribable to Turing machines. 'There can be no question of an isolated
    state or token possessing an intrinsic translational content; it will have a
    specific translational content only if, and only insofar as, it enjoys a
    specific set of relations to the other elements in a *system* of
    representations' (Paul M. and Patricia S. Churchland, 'Functionalism,
    qualia, and intentionality', *Philosophical Topics* 12 (1981), p. 140). The
    Churchlands think that mental phenomena which functionalists are
    criticized for not being able to account for, *either* (as in the case of
    qualia) can indeed be accounted for on machine models, or *do not need*

to be accounted for (as with intentionality) since they are 'mysteries' and what is not mysterious in the concept of them *can* be instantiated mechanically. As far as Searle's 'intrinsic intentionality' is concerned, since neither calibrational nor translational content are this, it can be concluded that 'there is ... no such thing as intrinsic intentionality, at least as Searle conceives it ... [Therefore f]unctionalists need not be concerned ... that computer simulations of human mentality fail to display it' (p. 142). Cf. p. 140: 'The correct strategy is to argue that our own mental states are just as innocent of "intrinsic intentionality" as are the states of any machine stimulation.' In general, it could be objected that the 'mystery' of intentionality is generated by the puritan ontology which finds no home for it.

34 For useful accounts see John Haugeland, *Artificial Intelligence: The Very Idea*, Cambridge, Mass./London: MIT Press/Bradford Books, 1987, pp. 133 ff., and (more elaborate) J. R. Nelson, *The Logic of Mind*, Dordrecht: D. Reidel, 1982, pp. 18ff.

35 See, e.g., Kathleen V. Wilkes, *Real Persons: Personal Identity without Thought Experiments*, Oxford: Clarendon Press, 1988, pp. 107, 154–6

36 See my 'Consciousness and the experience of freedom', in E. LePore and R. van Gulick (eds), *John Searle and his Critics*, Oxford: Basil Blackwell, 1990.

37 Cf. Paul M. Churchland, *Matter and Consciousness: A Contemporary Introduction to the Philosophy of Mind*, Cambridge, Mass./London: MIT Press/Bradford Books, rev. edn 1988, p. 66; cf. p. 31.

VI Practice

1 Hubert L. Dreyfus, 'Husserl's perceptual *noema*', in Hubert L. Dreyfus (ed.), *Husserl, Intentionality, and Cognitive Science*, Cambridge, Mass./London: MIT Press/Bradford Books, 1982, p. 120.

2 The quotations here are from a preliminary, manuscript version of Hubert L. Dreyfus's 'Commentary' on part one of Heidegger's *Being and Time*, kindly made available by the author. Heidegger's view, as presented, is interestingly close to that expressed by John Dewey in *Human Nature and Conduct*, New York: Modern Library 1930.

3 See Daniel C. Dennett, 'Cognitive wheels', in Christopher J. Hookway (ed.), *Minds, Machines and Evolution*, Cambridge: Cambridge University Press, 1984, for a clear exposition of a version of the 'frame' problem based on this view.

4 Cf. Hubert L. and Stuart E. Dreyfus, 'Coping with change: why people can and computers can't', in Z. W. Pylyshin (ed.), *The Robot's Dilemma: The Frame Problem in Artificial Intelligence*, Ablex, 1987, pp. 95–111.

5 A Spartan version of what the Dreyfuses could mean by the 'whole organism' which they propose as 'the minimum unit of analysis' (Hubert L. Dreyfus and Stuart E. Dreyfus, 'Making a mind vs. modeling the brain: AI back at a branch point', *Daedalus* 117 (1988), p. 39).

6 John Locke, *An Essay Concerning Human Understanding* (1690),

abridged and ed. John W. Yolton, London: Dent/New York: Dutton, 1976, p. 58.

7   Frederick A. Olafson, *Heidegger and the Philosophy of Mind*, New Haven: Yale University Press, 1987, p. 14.

8   ibid., p. 21.

9   ibid. p. 24.

10 W. G. Penfield, who conducted his experiments in Montreal, is also famous for his 'homunculus' showing the proportional representation of bodily parts on the surface of the cerebral cortex.

11 See Hubert L. Dreyfus and Jane Rubin, 'You can't get something for nothing: Kierkegaard and Heidegger on how not to overcome nihilism', *Inquiry* 30 (1987), pp. 47–8.

12 As expounded in Dreyfus's 'Commentary' (see note 2 above).

13 ibid. Dreyfus notes that this view 'defies common sense, our ordinary concepts and a long philosophical tradition'.

14 Dreyfus and Dreyfus, 'Making a mind', pp. 32 and 39.

15 Cf. Dreyfus, 'Husserl's perceptual *noema*', p. 122.

16 David Marr, *Vision: A Computational Investigation into Human Representation and Processing of Visual Information*, San Francisco: W. H. Freeman, 1982, e.g. pp. 36–7, 317, and the synopsis in ch. 6.

17 J. J. Gibson, *The Ecological Approach to Visual Perception*, Boston: Houghton Mifflin Co. 1979.

18 For a useful discussion of Gibson see Avrum Stroll, 'Wittgenstein's nose', in Brian McGuinness and Rudolf Haller (eds), *Wittgenstein in Focus/Im Brennpunkt: Wittgenstein*, Amsterdam: Rodopi, 1989, pp. 394–414. Stroll argues: (i) that the unprocessed stimulus, an unconditioned X, which mediationists imply is represented by the final event in the stimulus/visual-effect causal sequence, remains unsatisfactorily noumenal and therefore incomparable with its alleged representation; (ii) that the complex of distinctions we make in our everyday applications of concepts like 'picture' and 'representation' have entailments which have no application in statements of the opposing views of mediationists and 'direct' perceptionists, and so are inevitably misleading if not unintelligible in such contexts. The upshot of Stroll's arguments is that mediationists misapply terms when they give *their* interpretation of the causal processes of visual perception (or, rather, in assuming that the results of their experimentation entail the mediationist position). It is similarly a misapplication of terms to conclude that, since the mediationist position can't be coherently stated (though I am not sure Stroll would put it that strongly), the 'direct' perceptionist view stands vindicated. The term 'direct' doesn't add any realist element to 'seeing' that the latter doesn't already contain, and qualifying the seeing as 'direct' only introduces confusions derived from the ordinary-language implications of the 'direct/indirect' distinction.

19 Gibson, op. cit., p. 147.

20 ibid., pp. 28f., 83f., 189f., 160ff.

21 Locke, op. cit., pp. 135–6.

22 Thomas Nagel, *The View from Nowhere*, Oxford/New York: Oxford University Press, 1986.

23 Dreyfus and Dreyfus, 'Making a mind', p. 32.
24 T. L. S. Sprigge, 'The importance of subjectivity: an inaugural lecture', *Inquiry* 25 (1982), p. 151.
25 These remarks are the gist of a fuller treatment in a draft manuscript by Frederick Olafson which the author kindly made available to me.

VII Control

1 D. C. Dennett, 'The milk of human intentionality', *The Behavioral and Brain Sciences* 3 (1980), pp. 428–30.
2 ibid., p. 429, original emphasis.
3 Thus falling into the category of 'radically lesioned sceptics' according to P. N. Johnson-Laird, 'Dennett's ark', *London Review of Books*, 1 Sept. 1988, p. 18.
4 E. g. Jerry A. Fodor, *Psychosemantics: The Problem of Meaning in the Philosophy of Mind*, Cambridge, Mass./London: MIT Press/Bradford Books, 1987, pp. 135ff.
5 P. M. Churchland, *Matter and Consciousness: A Contemporary Introduction to the Philosophy of Mind*, Cambridge, Mass./London: MIT Press/Bradford Books, rev. edn 1988, p. 76; cf. P. S. Churchland, 'Replies to comments', *Inquiry* 29 (1986), p. 241.
6 For the notion of a 'cognitive map' see D. A. Olton, 'Mazes, maps and memory', *American Psychologist* 34 (1979), pp. 588–96.
7 See John Haugeland, 'Semantic engines: an introduction to mind design', in John Haugeland (ed.), *Mind Design: Philosophy, Psychology, Artificial Intelligence*, Cambridge, Mass./London: MIT Press/Bradford Books, 1981, pp. 21ff.
8 See Johnson-Laird, op. cit., p. 17.
9 G. R. Gillett, 'Representations and cognitive science', *Inquiry* 32 (1989), pp. 264–5). Gillett reports that monkeys with a certain kind of frontal-lobe lesion are unable to perform this task, though they can still perform simple alternation tasks by learning complex responses of choice-and-reorientation, rather than 'a temporal pattern of input present-ations' (p. 264).
10 ibid., p. 265. Gillett uses the substantive form 'representation' throughout. But he argues against the formal cognitivism of a view like Fodor's according to which representations are correlated with elements in a natural language on the one hand and identifiable elements in the world on the other, and which then take the underlying mechanisms to be computational. And in favouring the Parallel Distributed Processing (or Connectionist) paradigm (see D. E. Rumelhart and J. L. McClelland, *Parallel Distributed Processing: Explorations in the Microstructure of Cognition*, Cambridge, Mass./London: MIT Press/Bradford Books, 1986), because it offers a better explanation of the 'multiple informational constraints and . . . unsystematic and messy input' employed by human cognition and perception (ibid., p. 261, abstract), Gillett is in effect proposing something more dynamic than the substantive form conveys: 'It is because the cortex enables us to form complex links between stimuli and to assemble significant stimulus patterns which are

interwoven with action in a myriad different ways that we are compelled to speak of the brain representing the world' (ibid., p. 271).

11 See Christopher Peacocke, *Sense and Content: Experience, Thought, and their Relations*, Oxford: Clarendon Press, 1983, p. 77.

12 See Gillett, op. cit.

13 See C. A. Hooker's review of S. P. Stich: *From Folk Psychology to Cognitive Science*, in *British Journal for the Philosophy of Science* 37 (1986), pp. 238–9.

14 P. S. Churchland, 'Consciousness: the transmutation of a concept', *Pacific Philosophical Quarterly* 64 (1983), p. 92.

15 Hooker draws a parallel between these anomalous phenomena and the absence in thermodynamic theory of any adequate phenomenological theory for macroscopic states, as in quantum superconductivity (the absence of electrical resistance in certain substances at temperatures close to absolute zero) (op. cit., p. 239).

16 P. S. Churchland, 'Reduction and the neurobiological basis of consciousness', in A. J. Marcel and E. Bisiach (eds), *Consciousness in Contemporary Science*, Oxford: Clarendon Press, 1988, p. 310; cf. P. S. Churchland, 'Consciousness: the transmutation of a concept,' pp. 82, 86, and 92.

17 P. S. Churchland, 'Reduction', p. 274.

18 E.g. ibid. p. 281.

19 ibid., p. 310. The fact that classical, or 'smooth', reduction fails in such a case, says Churchland, should not be interpreted as indicating that some genuinely explanatory factor survives the best efforts of neurobiological research to accommodate the facts, but as showing that 'the folk-psychological categories lack sufficient integrity to stick'. The reduction is 'either a revisionary reduction – of revised psychological categories to neurobiological categories – or, more radically, an outright replacement of the old folk notion of consciousness with new and better large-scale concepts' (ibid.).

20 See Stephen Toulmin, 'The genealogy of "consciousness"', in P. F. Secord (ed.), *Explaining Human Behavior: Consciousness, Human Action, and Social Structure*, Beverly Hills, Calif.: Sage Publications, 1982, pp. 57–62.

21 op. cit., p. 278.

22 Kathleen V. Wilkes, 'Is consciousness important?', *British Journal for the Philosophy of Science* 35 (1984), p. 239.

23 N. Humphrey, *Consciousness Regained: Chapters in the Development of Mind*, Oxford: Clarendon Press, 1983.

24 John R. Searle, *Intentionality: An Essay in the Philosophy of Mind*, Cambridge: Cambridge University Press, 1983, p. 265, original emphasis.

25 ibid., pp. 265–6.

26 John R. Searle, *Minds, Brains and Science*, Cambridge, Mass.: Harvard University Press, 1984, p. 93.

27 See R. W. Sperry, 'An objective approach to subjective experience', *Psychological Review* 77 (1970), p. 589. Sperry uses the wheel example to illustrate how 'the component parts of . . . an excitatory neural process

are carried along thus controlled by the dynamic properties of the whole system'. Cf. Charles Ripley, 'Sperry's concept of consciousness', *Inquiry* 27 (1984), pp. 407–8.

28 Searle, *Intentionality*, p. 265.

29 My comments here owe much to Ripley's excellent reconstruction of Sperry's position as an 'emergent materialism' (see Ripley, op. cit., p. 415 *et passim*).

30 Searle, *Minds, Brains and Science*, p. 93.

31 P. M. Churchland, 'Reduction, qualia, and the direct introspection of brain states', *Journal of Philosophy* 82 (1985), p. 16.

32 T. L. S. Sprigge, 'The importance of subjectivity: an inaugural lecture', *Inquiry* 25 (1982), p. 153.

33 John Locke, *An Essay Concerning Human Understanding* (1690), abridged and ed. John W. Yolton, London: Dent/New York: Dutton, 1976, p. 38.

34 Cf. Charles Taylor, 'Self-interpreting animals', in C. Taylor, *Philosophical Papers*, I: *Human Agency and Language*, Cambridge: Cambridge University Press, 1985, pp. 48ff.

VIII Others

1 For comment and further references on certain implications of assimilating value to such states, particularly when values are understood as secondary qualities, see Colin McGinn, *The Subjective View: Secondary Qualities and Indexical Thoughts*, Oxford: Clarendon Press, 1983, pp. 145–55.

2 T. L. S. Sprigge, 'Utilitarianism and idealism: a rapprochement', *Philosophy* 60 (1985), p. 454.

3 Daniel C. Dennett, 'How to study human consciousness empirically', *Synthese* 53 (1982), p. 178, original emphasis.

4 N. Humphrey, *Consciousness Regained: Chapters in the Development of Mind*, Oxford: Clarendon Press, 1983, p. 186.

5 ibid., p. 8.

6 ibid., pp. 19–21.

7 ibid., p. 30.

8 See Anthony O'Hear's discussion, 'Evolution, knowledge, and self-consciousness', *Inquiry* 32 (1989), p. 142.

9 Humphrey, op. cit., p. 69.

10 ibid., p. 6, emphasis removed.

11 According to Humphrey, since non-social animals, such as frogs, snails, and cod, do not need to do psychology, they have no need for consciousness (op. cit., p. 37), any more than magnets, in order to function, need to have insight into their own powers of attraction and repulsion. Consciousness, for Humphrey, is *simply* the ability to have subjective feelings that are available to introspection.

12 See A. W. Burks, 'An architectural theory of functional consciousness', in N. Rescher (ed.) *Current Issues in Teleology*, New York: University Press of America, 1986, pp. 9–10.

13   Humphrey, op. cit., p. 19.
14   O'Hear, op. cit., p. 132.
15   See O'Hear, op. cit.
16   Humphrey, op. cit., p. 6.
17   ibid., p. 9.
18   ibid., p. 10.
19   ibid., p. 20.
20   Cf. Gregory Sheridan, 'Can there be moral subjects in a physicalist universe?', *Philosophy and Phenomenological Research* 43 (1983), p. 429.
21   Humphrey, op. cit., p. 25.
22   It is tempting to draw a parallel between Humphrey's example of a blind-sighted monkey, which might be able to use visual information in certain ways but wouldn't know what it is like for another monkey to see (op. cit., p. 40), and (for example) male (or for that matter female) chauvinists who might conceivably be partly excused for not knowing what it is like to be a member of the opposite sex.
23   See J. L. Mackie, *Ethics – Inventing Right and Wrong*, Harmondsworth: Penguin Books, 1977.
24   See Paul Feyerabend, *Farewell to Reason*, London: Verso, 1987.
25   Of course, as sadism proves, 'other-regarding' actions need not be altruistic; nor need self-regarding actions be selfish, as the ability to improve oneself as an 'other-regarder' proves.
26   Alastair Hannay, 'Propositions toward a humanist consensus in ethics', in M. B. Storer (ed.), *Humanist Ethics: Dialogue on Basics*, Buffalo, NY: Prometheus Press, 1980, e.g. pp. 189–90.
27   Sheridan, op. cit., p. 443.
28   ibid., p. 430.
29   ibid., p. 432.
30   ibid., p. 443. The critical version of physicalism here is a form of functionalism in which a person's overall teleological performance is accounted for by breaking it down into an inverted hierarchy of increasingly specialized and decreasingly 'intentional' agencies below what Dennett has labelled the 'personal' level. Types of mental state, classified in terms of 'institutional' purposes or responses, are then identified with constitutive activities at some scientifically relevant sub-personal level, as far down as one chooses, even to the subatomic level. Sheridan's argument is that, even at the information-processing level, functionalists are unable to 'speci[fy] exactly what activity, or combination of activities, is to be identified (strictly) with a tokening of pain' (ibid., p. 441).
31   G. Frege, 'On sense and reference', in P. T. Geach and M. Black (eds), *Philosophical Writings of Gottlob Frege*, Oxford: Basil Blackwell, 1960, p. 59. Quoted by Sheridan, op. cit., p. 445.
32   Sheridan, op. cit., pp. 445–6.
33   ibid., p. 446.
34   Cf. ibid., p. 446. If one can preserve the notion of a moral subject on the grounds that there is, as a matter of fact, something it is like to be in pain, denying at the same time that something lacking that subjective aspect is a moral subject, why should one not, if as a matter of fact (and suppose

204

for the sake of argument it is a fact) there is something it is like to act voluntarily, preserve the notion of a moral agent? It might be argued that there is an asymmetry. Phenomenological suffering calls for sympathy, while in terms of interpersonal relations phenomenological voluntariness is neither here nor there. On the other hand, considerable importance is attached to it in our institutions and self-understanding, and it would make quite a difference to these if we treated the feeling of voluntariness as merely an illusion. What makes the difference here, however, is whether voluntariness itself is present, and not just the feeling. But then again, it may be that the belief in its presence is unavoidable, a constituent rule of human thought.

35 See Wilfrid Sellars, 'Putting man into the scientific image', in *Science, Perception and Reality*, London: Routledge & Kegan Paul, 1963, pp. 38–40; cf. Sheridan, op. cit., p. 447.

IX Agenda

1 See Richard Rorty, 'Comments on Dennett', *Synthese* 53 (1982), pp. 183 and 186.

2 ibid., p. 183.

3 ibid., p. 187.

4 The idea implicit here of a universal science of fundamental events seems highly implausible. But there are these two opposing perspectives: (1) new scientific domains emerge as matter complicates, or as higher-order systems come into effect, perhaps due to evolutionary principles, so that a science of the fundamental events at stage 1 proves inadequate at stage 2; (2) since evolutionary principles are part of the universal science of fundamental events, nothing scientifically new emerges in the course of evolution, so that all subsequent stages are constrained by a set of laws that belong to stage 1. (1) seems to have the consequence that because of the 'native' possibility of evolution, science can predict its supersession though not determinately. (2) seems to have the consequence that no later-stage sciences can offer their own stage-specific causal explanations in terms of their special taxonomies of the events they are said to share with the fundamental science.

5 Richard Rorty, *Philosophy and the Mirror of Nature*, Princeton, NJ: Princeton University Press, 1979, p. 82.

6 William G. Lycan, *Consciousness*, Cambridge, Mass./London: MIT Press/Bradford Books, 1987.

7 ibid., pp. 5 and 22 ff.

8 Ray Jackendoff, *Consciousness and the Computational Mind*, Cambridge, Mass./London: MIT Press/Bradford Books, 1987, p. 20.

9 ibid., pp. 288 and 290.

10 See John R. Searle, *What's Wrong with the Philosophy of Mind?*, Cambridge, Mass./London: MIT Press/Bradford Books, 1990, ch. 6.

11 ibid., ch. 7. Quotations are from a preliminary draft kindly made available by the author. We should note that Searle's whole treatment is stamped by his determination to make it consistent with two aspects of

the 'overall contemporary world view' and which he takes to be 'no longer optional for reasonably well-educated citizens of the present era . . . [namely] the atomic theory of matter and the evolutionary theory of biology' (ch. 4). Consciousness is an emergent (neuro-biological) phenomenon whose 'underlying causal reality' is to be found in neurophysiological processes. The reason that consciousness cannot be ontologically reduced in the way, say, colours can, is that unlike the latter, where the subjective quality can be treated as of secondary importance – mere 'appearance' to the underlying reality – to be 'carved off', with conscious states such as pains the phenomena are the subjective experiences themselves, so in their case 'there is no way to carve anything off' (ch. 7). See Chapter VII above.

12 See Frederick A. Olafson's discussion of Heidegger in this respect, *Heidegger and the Philosophy of Mind*, New Haven: Yale University Press, 1987, e.g. pp. 60 and 102.

13 See p. 115 above.

14 Anthony O'Hear, *The Element of Fire: Science, Art, and the Human World*, London/New York: Routledge, 1988, p. 65. The book discusses the tension between the scientific conception of the world and our actual ways of experiencing it.

15 For further discussion see my 'The "what" and the "how" ', in D. F. Gustafson and B. L. Tapscott (eds), *Body, Mind, and Method*, Dordrecht: D. Reidel, 1979, pp. 17–36.

16 See O'Hear, op. cit., pp. 103ff.

17 Colin McGinn, 'Can we solve the mind–body problem?', *Mind* 98 (1989), p. 349.

18 T. L. S. Sprigge, *The Rational Foundations of Ethics*, London: Routledge & Kegan Paul, 1988, p. 252.

Bibliography

Aquila, R. E., Critical notice of Searle's *Intentionality*, *Journal of Philosophy and Phenomenological Research* 46 (1985), pp. 159–70.

Armstrong, D. M. *A Materialist Theory of the Mind*, London: Routledge & Kegan Paul, 1968.

Armstrong, D. M. 'Consciousness and causality', in D. M. Armstrong and N. Malcolm, *Consciousness and Causality: A Debate on the Nature of Mind*, Oxford: Basil Blackwell, 1984, pp. 103–91 and 205–17.

Austin, J. L. 'A plea for excuses', in J. L. Austin, *Philosophical Papers*, Oxford: Clarendon Press, 1961, pp. 123–52.

Austin, J. L. *Sense and Sensibilia*, Oxford: Clarendon Press, 1962.

Ayer, A. J. *The Foundations of Empirical Knowledge*, London: Macmillan, 1940.

Barrett, W. *Death of the Soul: From Descartes to the Computer*, Oxford/New York: Oxford University Press, 1987.

Bird, G. *William James*, Arguments of the Philosophers, London: Routledge & Kegan Paul, 1986.

Block, N. 'Are absent qualia impossible?', *Philosophical Review* 89 (1980), pp. 257–74.

Block, N. 'Troubles with functionalism', in N. Block (ed.), *Readings in Philosophy of Psychology* I, London: Methuen, 1980, pp.268–305.

Brentano, F. *Psychology from an Empirical Standpoint* (1874), ed. O. Straus and L. L. McAlister, London: Routledge & Kegan Paul, 1973.

Burks, A. W. 'An architectural theory of functional consciousness', in N. Rescher (ed.), *Current Issues in Teleology*, New York: University Press of America, 1986, pp. 1–14.

Burtt, E. A. *The Metaphysical Foundations of Modern Science*, Garden City, NY: Doubleday Anchor Books, 1955.

Caws, P. *Sartre*, Arguments of the Philosophers, London: Routledge & Kegan Paul, 1979.

Chisholm, R. M. *The First Person*, Hassocks: Harvester Press, 1981.

Churchland, P. M. *Matter and Consciousness: A Contemporary Introduction to the Philosophy of Mind*, Cambridge, Mass./London: MIT Press/ Bradford Books, 1984. (Rev. edn 1988.)

Churchland, P. M. 'Reduction, qualia, and the direct introspection of brain states', *Journal of Philosophy* 82 (1985), pp. 8–28.

Churchland, P. S. 'Consciousness: the transmutation of a concept', *Pacific Philosophical Quarterly* 64 (1983), pp. 80–95.

Churchland, P. S. *Neurophilosophy: Toward a Unified Science of the Mind–Brain*, Cambridge, Mass./London: MIT Press/Bradford Books, 1986.

Churchland, P. S. 'Replies to comments', *Inquiry* 29 (1986), pp. 241–72.

Churchland, P. S. 'Reduction and the neurobiological basis of consciousness', in A. J. Marcel and E. Bisiach (eds), *Consciousness in Contemporary Science*, Oxford: Clarendon Press, 1988.

Churchland, P. M. and Churchland, P. S. 'Functionalism, qualia, and intentionality', *Philosophical Topics* 12 (1981), pp. 121–45

Condillac, E. B. de *Traité des sensations* (Paris 1754; re-ed. 1778), *Œuvres philosophiques*, ed. G. Le Roy, Paris: Presses Universitaires de France, 1947–51, I.

Cummins, R. *The Nature of Psychological Explanation*, Cambridge, Mass./London: MIT Press/Bradford Books, 1983.

Davidson, D. 'Mental events', in L. Foster and J. W. Swanson (eds), *Experience and Theory*, London: Duckworth, 1970, reprinted in D. Davidson, *Essays on Actions and Events*, Oxford: Clarendon Press, 1980, pp. 207–27.

Davidson, D. 'The inscrutability of reference', *Southwestern Journal of Philosophy* 10 (1979), reprinted in D. Davidson, *Inquiries into Truth and Interpretation*, Oxford: Clarendon Press, 1984, pp. 227–41.

Davidson, D. 'Toward a unified theory of meaning and action', *Grazer Philosophische Studien* 11 (1980), pp. 1–12.

Davis, L. 'Functionalism and absent qualia', *Philosophical Studies* 41 (1982), pp. 231–49.

Dennett, D. C. *Brainstorms: Philosophical Essays on Mind and Psychology*, Brighton: Harvester Press, 1985.

Dennett, D. C. 'Cognitive wheels: the frame problem of AI', in C. J. Hookway (ed.), *Minds, Machines and Evolution*, Cambridge: Cambridge University Press, 1984, 129–51.

Dennett, D. C. *Content and Consciousness*, London/Boston/Henley: Routledge & Kegan Paul, 1969. (New pref. 1986.)

Dennett, D. C. *Elbow Room: The Varieties of Free Will Worth Wanting*, Oxford: Clarendon Press, 1984.

Dennett, D. C., Exchange with Searle in the *New York Review of Books*, 1982.

Dennett, D. C. 'How to study human consciousness empirically, or Nothing comes to mind', *Synthese* 53 (1982), pp. 159–80.

Dennett, D. C. 'Intentional systems', *Journal of Philosophy* 67 (1971), pp. 87–106, reprinted in D. C. Dennett, *Brainstorms: Philosophical Essays on Mind and Psychology*, Brighton: Harvester Press, 1985, pp. 3–22.

Dennett, D. C. 'On giving libertarians what they say they want', in D. C. Dennett, *Brainstorms: Philosophical Essays on Mind and Psychology*, Brighton: Harvester Press, 1985, pp. 286–99.

Dennett, D. C. 'The evolution of consciousness', The Jacobsen Lecture, London, 13 May 1988.

Dennett, D. C. *The Intentional Stance*, Cambridge, Mass./London: MIT Press/Bradford Books, 1987.

Bibliography

Dennett, D. C. 'The milk of human intentionality', *The Behavioral and Brain Sciences* 3 (1980), pp. 428–30.

Dennett, D. C. 'Three kinds of intentional psychology', in R. Healey (ed.), *Reduction, Time and Reality: Studies in the Philosophy of the Natural Sciences*, Cambridge: Cambridge University Press, 1981, pp. 37–60.

Dennett, D. C. 'Toward a cognitive theory of consciousness' in C. W. Savage (ed.), *Perception and Cognition: Issues in the Foundations of Psychology* 1978, reprinted in D. C. Dennett, *Brainstorms: Philosophical Essays on Mind and Psychology*, Brighton: Harvester Press, 1985.

Dewey, J. *Experience and Nature*, Chicago: Open Court 1925; 2d edn. New York: Dover Publications, 1929.

Dewey, J. *Human Nature and Conduct*, New York: Holt, 1922; New York: Modern Library, 1930.

Dreyfus, H. L., *Division I Being-in-the-World: A Commentary on 'Being and Time'*, forthcoming.

Dreyfus, H. L. *'Husserl's perceptual noema'*, in H. L. Dreyfus (ed.), *Husserl, Intentionality, and Cognitive Science*, Cambridge, Mass./London: MIT Press/Bradford Books, 1982, pp. 97–123.

Dreyfus, H. L. *What Computers Can't Do: A Critique of Artificial Reason*, New York: Harper & Row, 1972, 2nd edn 1979.

Dreyfus, H. L. and Dreyfus, S. E. 'Coping with change: why people can and computers can't', revised and reprinted in Z. W. Pylyshyn (ed.), *The Robot's Dilemma: The Frame Problem in Artificial Intelligence*, Norwood, NJ: Ablex, 1987, pp. 95–111.

Dreyfus, H. L. and Dreyfus, S. E. 'Making a mind vs. modeling the brain: AI back at a branchpoint', *Daedalus* 117 (1988), pp. 15–43.

Dreyfus, H. L. and Rubin, J. 'You can't get something for nothing: Kierkegaard and Heidegger on how not to overcome nihilism', *Inquiry* 30 (1987), pp. 33–75.

Ey, H. *Consciousness: A Phenomenological Study of Being Conscious and Becoming Conscious*, trans. John H. Flodstrom, Bloomington/London: Indiana University Press, 1978.

Feyerabend, P. *Farewell to Reason*, London: Verso, 1987.

Fichte, J. G. *Grundlage der gesamten Wissenschaftslehre*, in *Gesamtausgabe der Bayerischen Akademie der Wissenschaften*, ed. R. Lauth and H. Jacob, Stuttgart: Fromann, 1965, I, 4.

Flanagan, O. J. Jr. *The Science of the Mind*, Cambridge, Mass./London: MIT Press/Bradford Books, 1984.

Fodor, J. A. *Psychosemantics: The Problem of Meaning in the Philosophy of Mind*, Cambridge, Mass./London: MIT Press/Bradford Books, 1987.

Fodor, J. A. *The Language of Thought*, Hassocks: Harvester Press, 1976.

Frege, G. *Collected Papers on Mathematics, Logic, and Philosophy*, ed. B. McGuinness, trans. M. Black, V. H. Dudman, P. Geach, H. Kaal, E.-H. W. Kluge, B. McGuinness, and R. H. Stoothoff, Oxford: Basil Blackwell, 1984.

Frege, G. 'On sense and reference', in P. T. Geach and M. Black (eds), *Philosophical Writings of Gottlob Frege*, Oxford: Basil Blackwell, 1960, pp. 56ff.

Frege, G. *Posthumous Writings*, ed. H. Hermes, F. Kambartel, and

F. Kaulbach, trans. P. Long and R. White, Oxford: Basil Blackwell, 1979.

Frege, G. *Translations from the Philosophical Writings of Gottlob Frege*, ed. P. Geach and M. Black, 3rd edn, Oxford: Basil Blackwell, 1980.

Gadamer, H.-G. *Truth and Method*, trans. William Glen-Doepel, London: Sheed & Ward, 1975.

Gibson, J. J. *The Ecological Approach to Visual Perception*, Boston: Houghton-Mifflin Co., 1979.

Gillett G. R. 'Brain bisection and personal identity', *Mind* 95 (1986), pp. 224–9.

Gillett, G. R. 'Representations and cognitive science', *Inquiry* 32 (1989), pp. 261–76.

Gillett, G. R. 'The generality constraint and conscious thought', *Analysis* 47 (1987), pp. 20–4.

Globus, G. C., Maxwell, G. and Savodnik, I. (eds), *Consciousness and the Brain: A Scientific and Philosophical Inquiry*, New York/London: Plenum Press, 1976.

Graham, G. and Stephens, G. L. 'Are qualia a pain in the neck for functionalists', *The American Philosophical Quarterly* 22 (1985), pp. 73–80.

Grossmann, R. *Phenomenology and Existentialism: An Introduction*, London: Routledge & Kegan Paul, 1984.

Hannay, A. 'The claims of consciousness', *Inquiry* 31 (1988), pp. 395–434.

Hannay, A. 'Consciousness and the experience of freedom', in E. LePore and R. van Gulick (eds), *John Searle and his Critics*, Oxford: Basil Blackwell (forthcoming).

Hannay, A. 'Mental illness and the *Lebenswelt*: a discussion of Maurice Natanson (ed.), *Psychiatry and Philosophy*', *Inquiry* 15 (1972), pp. 208–30.

Hannay, A. *Mental Images – A Defence*, London: Allen & Unwin/New York: Humanities Press, 1971.

Hannay, A. 'Propositions toward a humanist consensus in ethics', in M. B. Storer (ed.), *Humanist Ethics: Dialogue on Basics*, Buffalo, NY: Prometheus Press, 1980, pp. 179–92.

Hannay, A. 'The "what" and the "how"', in D. F. Gustafson and B. L. Tapscott (eds), *Body, Mind, and Method*, Dordrecht: D. Reidel, 1979, pp. 17–36.

Haugeland, J. *Artificial Intelligence: The Very Idea*, Cambridge, Mass./London: MIT Press/Bradford Books, 1987.

Haugeland, J. 'Semantic engines: an introduction to mind design', in J. Haugeland (ed.), *Mind Design: Philosophy, Psychology, Artificial Intelligence*, Cambridge, Mass./London: MIT Press/Bradford Books, 1981, pp. 1–34.

Hegel, G. W. F. *Phenomenology of Spirit*, trans. A. V. Miller, Oxford: Clarendon Press, 1979.

Hegel, G. W. F. *Philosophy of Right*, trans. T. M. Knox, Oxford: Oxford University Press, 1967.

Hegel, G. W. F. *Sämtliche Werke*, ed. H. Glockner, Stuttgart: Fromann, 1927–30.

Heidegger, M. *Being and Time*, trans. J. Macquarrie and E. Robinson, New York: Harper & Row, 1962.

Heidegger, M. *History of the Concept of Time: Prolegomena*, trans. T. Kisiel, Bloomington: Indiana University Press, 1985.

Honderich, T. *A Theory of Determinism: The Mind, Neuroscience, and Life-hopes*, Oxford: Clarendon Press, 1988.

Honderich, T. 'Nomological dualism: reply to four critics', *Inquiry* 24 (1981), pp. 419–38.

Honderich, T. 'Psychological lawlike connections and their problem', *Inquiry* 24 (1981), pp. 277–303.

Hooker, C. A., Review of S. P. Stich: *From Folk Psychology to Cognitive Science*, *British Journal for the Philosophy of Science* 37 (1986), pp. 238–42.

Hume, D. *A Treatise of Human Nature*, London: Dent, 1977.

Humphrey, N. *Consciousness Regained: Chapters in the Development of Mind*, Oxford: Clarendon Press, 1983.

Husserl, E. *Cartesian Meditations: An Introduction to Phenomenology*, trans. D. Cairns, The Hague: Martinus Nijhoff, 1970.

Husserl, E. *Ideas: General Introduction to Pure Phenomenology* (1931), trans. W. R. Boyce-Gibson, New York: Crowell Collier & Macmillan, 1962.

Hutcheson, F. *Illustrations on the Moral Sense*, ed. B. Peach, Cambridge, Mass.: Harvard University Press/Belknap Press, 1971.

Jackendoff, R. *Consciousness and the Computational Mind*, Cambridge, Mass./London: MIT Press/Bradford Books, 1987.

Jackson, F. 'Epiphenomenal qualia', *Philosophical Quarterly* 32 (1982), pp. 127–36.

James, W. 'Does "consciousness" exist?', *Journal of Philosophy, Psychology and Scientific Methods* 1 (1904), reprinted in W. James, *Essays in Radical Empiricism*, London: Longmans Green & Co., 1912, pp. 1–38.

James, W. *Essays in Radical Empiricism*, London: Longmans Green & Co., 1912.

James, W. *The Principles of Psychology*, 2 vols, London: Constable, 1950.

James, W. *The Works of William James: Manuscript Essays and Notes*, Cambridge, Mass.: Harvard University Press, 1988.

John, E. R. 'A model of consciousness', in E. Schwartz and D. Shapiro (eds), *Consciousness and Regulation: Advances in Research* I, London/New York/Sydney/Toronto: Wiley & Sons, 1976, pp. 1–50.

Johnson-Laird, P. N. *Mental Models: Towards a Cognitive Science of Language, Inference, and Consciousness*, Cambridge: Cambridge University Press, 1983.

Johnson-Laird, P. N. 'Dennett's ark', *London Review of Books*, 1 Sept. 1988.

Johnson-Laird, P. N. *The Computer and the Mind: An Introduction to Cognitive Science*, Cambridge, Mass.: Harvard University Press, 1988.

Kant, I. *Critique of Pure Reason*, trans. N. Kemp Smith, London: Macmillan, 1929. (2nd imp. with corr. 1933, repr. 1980.)

Kierkegaard, S. *The Sickness Unto Death*, trans. A. Hannay, Harmondsworth: Penguin Books, 1989.

Kim, J. 'Honderich on mental events and psychoneural laws', *Inquiry* 32 (1989), pp. 29–48.

Kim, J. 'Psychophysical laws', in E. LePore and B. McLaughlin (eds), *Actions and Events: Perspectives on the Philosophy of Donald Davidson*,

Oxford: Basil Blackwell, 1986, pp. 369–86.

Landesman, C. 'Consciousness', in P. Edwards (ed.), *The Encyclopedia of Philosophy*, London: Collier-Macmillan, 1967.

Leibniz, G. W. *New Essays Concerning Human Understanding* (1765), in *G. W. Leibniz: Sämtliche Schriften und Briefe*, Darmstadt: German Academy of Sciences, 1923–, series VI, vol. 6.

Levine, J. '*The Nature of Psychological Explanation* by Robert Cummins: a critical notice', *Philosophical Review* 96 (1987), pp. 249–74.

Locke, J. *An Essay Concerning Human Understanding* (1690), abridged and ed. John W. Yolton, London: Dent/New York: Dutton, 1976.

Lycan, W. G. *Consciousness*, Cambridge, Mass./London: MIT Press/Bradford Books, 1987.

Lycan, W. G. 'Form, function, and feel', *Journal of Philosophy* 77 (1981), pp. 24–50.

Lyons, W. *The Disappearance of Introspection*, Cambridge, Mass./London: MIT Press/Bradford Books, 1986.

McCulloch, G. 'What it is like', *Philosophical Quarterly* 38 (1988), pp. 1–19.

McGinn, C. 'Can we solve the mind–body problem?', *Mind* 98 (1989), pp. 349–66.

McGinn, C. *The Subjective View: Secondary Qualities and Indexical Thoughts*, Oxford: Clarendon Press, 1983.

MacIntyre, A. *Whose Justice? Which Rationality?*, London: Duckworth, 1988.

Mackie, J. L. *Ethics – Inventing Right and Wrong*, Harmondsworth: Penguin Books, 1977.

Mackie, J. L. 'The transcendental "I"', in J. L. Mackie, *Selected Papers* II: Persons and Values, Oxford: Clarendon Press, 1985, pp. 15–27.

Madell, G. *Mind and Materialism*, Edinburgh: Edinburgh University Press, 1988.

Madell, G. 'Neurophilosophy: a principled sceptic's response', *Inquiry* 29 (1986), pp. 153–68.

Madell, G. 'Physicalism and the content of thought', *Inquiry* 32 (1989), pp. 107–21.

Malcolm, N. 'Consciousness and causality', in D. M. Armstrong and N. Malcolm, *Consciousness and Causality: A Debate on the Nature of Mind*, Oxford: Basil Blackwell, 1984, pp. 1–101 and 193–204.

Marr, D. *Vision: A Computational Investigation into Human Representation and Processing of Visual Information*, San Francisco: W. H. Freeman, 1982.

Matson, W. I. *Sentience*, Berkeley/Los Angeles/London: University of California Press, 1976.

Merleau-Ponty, M. *Phenomenology of Perception*, trans. C. Smith, London: Routledge & Kegan Paul, 1962.

Mill, J. S. *Collected Works* IX, London: Routledge & Kegan Paul, 1979.

Miller, I. *Husserl, Perception, and Temporal Awareness*, Cambridge, Mass.: MIT Press, 1984.

Miller, J.-A. (ed.), *The Seminar of Jacques Lacan* Bk II: *The Ego in Freud's Theory and in the Technique of Psychoanalysis 1954–1955*, trans. S. Tomaselli, Cambridge: Cambridge University Press, 1988.

Moore, G. E. *Some Main Problems of Philosophy*, London: Allen & Unwin/

New York: Macmillan, 1953.

Moore, G. E. 'The subject-matter of psychology', *Proceedings of the Aristotelian Society* (1909–10), extracts reprinted in G. N. A. Vesey (ed.), *Body and Mind: Readings in Philosophy*, London: Allen & Unwin, 1964, pp. 236–45.

Nagel, T. *Mortal Questions*, Cambridge: Cambridge University Press, 1979.

Nagel, T. *The View from Nowhere*, Oxford/New York: Oxford University Press, 1986.

Nagel, T. 'What is it like to be a bat?', *Philosophical Review* 83 (1974), reprinted in T. Nagel, *Mortal Questions*, Cambridge: Cambridge University Press, 1979, ch. 12.

Nelson, J. R. *The Logic of Mind*, Dordrecht: D. Reidel, 1982.

Neumann, E. *The Origins and History of Consciousness*, foreword by C. G. Jung, trans. R. F. C. Hull, Princeton: Princeton University Press/London: Routledge & Kegan Paul, 1954 (pb. 1970).

O'Hear, A. 'Evolution, knowledge, and self-consciousness', *Inquiry* 32 (1989), pp. 127–50.

O'Hear, A. *The Element of Fire: Science, Art, and the Human World*, London/New York: Routledge, 1988.

Olafson, F. A. *Heidegger and the Philosophy of Mind*, New Haven: Yale University Press, 1987.

Olton, D. A. 'Mazes, maps and memory', *American Psychologist* 34 (1979), pp. 588–96.

Peacocke, C. *Sense and Content: Experience, Thought, and their Relations*, Oxford: Clarendon Press, 1983.

Peacocke, C. and McGinn, C. 'Consciousness and other minds', *Proceedings of the Aristotelian Society*, suppl. vol. 58 (1984), pp. 97–137.

Penfield, W. G. *The Mystery of Mind: A Critical Study of Consciousness and the Human Brain*, Princeton: Princeton University Press, 1975.

Place, U. T. 'Is consciousness a brain process?', *British Journal of Psychology* 47 (1956), pp. 44–50.

Popper, K. R. and Eccles, J. *The Self and its Brain*, Berlin: Springer, 1977.

Post, J. F. *The Faces of Existence: An Essay in Non-reductive Metaphysics*, Ithaca, NY: Cornell University Press, 1987.

Pribram, K. H. 'Problems concerning the structure of consciousness', in G. C. Globus, G. Maxwell, and I. Savodnik (eds), *Consciousness and the Brain: A Scientific and Philosophical Inquiry*, New York/London: Plenum Press, 1976, pp. 297–313.

Quine, W. V. *Quiddities: An Intermittently Philosophical Dictionary*, Cambridge, Mass.: Harvard University Press/Belknap Press, 1987.

Quine, W. V. *Word and Object*, Cambridge, Mass.: MIT Press/New York: Wiley, 1960.

Rankin, K. W. 'The role of imagination, rule-operations, and atmosphere in Wittgenstein's language-games', *Inquiry* 10 (1967), pp. 279–91.

Reid, T. *An Inquiry into the Human Mind*, ed. with intro. by T. Duggan, Chicago: University of Chicago Press, 1970.

Reid, T. *Essays on the Intellectual Powers of Man* (1785), ed. Baruch Brody, Cambridge, Mass.: MIT Press, 1969.

213

Rey, G. 'A reason for doubting the existence of consciousness', in R. J. Davidson, G. E. Schwarz, and D. Shapiro (eds) *Consciousness and Self-regulation*, New York: Plenum Press, 1983, pp. 1–39.

Ripley, C. 'Sperry's concept of consciousness', *Inquiry* 27 (1984), pp. 399–423.

Rorty, R. 'Comments on Dennett', *Synthese* 53 (1982), pp. 181–7.

Rorty, R. *Philosophy and the Mirror of Nature*, Princeton, NJ: Princeton University Press, 1979.

Rumelhart, D. E. and McClelland, J. L. *Parallel Distributed Processing: Explorations in the Microstructure of Cognition*, Cambridge, Mass./ London: MIT Press/Bradford Books, 1986.

Russell, B. *The Analysis of Mind*, London: Allen & Unwin, 1921.

Ryle, G. *The Concept of Mind*, London: Hutchinson's University Library, 1949.

Sartre, J.-P. *Being and Nothingness: An Essay on Phenomenological Ontology* (1943), trans. H. Barnes, New York: Philosophical Library, 1956.

Sartre, J.-P. *L'Imagination* (1936), Paris: Presses Universitaires de France, 1956.

Sartre, J.-P. *The Transcendence of the Ego: An Existentialist Theory of Consciousness*, trans F. Williams and R. Kirkpatrick, New York: Noonday Press, 1957.

Savodnik, I. 'Mind, brain, and the symbolic consciousness', in G. C. Globus, G. Maxwell, and I. Savodnik (eds), *Consciousness and the Brain: A Scientific and Philosophical Inquiry*, New York/London: Plenum Press, 1976, pp. 73–98.

Searle, J. R. *What's Wrong with the Philosophy of Mind?*, Cambridge, Mass./ London: MIT Press/Bradford Books, 1990.

Searle, J. R. 'Indeterminacy, empiricism, and the first person', *Journal of Philosophy* 84 (1987), pp. 123–46.

Searle, J. R. 'Intentionality and the use of language', in A. Margalit (ed.), *Meaning and Use*, Dordrecht: D. Reidel, 1979, pp. 181–97.

Searle, J. R. *Intentionality: An Essay in the Philosophy of Mind*, Cambridge: Cambridge University Press, 1983.

Searle, J, R. 'Minds, brains, and programs', *The Behavioral and Brain Sciences* 3 (1980), pp. 417–57, with commentaries and reply. Reprinted without commentaries in J. Haugeland (ed.), *Mind Design: Philosophy, Psychology, Artificial Intelligence*, Cambridge, Mass./London: MIT Press/Bradford Books, 1981, pp. 282–306.

Searle, J. R. *Minds, Brains and Science*, Cambridge, Mass.: Harvard University Press, 1984.

Searle, J. R. 'What is an intentional state?', *Mind* 88 (1979), pp. 74–92.

Secord, P. F. (ed.), *Explaining Human Behavior: Consciousness, Human Action and Social Structure*. Beverly Hills/London/New Delhi: Sage Publications, 1982.

Sellars, W. *Science, Perception and Reality*, London: Routledge & Kegan Paul, 1963.

Sheridan, G. 'Can there be moral subjects in a physicalist universe?', *Philosophy and Phenomenological Research* 43 (1983), pp. 425–47.

214

Shoemaker, S. 'Absent qualia are impossible – a reply to Block', *Philosophical Review* 90 (1981), pp. 581–99.

Shoemaker, S. 'Functionalism and qualia', *Philosophical Studies* 27 (1975), pp. 291–315.

Shoemaker, S. 'Phenomenal similarity', *Critica* 7 (1975), pp. 3–37.

Shoemaker, S. *Self-knowledge and Self-identity*, Ithaca, NY: Cornell University Press, 1963.

Sluga, H. 'Foucault, the author, and the discourse', *Inquiry* 28 (1985), pp. 403–15.

Smart, J. J. C. 'Sensations and brain processes', *Philosophical Review* 68 (1959), pp. 141–56.

Sperry, R. W. 'An objective approach to subjective experience', *Psychological Review* 77 (1970), pp. 587–9.

Sperry, R. W. 'Forebrain commissurotomy and conscious awareness', *Journal of Medicine and Philosophy* 2 (1977), pp. 101–22.

Sperry, R. W. 'Neurology and the mind–brain problem', *American Scientist* 40 (1952), pp. 291–312.

Sprigge, T. L. S. 'Final causes', *Proceedings of the Aristotelian Society* suppl. vol. 45 (1971), pp. 149–70.

Sprigge, T. L. S. 'Intrinsic connectedness', *Proceedings of the Aristotelian Society* 88 (1987–88), pp. 129–45.

Sprigge, T. L. S. 'Metaphysics, physicalism, and animal rights', *Inquiry* 22 (1979), pp. 101–43.

Sprigge, T. L. S. 'Non-human rights: an idealist perspective', *Inquiry* 27 (1984), pp. 439–61.

Sprigge, T. L. S. 'Personal and impersonal identity', *Mind* 97 (1988), pp. 29–49.

Sprigge, T. L. S. 'The importance of subjectivity: an inaugural lecture', *Inquiry* 25 (1982), pp. 143–63.

Sprigge, T. L. S. *Theories of Existence: A Sequence of Essays on Fundamental Positions in Philosophy*, Harmondsworth: Penguin Books, 1985.

Sprigge, T. L. S. *The Rational Foundations of Ethics*. The Problems of Philosophy: Their Past and Present, London: Routledge & Kegan Paul, 1988.

Sprigge, T. L. S. 'The self and its world in Bradley and Husserl', in A. Manser and G. Stock (eds), *The Philosophy of F. H. Bradley*, Oxford: Clarendon Press, 1984, pp. 286–302.

Sprigge, T. L. S. *The Vindication of Absolute Idealism*, Edinburgh: Edinburgh University Press, 1983.

Sprigge, T. L. S. 'Utilitarianism and idealism: a rapprochement', *Philosophy* 60 (1985), pp. 447–63.

Stemmer, N. 'Physicalism and the argument from knowledge', *Australasian Journal of Philosophy* 67 (1989), pp. 84–92.

Strawson, G. 'Consciousness, free will, and the unimportance of determinism', *Inquiry* 32 (1989), pp. 3–27.

Strawson, P. F. *Individuals: An Essay in Descriptive Metaphysics*, London: Methuen, 1959.

Stroll, A. 'Wittgenstein's Nose', in B. McGuinness and R. Haller (eds),

Wittgenstein in Focus – Im Brennpunkt: Wittgenstein, Amsterdam: Redopi, 1989, pp. 394–414.

Sullivan, J. W. N. *The Limitations of Science*, New York: Viking Press, 1933.

Swinburne, R. *The Evolution of the Soul*, Oxford: Clarendon Press, 1985.

Taylor, C. 'Self-interpreting animals', in C. Taylor, *Philosophical Papers 1: Human Agency and Language*. Cambridge: Cambridge University Press, 1985, pp. 45–75.

Toulmin, S. 'The genealogy of "consciousness"', in P. F. Secord (ed.), *Explaining Human Behavior: Consciousness, Human Action and Social Structure*, Beverly Hills/London/New Delhi: Sage Publications, 1982, pp. 53–70.

Tugendhat, E. *Self-consciousness and Self-determination*, trans. P. Stern, Cambridge, Mass./London: MIT Press/Bradford Books, 1986.

Vendler, Z. *The Matter of Minds*, Oxford: Clarendon Press, 1984.

Vesey, G. N. A. (ed.) *Body and Mind: Readings in Philosophy*, London: Allen & Unwin, 1964.

Weiskrantz, L. *et al.* 'Visual capacity in the hemianopic field following a restricted occipital ablation', *Brain* 97 (1974), pp. 709–28.

White, A. R. 'Seeing what is not there', *Proceedings of the Aristotelian Society* 70 (1969–70), pp. 61–74.

Wilkes, K. V. 'Is consciousness important?', *British Journal for the Philosophy of Science* 35 (1984), pp. 223–43.

Wilkes, K. V. 'Nemo psychologus nisi physiologus', *Inquiry* 29 (1986), pp. 169–85.

Wilkes, K. V. *Real Persons: Personal Identity without Thought Experiments*, Oxford: Clarendon Press, 1988.

Williams, B. 'Imagination and the self', British Academy Annual Philosophical Lecture, 1966, reprinted in B. Williams, *Problems of the Self*, Cambridge: Cambridge University Press, 1973.

Wittgenstein, L. *Notebooks 1914–1916*, 2d edn, Oxford: Basil Blackwell, 1979.

Wittgenstein, L. *Philosophical Investigations*, trans. G. E. M. Anscombe, Oxford: Basil Blackwell, 1958.

Wittgenstein, L. *Remarks on the Philosophy of Psychology* II, ed. G. H. von Wright and H. Nyman, trans. C. G. Luckhardt and M. A. W. Aue, Oxford: Basil Blackwell, 1980.

INDEX

A and *see* spirit
accountability 4; *see* moral
analytical realism, the fallacy of 141
anomalous monism 84, 86
Antipodeans *see* Rorty
apperception: transcendental unity
  of 29–30, 33; unity of 16, *see*
  consciousness, unity of
Aquila, R. E. 91, 95, 198
Aristotle 21, 31, 72, 123, 189
Armstrong, D. M. 192
Austin, J. L. 19, 189
aware, awareness 1, 25, 17, 55, 76,
  95, 133, 138, 188; *see* self-
  awareness
Ayer, A. J. 198

behaviourism, behaviourist 4, 44,
  108, 117, 139, 179
Berkeley, G. 24
Bird, G. 191
blind-sight 105, 204
Block, N. 192
Bradley, F. H. 125
brain 4; brain bisection 65, 79–82
Brentano, F. 64, 74, 78, 87, 194,
  196, 197
Burks, A. W. 203
Burtt, E. A. 189

Cartesian *see* Descartes
Caws, P. 191
Chisholm, R. 195

Churchland, P. M. 54, 55, 192, 193,
  198–9, 201, 203
Churchland, P. S. 138, 142, 198–9,
  201, 202
cognitive maps 133, 201
cognitivism, cognitivist 101, 104,
  135
comportment 108, 112
computer *see* machine intelligence
conceptual: ability 136; structure
  175
concrete universal *see* self
Condillac, E. B. de 53, 192
conditions of satisfaction 66, 75, 88,
  90–1, 94, 121
confabulation 98
conscious, consciousness *passim*;
  abandonment of 13; acts of 27–
  8, 64–5, 67–8, 78, 98, 194, 195;
  connection with conscience 15,
  62, 188; conscious control 43,
  126–52, 159; etymology of 14–
  16, 187–8; as inner sense 14;
  inside character of 124, 171–2,
  179, 181–2; nature of 2; as
  nonentity 35; reflexive 157–61,
  164, 166, 178, 188; and social life
  144, 153–70, 184–5; subject/s of,
  8, 21–34, 37, 46, 47, 58, 64–82,
  71, 76, 77, 79–82, 101; unity of
  16, 35, 46, 78–82, 161; *see* self-
  consciousness
consequentialist 166
Constantinople, Council of 21

217